UNDERSTANDING CLASSICAL PSYCHOANALYSIS

Understanding Classical Psychoanalysis gives a clear overview of the key tenets of classical Freudian psychoanalysis, and offers a guide to how these might be best understood and applied to contemporary psychoanalytic theory and practice.

Covering such essential concepts as the Oedipus complex, narcissism and metapsychology, Fayek explores what Freud's thinking has to offer psychoanalysts of all schools of thought today, and what key facets of his work can usefully be built on to develop future theory.

The book will be of interest to psychoanalysts and psychoanalytic psychotherapists in practice and training, as well as teaching faculties and postgraduate students studying Freudian psychoanalysis.

Ahmed Fayek is a member of the IPA, the APsaA, and division 39 APA. After fifty-five years in the field – practising, teaching, and training in psychoanalysis – Ahmed retired to focus on his psychoanalytic writings. His interest in German Idealistic Philosophy led him to Freud's manner of thinking and from there to the theory of psychoanalysis.

"This is a very timely book: Psychoanalysis is in crisis. Many attribute the crises to external factors changes in the zeitgeist and the culture, but Fayek contends the crisis is of our own making and I agree. The fault is not in our stars it is in ourselves. He confronts the crisis head on, considering what is foundational for psychoanalysis, what needs to be preserved and what needs to be changed. This book should be read widely because it is a credo for what it means to be a psychoanalyst. The final chapter on organizational structure and its negative impact on the field is very timely and important."

— Arnold Richards, editor of internationalpsychoanalysis.net and publisher of ipbooks.net

"Ahmed Fayek's call for a revision of psychoanalytic theory is as brave as it is necessary. Renovation, expansion, deletion, in all facets of our body of knowledge, from how the psychoanalyst understands the analysis to the technique he/she uses, is the scope of Dr. Fayek's scholarly book. This challenge to revise theory and education along with the institutions that support psychoanalysis as it is now, says Fayek, must include psychologists, child psychologists, philosophers, sociologists, and linguists working together. I applaud Dr. Fayek for paving the way for a revolutionary project. His knowledge of Freud is deep and respectful but he encourages us to move ahead so that Freud's discoveries will not fade away."

—Jane S. Hall, LCSW, FIPA, Past President of the Contemporary Freudian Society, author of *Deepening the Treatment* (1998) and *Roadblocks on the Journey of Psychotherapy* (2004)

UNDERSTANDING CLASSICAL PSYCHOANALYSIS

Freudian concepts in contemporary practice

Ahmed Fayek

Routledge
Taylor & Francis Group
LONDON AND NEW YORK

First published 2017
by Routledge
4 Park Square, Milton Park, Abingdon, Oxon, OX14 4RN

and by Routledge
605 Third Avenue, New York, NY 10158

Routledge is an imprint of the Taylor & Francis Group, an informa business

British Library Cataloguing in Publication Data
A catalogue record for this book is available from the British Library

Library of Congress Cataloging in Publication Data
Names: Fayek, Ahmed, author.
Title: Understanding classical psychoanalysis : Freudian concepts in contemporary practice / Ahmed Fayek.
Description: Abingdon, Oxon ; New York, NY : Routledge, 2017. | Includes bibliographical references.
Identifiers: LCCN 2016026541| ISBN 9781138218260 (hardback) | ISBN 9781138218277 (pbk.) | ISBN 9781315437897 (ebook)
Subjects: LCSH: Freud, Sigmund, 1856-1939. | Psychoanalysis.
Classification: LCC BF173.F85 F3943 2017 | DDC 150.19/52--dc23
LC record available at https://lccn.loc.gov/2016026541

ISBN: 978-1-138-21826-0 (hbk)
ISBN: 978-1-138-21827-7 (pbk)
ISBN: 978-1-315-43789-7 (ebk)

Typeset in Bembo
by HWA Text and Data Management, London

CONTENTS

PREFACE

Psychoanalysis is already discovered. Like all the great discoveries it led to the details of that discovery engendering a comprehensive theory of the psyche and the psychology of the individual. The theory, identified as the *Freudian Doctrine*, kept growing, expanding, changing to some extent, during Freud's life and by his own creative mind, without losing its special status as the only theory that is, in the field of psychological phenomena. After his passing, and for several decades, analysts aspired to contribute, modify, improve, reformulate that doctrine and even replace it all together. The result was a crisis that is seriously threating psychoanalysis as whole (Fayek, 2010, 2015).

A discovery cannot be rediscovered. It could only be revisited, explored, redefined, because there is an inherent novelty in the discovery that cannot be repeated. The novelty of discovering the unconscious cannot be experienced once again. However, after more than a century of that discovery and the reformulation(s) of its theory over the years, it is natural that the theory would need revision. If not because some of its limitations are exposed, or its informative aspects could be better reconfigured, it would be because its success in dealing with its subject matter over time represents and allows a more penetrating understanding of it. In better terms, a successful theory leads with time to the need to revise its main propositions.

Revising the Freudian doctrine is a natural result of its success, which is proven by its resiliency and its survivability in spite of constant criticisms, even from psychoanalysts. Revising some main propositions is meant to give them a better explanation that befits what they have originally allowed us to understand. It is an act of correcting previous misunderstandings – corrections stemming from those same relatively flawed misunderstandings. This process was undertaken by Freud regarding some of his basic conceptions, as will be stated later. Thus, revising some of Freud's main propositions is a need that came from their success, which demands maintaining their fundamentality and significance.

I use the masculine pronoun He throughout this book to refer to the human subject irrespective of gender.

INTRODUCTION

Deviation or revision

Psychoanalysis is the first theory of the psyche, and it happened to be a theory of the dynamics of the intrapsychic. It took Sigmund Freud many years and several attempts to find the prompting stimulus for those dynamics; hence psychoanalysis and the conception of the intrapsychical eventually became synonyms. For reasons I explained in other works (Fayek, 2010, 2013) some psychoanalysts tried to replace Freud's intrapsychical propositions with different ones, but they were only able to make the change from an intrapsychical theory to an interpersonal one. The psychoanalytic scene began to unravel. As a result, The International Psychoanalytic Association (IPA) recognized theoretical plurality and accepted the notion of schools of psychoanalysis (Wallerstein, 1989), and that was for political expediency as Wallerstein himself has stated (2005). This was a main shift in the field. After more than a century of psychoanalysis being a unitary theory of the intrapsychical and the trademark of the Freudian doctrine, it started to have diverse denotations. Instead of declaring the original theory of psychoanalysis obsolete and inadequate they claimed theoretical novelties and appropriated the term and title 'psychoanalysts'. The general but undeclared reason for that is none of those schools had any substance that could identify them to coin as their title. Another reason is that most of those who claimed coming up with novel theories were formerly trained psychoanalysts and derived a great deal of narcissistic gain from being known as such. It was one of those unethical professional gestures on a big scale. Despite Freud's few revisions and the additions of few talented analysts in his time and after he passed, the core of the theory did not change. It also proved that it could not be changed without becoming distorted; nevertheless it could be revised without losing its core. There is only one psychoanalysis: a theory of the intrapsychic, or any theory of the intrapsychical, is psychoanalytic.

Psychoanalysis is one of the major cultural feats of the nineteenth and twentieth century. It highlighted and developed the notion that the human subject is a topic of curiosity in his own right, and there is a great deal to discover about him outside his socio-moral-economic manifestations. Freud started responding to that curiosity and initiated the first purposive research in the nature of the human subject as such. Although there is an implicit concurrence on the existence of a theory of psychoanalysis, even relating it solely to Freud's conceptions, there are many disagreements on which of his writings institutes and presents that theory. In the American way of regarding things his most recent formulations (ego-psychology) must be the representative of his theory. The European way was different: it was the formulation most related to the intrapsychical core that should be considered representative of psychoanalysis. Therefore, any attempt at expounding or making any *revision* of the presumed theory could be mistakenly considered moving away from its purely classical Freudian format, or manipulating aspects of it to serve a biased objective. Like all the great theories of the last three or four centuries psychoanalysis demands being revised to maintain its prominent place in a new age.

The main and unchallenged fact about the great theories of mankind is that they are all products of *intuitions* and not of deductive thinking. The heliocentric conception was an intuitive idea (an intuitive inductive conception), which had to be followed by the search for its validity. Copernicus' notion was left to Kepler to validate. He had the *insight* that its validation would come deductively from astronomical evidence. His insight, which was proven correct, led to Newton's insight about gravity. His theory of gravity triggered – in turn – Einstein's intuition about relativity. Psychoanalysis was also the brainchild of an intuition. But Freud himself provided the most significant insights that proved it. His insights were instrumental in expanding the original intuitive conception that he had, and the bases for further intuitions followed by more useful insights. Different from the other great theories, psychoanalysis was initiated and evolved for more than half a century by the same person. Freud's intuitions and insights were more spectacular and productive than the rest of his disciples were able to provide. Hence, it is true to say that psychoanalysis was Freud's discovery and its theory was and still is essentially his.

During the long time Freud lived and worked on his theory, he made few substantial revisions to it. He seemed to have run out of steam in the very last few years of his life when he just applied his theory to aspects in the field. However, after his passing we did not receive any significant intuitions from other seemingly good psychoanalysts, and only very few insights that looked promising at the beginning (Melanie Klein, Bion, Lacan, and maybe Kohut). It is possible that it was not Freud himself who ran out of steam, but the theory as he left it. Another fact has to be considered. The new versions of psychoanalysis shed a shadow of doubt on the doctrine and weakened its status. However, something important has been missed in the puzzle of the weakened state of the theory of psychoanalysis at the present time. The recent changes in the humanities owe psychoanalysis the premise that anything human is subject to explorations and discoveries. The Freudian doctrine is a clear originator of our modern conceptions of the human being. Any modern human science has an aspect of Freudianism in it. Psychoanalysis is now permeating the life of the regular guy in the street and our attitudes towards everything human. Therefore, we should not miss that psychoanalysis has to evolve to catch up with the evolution, if not the revolution. It began in the humanities. It is common knowledge in most of the cultured world that a person's personality is basically structured and formed in childhood. This knowledge is still founded on functional evidence derived from passed observations. My endeavour is to revise this Freudian proposition by getting to is structural core and leave aside those functional observations. The functional meaning of those propositions was natural in a growing informative theory about the psyche and the individual (Fayek, 2015), but they became issues of contention when the information in them lost its novelty or its support by new observations. Some psychoanalysts suggested replacing them with others. In my opinion, the problem is not in the content of the theory of psychoanalysis, but the lack of a clear structural core.

Structuralism is defined in many ways, but I prefer to identify it relative to its antithesis: functionalism. The main objective in the preliminary stage of a human science was always gathering as many observations as possible, to build a comprehensive theory of causality. After that, scientists usually looked for comprehensive formula, which explains the abundant material they gathered. The first and most demanding task was to formulate an explanatory theory that would reduce the 'plenty' of information to 'few' rules. They usually achieved this by using a social phenomenon to explain another – i.e., making one a function of the other. For instance, in anthropology the anthropologist encountered many different familial formations in the different societies they visited and studied. After mastering the art of observing and classifying family types they tried to relate the familial structure to a common cause. Some found that the mode of production in that society could be a useful functional explanation. For instance, the tribe was a familiar functional organization. The tribe as the umbrella to its familiar branches gives the head of the tribe an absolute authority, which he could delegate to the heads of the branches. This functional system was essential to keep the property of the branches secure within the total property of the tribe. Theories continued to be functional in regard to finding causal explanations to the different social phenomena. But after years of recorded work and a plethora of studies, it became clear that functional theories miss something basic in their theorizing. Although it is true that familial types in all societies are functions of the mode of production there is no clear unified explanation for the existence of marriage as a social stipulation and marriage as the precondition of familial life. Everything that has been studied and explained had to be done by marriage. Thus, marriage is a precondition to those familial types. Functional thinking could not answer that question – at least in a general satisfying way. Levi-Strauss (1971) uncovered a basic rule in marriage of any marital system.

It is the regulation of the incestuous taboo. In other terms, all human societies have incestuous taboos, and marriage regulates that taboo and preserves it. Thus, marriage and its different specifications in different societies is the safeguard of the breakdown of the rules of incest. Therefore, the family is structurally the regulator of the incestuous taboo, which in turn functions as the guardian of the modes of production in each society. Marriage structures the society. Levi-Strauss called his approach Structural anthropology, as Piaget (1970) identified some of the structural psychologies before him. *The main attribute of a structural theory is bringing out the inner interrelationships of the theoretical formulations instead of exposing causal links between elements of the informative aspect of the theory*. It is curious that Freud (1912–1913) uncovered the significance of that taboo in relation to the origin of building the intrapsychical core of the human individual.

In terms of a psychoanalytic theory, a structural theory of psychoanalysis is one that is based on psychical processes: the representation of the *Ucs.*, instead of naming its content, and uncovering the working of the primary process instead of lifting the repression of objectionable urges or thought. In other terms, a functional psychoanalytic theory would be about protecting the ego from the pressures of the id, when the same thing expressed structurally would be: to decipher a metonymy in the patient's symptom in order to reconstruct previous incoherent and fragmented childhood memories.

A structural theory of psychoanalysis needs structural proposition to give it a comprehensive status and quality. For instance, the Oedipus complex, as Freud thought of it, came from his self-analysis (Letter, October 15, 1897c). He had it in mind all along as a manifestation of a general formative process emanating from the relationships between the parents and their offsprings' regarding infantile sexuality. He gave it the name of a Greek tragedy (1910h) and considered it universal. It was a functional proposition because he used it to explain a host of psychical phenomena, both normal and pathological. Evidently, the function it served then would not stand now, when we consider the changes in the role of the father in the family after the Second World War (1939–1945). Unless we conceive of its structural nature analysts would not consider it in their practice or theory, as it is actually happening now. The Oedipus is a proposition of the interfamilial dynamics at a certain time, which has a major impact on the formation of the intrapsychic. Thus, it is universal but could take different forms depending on the time and the society. Having said that, I believe it would be useful to make a distinction between intuitions and insights, because Freud's doctrine is founded on intuitions like the mixture of primary and secondary processes in every psychical phenomenon, and insights like symptoms, dreams, and parapraxes are structured the same. Intuitions are not repeatable; they stand out as something – as Freud has said – that does not come twice in a lifetime. They are, in terms of types of thinking, inductive thinking – i.e., eliciting a general principle from seemingly unrelated details. In terms of the content of inductive thinking ideas seem at first to be of no particular importance, but when they are properly arranged later they prove to be the bearers of limitless possibilities and unexpected discoveries. Because all great theories are borne within intuitions, they are unrepeatable and irreplaceable. Insights are about concrete issues that transpire after some concentrated deductive work. They provide material information, have concrete content, and look at first sight to be discoveries, but they are merely extensions of the intuitions. Therefore, when and if we keep Freud's intuitions in focus we will see that we could only revise them, while the insights they generated could with time fall behind. Freud's insight could be changed, dismissed, negated, while his intuitions are his unique stamp on the discovery of the human subject.

Psychoanalysis occupies a significant place in the tapestry of human sciences. It was the first to introduce two important contributions to those sciences. First, it complemented the cognitive theories of psychology in the nineteenth century with the concept of the unconscious, which eventually revealed that some mental processes happen a-consciously. The human subject didn't seem too complex to study anymore. It also put human sciences face to face with the need to explore the nature of the human subject, because it revealed aspects of the human subject that were, for centuries, framed in socio-religious conceptions that had little meaning or explanatory value. Those aspects relate to what evolution has changed in him, hence separated humans from the other species of sapiens, which vanished before our species dominated earth. Psychoanalysis demystified the human subject, so it changed the subject matter of all the humanities. The humanities owe psychoanalysis its modern subject matter. Human sciences progress in leaps and not in steps. A human scientist or an intuitive thinker could become suddenly aware of a human phenomenon, which has been taken for granted for a long time or did not seem to relate to anything in particular, and gains an explanation that could reveal its unexplored core configuration. For instance, Everett's observation (2012) showed that family structures in some primitive societies, based on the rules of incest, affect the usage of pronouns in the language of that society, and have a role in structuring the grammar of that language.

Once an intuition is out, other scientists of the humanities work on unfolding it into insightful details. They embark on a process of developing and expanding the issues raised by that intuition. Detailing the intuitive observation goes through a period of theorizing about the new gathered information. Gradually, those expansions slow down when the informative aspects of the original intuition reaches its limits. As a result, theoretical evolution in human sciences requires *periodical revisions* of its implicit propositions to stimulate the birth of new intuitions. This is the history of the theory of our origins; moving from the fictional and mythical stories as depicted in religions and expanded in theology, we went on in our present way to know their origins. Studying those changes in the developmental course of a human science requires tracing several intuitions of a number of thinkers, and the many insights they engendered, which sometimes expand over a long period of time making it difficult to specify – especially when the insights are distant from the intuitions that instigated them in the first place. Fortunately, this is not the case with psychoanalysis, because *reading Freud's text in its chronological sequence has the advantage of making one follows this man's exceptional mind weaving the psychoanalytic discovery; giving intuitions that we can see in hindsight their origins, getting false insights, correcting them – all that without losing his way towards an unidentified objective.* He had few major intuitions about the material he was dealing with, which led to noteworthy revisions of the theory and he was the one who did the revising. He also had several very significant insights that advanced his intuitions.[1] In revising the main Freudian propositions I will try to reveal the structural core of the conceptions in those propositions. However, in doing that I could probably deviate unintentionally from the basics of the propositions. Hopefully, reaching the structural core of the intuition would show me – and others – if I have deviated from the original discovery. After identifying the structural core of a proposition it will become possible to look at the original insights it generated and revise them to reconnect properly with that structural core of the intuitions. Previously (Fayek, 2013), I tried something similar by showing that Freud has built a principal *structural* theory of processes and meaning, which should replace his *functional* theory of abreaction and catharsis. I did that following a sequential line of evolution. In 2014, I attempted to revise the informative side of the theory (the functional theory) in order to reveal the structural core of psychoanalysis that could become its future; I did this in sections.

As a preliminary idea of my revisions I will show that the Freudian doctrine is a product of a very simple but extremely basic intuition, which permeated the rest of his intuitions. If there is anything new in my attempt it will be focusing attention on the nature of 'that foundational intuition' that was behind Freud conceiving of psychoanalysis. He averred it to Jones in a casual way and close to the end of his life. Jones wrote (1954):

> I asked him [Freud] once which were his favourites among his writings, and he fetched from the shelves *The Interpretation of Dreams* and the *Three Essays on the Theory of Sexuality* saying: "I hope one will soon be out of date [*The Three Essays*] through being generally accepted, but the other one should last longer." Then with a quiet smile, he added: "It seems to be my fate to discover only the obvious:[2] that children have sexual feelings, which every nurse-maid knows; and that night dreams are just as much a wish-fulfilment as day dreams." Shall we call this a catachrestic meiosis?
>
> (p. 384)

He was absolutely right. If there is a classic example of understating something, his statement of what fate apportioned for him is the best. Those two books were considered by Freud two separate insights: one is dreams are *wish fulfilment*, and the other is *infantile sexuality*. He did not understate the value of those two insights, but he did not notice that they were the outcome of one intuition, which is important to articulate and underscore now, because we will encounter this in all his works and we should not miss it in any attempt at revising the theory. When this insight is not present in an analyst's work the analyst is likely to have deviated from psychoanalysis. Until the time Freud came up with the theory of dreams, psychical phenomena were examined and explained as isolated ontological entities that could have explanations but not necessarily meanings. Thus, there was no notion of common ground shared by them and they were treated as isolated states. Freud had the intuition that psychical phenomena are *manifestations* of something latent – i.e., they have meanings within their manifest content. This intuition inferred that a latent content has been transformed into a manifest state; therefore, the manifest aspect of the phenomena, which is the psychical phenomena, is a result of a process which constitutes that transformation. The transformation of the latent is the birth of the psychical. In other terms, the manifest dream is a product of a process that transformed 'some latent content' into the reported dream. This sounds now like a banal discovery, but when we go back to before Freud we would notice its significance. Dreams were taken as premonitions or considered nonsensical. Hysterical patients were sent to health spas that had some water source for a 'cure'. The link between the manifest (hysterical malaise) and the *cure* is unfathomable in that kind of psychiatry. Freud's intuition about the manifest, the latent, and the process that transforms the former into the latter created the duality of manifest/latent and generated several other dualities. The duality of manifest/latent came with the dualities of condensation (metaphor) and displacement (metonymy), the primal (Ur)/primary (Primare), phylogenetic/genetic. However, Freud's dualities were dissimilar to Descartes's duality because it postulated a link and not separation between the deuce. Thus, other fields of the humanities adopted Freud's duality as it happened in the field of language where the terms of signifier/signified and contiguity/similarity took a new perspective. In the link between those dualities and the process of transformation resided the subjects of interest in a host of other sciences.

Freud's intuition implied the existence of a particular psychological process that initiates and creates the way the transformation of the latent into a manifest will happen. The central part in the intuition was identifying that psychological process. He made a very peculiar but fortunate connection between Breuer's conception of *Free* and *Bound* neurological energy, which was used in the *Studies on Hysteria* (1895d)[3] a cognitive equivalent to that duality. He made a distinction between a *primary* cognitive process, which has the mental function in a state of flux, and a secondary process that is responsible for organizing thought processes according to the demands of reality. From this starting point the study of the psychical phenomena has begun. The transformation of the latent content into a manifest phenomenon happens under the influence of the primary process but has finally to abide by the demands of the secondary process. Considering that the psychical is a manifest that has a latent meaning was paramount in the psychoanalytic discovery. Just as a reminder, the notion of the day residues and the infantile wish as the constituents of the dream and its format as wish fulfilment is the same as the precipitating factors and childhood experiences as the constituents of symptoms and character disorders. The notion of the *after-*

effect is anchored in the intuition of the manifest and the latent with the primary process interceding between the two.

Freud's publications before the two insights (1892–1895) were showing a budding interest in the sexual aetiology of hysteria. However, his publication with Breuer in 1895 and his correspondence with Fliess (1887–1904) show a subtle but very determined change in his outlook on the role of sexuality in hysteria. He became curious about the structure of the phenomena associated with sexual life – i.e., the nature of sexuality encountered in the psychoneuroses. He was also curious about the psychical structures that could explain the fate of the repressed (1894a, 1896c). He had the insight that dreams will be the road to discovering the issues pertaining to sexuality in the psychoneuroses. He wrote to Fliess saying (January 3–4, 1899): "I have not yet finished the dream-book. If I wait a little longer, I shall be able to describe the mental process in the dreams in such a way that it also includes the process in the formation of hysterical symptoms." This was a clear indication that he had a link in mind between dreams and sexuality in the neuroses. On October 11 of the same year he says to Fliess: "A theory of sexuality maybe the immediate successor to the dream book." This did not happen because as he said a few months later (letter, January 26, 1900): "I am putting together material for the theory of sexuality and waiting till some spark can set what I have collected ablaze." The two insights were obviously connected but the connection was not clear in Freud's mind, because he was not yet close to finding out how the primary process connects the manifest sex with a known content.

The significance of the subtle change in Freud's interest was far reaching. First, he became familiar with the workings of the primary process in forming the manifest dream. He knew its role was creating confusing manifestations of the psychical phenomena, which 'conceals' the latent. He called that repression at the time. Second, he "somehow" realized that the primary processes are not pathological, as such, but could cause psychopathology to form under certain circumstances; as they could also create some great and healthy non-pathological phenomena. He previously indicated in a letter to Fliess that "a satisfactory general understanding of neuro-psychotic disturbance is not possible unless one can make a connection with clear presuppositions about normal psychical processes" (May 25, 1895). Sure enough, he spent five years during that critical period in his practice studying and writing about the normal: slips of the tongue, dreams, jokes, and screen memories, with a few short accounts on psychopathology (1901b, 1905c). He worked on that before the spark that ignited the book on sexuality came by (1899a, 1901b, 1905c). When the spark came he realized that the concept of *Trieb* would have the solution to the problem of sexuality, and he found the link between sexuality and its role in in psychical life in general. He no longer looked at sexuality as a simple urge but as a *Trieb* that has a *source*, *pressure*, *aim* and *object*. He was able to connect his curiosity about the varied sexual manifestation in the psychoneuroses and his intuition about the manifest and the latent. *Sexuality was a translation of a link between the aim and the object of the sexual urge*. Additionally, adult sexuality was manifesting infantile sexuality in different degrees and forms of immaturity.

The intuition of the manifest and the latent mediated by the primary process is the first, the starting point in the discovery of psychoanalysis, and the most fundamental in the discovery. Dreams, symptoms, transference, after effect, narcissism, art, war, social phenomena, etc., have manifest and latent sides, with the same primary process connecting them. Thus, deviating from the original, traditional, classical, Freudian theory could happen in two ways: first, ignoring the duality of the manifest and latent, and the working of the primary process in linking them, suggesting a different way of looking at psychical phenomena; and second, coming to a different conception as a more fundamental latent and better one than Freud's or the classical one. Those two possibilities boil down to either deviating from a basic intuition, which would create a major and obvious departure from psychoanalysis, or deviating from one or more of the insights in the theory, which would result in discrepancies in the conclusions we reach, but not a major departure from the theory. For instance, the shift from the centrality of the intrapsychical in the formation of all psychical phenomena is a breach of the original intuition about the structure of the psychical phenomena. Though, dealing with narcissism as a problem in the formation of the identity rather than a phenomenon of libidinal nature would not be a departure from the theory because the rest of the theory remains intact. However, it is impossible to revise some of Freudian doctrine without seeming to be deviating.

The limits of deviating from the Freudian doctrine

How much deviation from Freud's doctrine is permissible before we are no longer Freudians or even psychoanalysts? I think the best yardstick to measure deviating from classical psychoanalysis is Freud's own yardstick. He revised his own theory four obvious times, and the theory still remained intact and kept its 'Freudian' trademark. If we could identify the reasons for his revisions of the theory and what the revisions did to maintain its integrity we could certainly learn from that what we could do in revising the theory, so that it would not lag behind. We know that – at least – Freud never ceased to have insights, and some of them were definitely opposing previous ones. His theory of anxiety remained the same from the period of hypnosis until 1926. Anxiety in that theory was a *symptom* of the 'repressed' trying to break through the defensive mechanisms, thus threating the stability of the ego. The new theory (1926d) reversed the relationship between anxiety and the repressed: anxiety was no longer a symptom of the repressed but the instigator of symptom formations – i.e., it became the originator of the defences and not their product. The new insight, which revised the theory in a major way, still maintained the link between anxiety and symptom formation. The subtle, but an actual reason for this revision, was the negative effect the structural point of view had on the 'dynamic' nature of the psychoanalytic theory. *The Ego and the Id* (1923b) reified the process of symptom formation, depicting it a mechanical interplay of agencies that stand for aspects of the subject. Some of Freud's other revisions looked like doing away completely with a central conception in the theory, and replacing it with another. For instance, Freud replaced the *Triebhaft* duality of sexual vs. self-preservation with the new duality of life vs. death (1920g). Nevertheless, the concept of *Trieb* was maintained and its upshot concept of *representation* remained as the base of the psychical phenomena. As mentioned earlier, there is a difference between deviating from a Freudian insight like anxiety, and deviating from an intuition like *Trieb* and representation. The consistency of the Freudian theory comes from the continuance of the intuitions, *in addition to* the ease of changing or getting rid of some irrelevant or incorrect insights.

Before 1914 Freud's theory was a theory of repression (forgetting) and catharsis (remembering). Everywhere one looked at that theory with all its rich concepts like libido, defence mechanisms, the dynamic unconscious, sexual *Trieb*, etc. one would have realized that it was a theory of 'explaining' psychical phenomena. Psychoanalysis was a theory of functions: the unconscious a function of repression, repression a function of defence, defence functions as holding back disturbing memories from affecting the neurotic; thus the duality of sexual *Trieb* vs. self-preservation *Trieben* fitted that type of theorizing. The theory of catharsis managed to turn the irrationality of the neuroses into an explainable and rational matter, by a system of causal explanations. We could add that psychoanalysts were under the impression that they have a theory of 'content' and they were dealing with material issues. The unconscious was a *substantive* entity, not merely of an adjectival quality, thus they both echoed Freud's allegory of making the unconscious conscious, as a mantra. The ego was to them a location and a place where certain things happen.

In 1914 Freud made a very significant revision of the theory. He wrote his paper on Narcissism (1914c). In that paper the libido concept, the cornerstone of the catharsis theory, underwent two important changes. First, the division of sexual-instinct and ego-instinct (self-preservation) was pushed aside to give way to a new insight: psychical life starts with the activity of one libido, which branches out to invest in the self and in its objects too. Second, the nature of the libido (sexual or life-preserving) is no more an issue; rather, the issue is what happens to it when it differentiates into ego-libido and object-libido. This revision of the theory changed the old insight about repressing the objectionable urges or thoughts, and replaced it with a new insight. The libido was no longer the means by which we explain psychical phenomena; it became subject to explaining. Narcissism replaced repression as the dominion where libidinal activity was enacted; yet still as an explanatory concept.

Freud realized that keeping psychoanalysis captive of a functional theory based on libidinal cathecting, contents, and causation demanded a correction. The correction came as a result of his insight that the conception of psychical phenomena goes beyond forgetting and abreacting. The one libido that could be invested in the self or its objects revealed that the psychical has an infrastructure composed of the dynamics of ego-libido and object-libido, which are interacting and creating the subject. Freud was moving towards a new field of insights about the structuring processes of the intrapsychic. The main issue was: *what is the beginning of being a psychological being?* How do we evolve to become the human being that we are? In better words: psychoanalysis was no more the search for the bad repressed things, and to make them material for consciousness so that they could be dealt with. It became the act of discovering what decides that something deserves and demands repression.[4] *Freud revised the functional formulation of the psyche and replaced it with the structural nature of the psyche!* By doing that, he changed the theory from a theory of psychical phenomena as entities that needed explaining to a theory of psychical processes that need analysing.

Evading building a psychological theory on a functional basis might look like deviating from the psychoanalytic theory, because structural concepts bypass the content of the subject and configure the processes which build the psychical nature of the subject. Freud's functional concept of narcissism makes narcissism a function of a type of libidinal investment (interest), while as a structural concept, narcissism makes the distinction between the subject and his objects as the basis of all the manifestations of narcissism. The attempts made by the contemporary schools of psychoanalysis to improve the theory of psychoanalysis by replacing its functional concepts with other 'better' functional ones resulted in making many other changes to the original doctrine and ended up with distorting it completely. Kohut's (1987) changing the subject of the analysis from the guilty person to the tragic person resulted in changes to the concept of narcissism, and turning it into a 'condition' of pathology, giving birth to the diagnosis of narcissistic disorders, and looking at the act of psychoanalysis as the restoration of a narcissistic self. The structure of narcissism in the Freudian doctrine is found in the interplay of identification that would differentiate between the subject and his objects; it is not a condition but rather *the state of affairs in the human condition* (see Chapter 4). Freud realized that libidinal investments, whether in the self or in the objects, deserve exploring because they constitute the way we become the human beings that we are. Structuralism in the humanities (ideographic sciences) is an advanced point in understanding humanistic phenomena. However, there is always the chance that a structural quality in a human phenomenon could become calcified after using it for a period and turning it into content, it becomes a relic of sorts. For instance, Lacan's ingenious intuition that language and the unconscious are similarly structured highlighted the distinction between speech (parole) and language (langue) and helped him to arrive at his maxim of 'the unconscious is structured as language'. It did not take long for that maxim to become an epithet and a relic in its own right. The placement of the primary process which is central in that arrangement has almost vanished. Even Lacan sometimes fell in love with his own intuitions and turned them into fossils.

Narcissism, as Freud suggested, has a primary state and a secondary state. The significance of that insight is very much part of the foundational intuition of the manifest and the latent and the centrality of the process of transformation and representation. As a result of this intuition Freud had to revise three basic concepts: repression (primary repression and repression proper), the theory of *Trieb* (reversal of aim, and displacement of object), and of the unconscious (a systemic unconscious and a dynamic unconscious that creates the preconscious). He examined those three psychical concepts and brought out their structural characteristics and their makeup. The rest of his work on the psychoanalytic theory after shifting gears from functions to strictures was mainly correction of the catharsis theory, with some very novel insight such as the ones in the papers on 'Negation' (1925h) and the 'Uncanny' (1919h).

Some analysts missed the point completely in regard to Freud's revisions, or what is called in the psychoanalytic circle 'turning points'. They took the three revisions as new (better) versions of the original catharsis theory, or merely some improvement to them. This way they believed, justifiably so, that if they could come up with another more *interesting* functional theory they could displace or replace the Freudian doctrine. Self-psychology was the first deviation from Freud's doctrine although it came from within psychoanalysis. Relational psychology (Stephen & Aron, 1999) and intersubjectivity (Stolorow & Atwood, 2002) are also deviations from psychoanalysis, but they came from outside psychoanalysis and were forced on it. They refuted its basic intuition that the 'intrapsychical' governs both the interpersonal and the intersubjective. Some analysts such as Green (*The Work of the Negative*, 1999b), Laplanche ('The theory of seduction and the problem of the other', 1997), Bion (1963), Matte-Blanco (1975) and a few others, came up with structural conceptions of some of Freud's basic concepts. Their works were extensions of the Freudian doctrine and applications of his inductive thinking in examining those concepts. They were insights in the same structural vane, not refutations of its basic premise.

The Freudian doctrine comprises his intuitions and his insights that emanated from those intuitions. His insights were subject to his revisions and are subject to new revisions. As long as they derive from his intuitions and are corroborated by them they could still be revisions of the Freudian propositions. But if the new insights have their own source (like some interpersonal theories), they would not and should not usurp the term 'psychoanalysis'. Freud's theory has the attribute of superior theories like Copernicus's heliocentric theory. Copernicus was off in calculating the orbits of the planets around the sun. Kepler corrected them from examining planetary charts made by Brahe, the astronomer. Newton changed Kepler's astronomical method into mathematical laws. Einstein did not change Newton's laws of gravity but explained them differently. None of those changes refuted that the sun is the centre of our planetary system; they only made sense of it. Freud's theory is of the same nature; it could be corrected in some of its details, refuted in some of its insights, and be added to with some new ones – even from other human sciences – without losing its integrity and uniqueness.

I will try my approach in revising six Freudian propositions, which cover the main issues in the theory. I will try to show that uncovering the structural core of the intuition in the proposition maintains its viability, but requires revising some of its insights and their internal dynamics. Hopefully, this exercise would encourage other analysts to do something similar so psychoanalysis would overcome its present stagnation. The interest in unfolding the main psychoanalytic propositions will also stimulate the interest of the other branches of the humanities in building a new and more comprehensive view of the human subject.

Notes

1 Freud's insights have been very consistent with his intuition; a characteristic we find missing in the insights of the contemporary schools of psychoanalysis.
2 This is the true nature of the intuition, which is discovering in the most obvious its most important attribute.
3 This change does not mean anything regarding the function of the super ego. On the contrary, discovering what is destined to be repressed *could* be interpreted as the process that discovered a new function of the Ego.
4 Strachey called Freud's three papers – *Trieben* and their vicissitudes, Repression, and the Unconscious–metapsychological papers. The three papers have nothing to do with the topographic, dynamic, and economic points of view, which are the framework of metapsychology. Strachey's misnaming of the three papers attests to misunderstanding their place in the evolution of the theory (1957a).

1

THE OEDIPUS COMPLEX

Keep or abandon?

Freud's conception of the Oedipus complex was a shocking psychoanalytic discovery because it was a condensation of all the fragmentary and disconnected repressed material at that time. It comprised the sexual in its most unacceptable form, which was incestuous. It also stipulated that the intrapsychical is structured around the dynamics of the forbidden and asocial. It depicted the child, who was considered till then just an innocent and ignorant entity as a 'being' who could be very much different in his intentions and desires from the moral person he was believed to be. Most of all, the Oedipus challenged all the moral convictions that humanity took centuries to build and instil in people.[1] The Oedipus shocked the world because it was a good conception to explain most of the previous discoveries and open the eyes to new unexpected ones. It was considered in the first few decades in the history of psychoanalysis as a conclusive psychoanalytic statement. The Oedipus stood out in the psychoanalytic literature as a yardstick to measure the deviation from the essence of psychoanalytic insights.

Psychoanalysts who were trained in the 1950s and 1960s never questioned the status of the Oedipus complex in the theory. There was a minor difference about that status between the Europeans and the North Americans. In Europe the Oedipus had an *explicit* place in the theory and the psychoanalytic way of thinking. It was hallowed and maintained a significant place, demonstrated by Klein's unsuccessful attempt to give it an existence in the first year of life. In France, it was kept as the measure of classism versus Lacanianism, although Lacan did not lack the ability to show that the Oedipus has a better explication in his theory than in the classical one. In the USA, the preoccupation with ego-psychology pushed the Oedipus to the background, but kept it as an *implicit* conception. Although very few analysts, mostly of a classical bent, and only in some circles in Europe (for instance, J. Kristeva) still talk about the

Oedipus complex occasionally (Crownfield, 1992) this conception does not have a significant place in the theory of psychoanalysis anymore, as the current psychoanalytic literature shows. Therefore, the Oedipus is no longer one of the main staples of psychoanalytic training; nevertheless, we can hardly find in the literature any open criticism of that conception. *I treat the conception of the Oedipus as a Freudian proposition and not just a conception for reasons I will present shortly and in the revision of that proposition.*

The proposition of the Oedipus

It was one of Freud's early intuitions that came to him first through his process of self-analysis and later he extrapolated it clinically in an intelligent way. In a letter to Fliess (October 15, 1897c) he says:

> I have found, in my own case too, falling in love with the mother and jealousy of the father, and I now regard it as universal event of childhood … if that is so, we can understand the riveting power of *Oedipus Rex*, in spite of all the objections raised by reason against its presupposition of destiny.

Mentioning the *Oedipus Rex* in the letter came as a weak link between his insight of the interfamilial dynamics and the Greek myth. In a paper, thirteen years later (1910h) Freud turns that particular interfamilial setting into a complex – moving it from the universal, which means in a way 'usual', to the problematic and the seat of possible psychopathology. In the next thirteen years Freud went back to the Oedipus complex occasionally. But, he made it a central piece in the *Ego and the Id* (1923b). In that work one could get confused about the significance of the complex to psychoanalysis, because in some places he explained it in terms of ego-psychology, and in other places he explained ego-psychology using it. He said: "*The broad general outcome of the sexual phase dominated by the Oedipus complex may, therefore, be taken to be the forming of a precipitate in the ego, consisting of these two identifications* [Father-identification and mother-identification] *in some way united with each other*" (ibid., 34). In those words, the Oedipus complex is the creator of the agencies of ego-psychology. But shortly after he says: "By setting up the ego ideal, the ego has mastered the Oedipus complex" (ibid., 36), which makes the new agencies responsible for the case of the Oedipus complex. There are other similar confusing statements in that regard, which in taking them seriously, we can conclude that the Oedipus complex was a misnomer of a very significant Freudian intuition. For now, I would say that his choice of the Greek Myth as the *name* of the interfamilial dynamics was unfortunate, although the *structure* of that myth was and still is merely an insight of the Greek myth. However, neither structuralism nor any structural analysis of the myth was available to Freud or later until Levi-Strauss had done it (1963).

Freud continued using the Oedipus as a conception that bordered the universal and the individual on one side and the normal and the pathological on the other. This intuition led him to think more, specifically about the destiny of the complex, because it could be the base of the normal and the abnormal. He talked about the types of dissolution of the Oedipus (Freud, 1924d) as the basis of creating the subject's character. Nevertheless he says:

> Although the majority of human beings go through the Oedipus complex as an individual experience, it is nevertheless a phenomenon which is determined and laid down by heredity and which is bound to pass away according to a programme when the next pre-ordained phase of development sets in. This being so, it is of no great importance what the occasions are which allow this to happen, or, indeed, whether any such occasion be discovered at all.
>
> (1924d, 174)

In light of the obvious hesitation he had about committing to one point of view about his intuition, we have to ask: what made the Oedipus complex the most popular conception in the history of the psychoanalytic discovery, and then fade away to oblivion? Why do some psychoanalysts – at that time, and still now – consider this a landmark conception? Would we be deviating from the Freudian doctrine if we denied or even just ignored it?

After Freud's death the conflict between Anna Freud and Melanie Klein was – in a major part – about the Oedipus complex (though it was also a personal conflict). The most basic difference between the two stands was the place of sexuality in the formation of the Oedipus situation. Freud and his daughter referred the Oedipus complex to the role of sexuality in creating a conflictual situation between father and son (daughter and mother). The Oedipus to them had a sexual content. Klein gave the Oedipus an earlier start that preceded the emergence of any infantile sexuality. It was based on the presence of the father within the relationship with the mother as soon as the infant is able to relate to full objects (the depressive phase), after the part-object stage (the schizoid phase). In Great Britain the Oedipus remained an ontological entity within clinical arguments between the three schools of the British society (the Freudian, the Kleinian and the independent group).

In France, the adoption of psychoanalysis by the intellectual community saved it from a narrow clinical understanding, obliged psychoanalysts to open their minds to the new rich comprehension of its theory, and fertilized psychoanalysis with the *thinkers*' flare of understanding the Oedipus myth. The birth of structuralism as a new trend of thinking, which emerged with the new works in linguistics, encouraged the human science people to 'structuralize' the phenomena they were studying. It was most obvious in anthropology in the work of Levi-Strauss (1978). He eventually structuralized the study of myths (1955) and the Oedipus myth in particular. He concluded that the myth of Oedipus "provides a kind of logical tool which relates the original problem-born from one or born from two? ... born from different or born from the same" (1963, 216).

The structuring of the myth this way puts sex within the interfamilial dynamics rather than as an isolated desire or urge. The structure of the myth reveals that if the child kills the father (in Freud's version of the complex, eliminating him) he will discover that the woman he married was his mother (in Freud's version, the woman he wants for himself is *a* mother). Lago and Thompson conclude (1996): "It is clear that analysis of this kind will quickly find itself reaching to the level of those unconscious categories of thought which underpin and formulate our total view of the world" (17). The structural understanding of the myth suggests that sexuality is not its motivating force but in fact is resultant of the familial structure. It has nothing to do with a sexual desire for the mother or a murderous wish towards the father. It pertains to the interfamilial situation in which the child's identity is defined by realizing his position between the man and the woman in that family. The Oedipus, structurally speaking, is the natural childhood event in which the subject's identity meets its different possibilities of formation, and not – as Freud originally presumed – a conflictual set up of the family. It later became the structuring force of the human attribute – the structuring force that creates and builds the *impossible* within human subject, which is an intrinsic aspect of human nature. Analysts-thinkers in France weaved the Oedipus into this new insight about the subject.

In the USA, the situation was quite different. The Oedipus complex was not denied but had no significant place in a non-dynamic psychology because ego-psychology precluded the interest in the processes that lead to the formation of the sense of identity: the ego as an agency that replaced the pronoun *I*. Analysts felt more at ease talking about the agency instead of the speaking of the subject. The literature on the subject shows the same sense of confusion which infiltrates Freud's writings about the subject. There was a tendency to separate the interfamilial core of the complex from its link to the myth. Eisold (2008) examined the result of replacing the myth of Oedipus with that of Orestes and the effect that would have had on understanding the interfamilial dynamics in terms of succeeding the parents instead of conflicting with them. Clark (2009) suggested the same thing, but added an interesting angle to that replacement. She suggested that if Freud opted to put Orestes as the core of interfamilial structure instead of Oedipus, psychoanalysis and even Western society would have had a different outlook on the psychological understanding of family structure – and maybe its function too. This viewpoint presumes that Freud has 'chosen' and determined a name for the family structure, not that family structure made Freud revive Oedipus drama.

There was a gradual relinquishing of the Oedipus complex for two underlying and unclearly articulated reasons. The first was that neither its universality nor its generality in the Western type of family is verified or verifiable. The complex was seen by many analysts as an exaggeration of some preconceived ideas. Freedman and Downey (1995) pointed out that the complex comprises two component parts that could be considered separately. They suggested that the part about the incestuous wish is unconfirmed, while the competitive part with the parent of the same sex is feasible. Nonetheless, this part should be considered within the biological differences between the sexes because it could be just a separate line of development. Kancyper (2006) suggested that it is necessary to leave behind a limited reading of the Oedipus nuclear complex and pay attention to Laius and Jocasta's histories and traumatic experiences with the murder of their son Oedipus. He added that the narrative of the myth creates phantasies made of passions and beliefs, scandals and secrets, which give shape to repeatable Oedipal structure in each individual subject – a structure that articulates the effects of the narcissistic and fraternal dynamic and may determine the subject's fate. Thus, the sanctity of the myth could be ignored to allow other views of its function. Masling et al. (2002) questioned the Oedipus from a different point of view: does it account equally for boys (men) and girls (women)? They reviewed the literature carefully to imply that the psychoanalytic bias towards the sexes is partially due to adopting the classical Oedipus complex and that bias for males has a direct effect on understanding the interfamilial structure. The second unarticulated reason for relinquishing the Oedipus complex was the radical and evident changes in the stereotypical perception of females in the society.

Blass (1994), in reviewing the Dora case, decided that Freud was wrong in concluding that the patient was experiencing the difficulties of a 'positive Oedipus position'. Green (1993) on the other hand used the Freudian concept of the Oedipus to support one of his clinical concepts – the dead mother. He concluded that it is a structuring function of the psychical apparatus similar to the functions attributed to the dead father in Freud's *Totem and Taboo* (1912–1913), and places the dead mother side by side with the Oedipus. The literature on the Oedipus complex is clearly undecided on whether it is the actual situation we encounter in the formation of the family or if it was just a fortunate (or unfortunate) choice of Greek myth to describe it. However, the most significant push to retire the Oedipus complex came from outside psychoanalysis. It came from anthropology and sociology.

Malinowski (1955) concluded from his anthropological studies that the Oedipus is not a universal complex, and it is simply a concern of Western culture because in the *avunculate* structure the mother's brother takes the father's status and function in interfamilial structure despite the presence of the biological father in the family. This familial type suggests that the universality of the Oedipus is not conditional on the presence of the biological father. Therefore, to decide if it is replaced with something else we have to examine its significance away from its content, because it seems that the biological link with two biologically different parents as Levi-Strauss clarified earlier (1963, 16), and the sexual content involved, make it too functional and concrete to fit within a structural theory of the subject. Family and family structure are very old social concepts (Frazer, 2012). They were recognized as one of the important social instruments in shaping and developing a child. However, before Freud proposed the Oedipus complex there was no conception of what takes place in the family (if there even was a conception of something taking place) to make those things happen. Freud's insight – limited as it was to the middle-class European family of the nineteenth century – was not about the Oedipus complex but about the existence of psychological interplay of forces that result in influencing the development of kids, till adulthood. In other words, Freud had the intuition that the relationship between father, mother and child has an operational influence in child rearing. His choice of the Oedipal model should not conceal the key idea that family dynamics have a structural core. Thus, the Oedipus was convenient and a relevant formation that could give it a structure. It also defines – in a familiar way – the interfamilial dynamics and what we deal with clinically.

The Oedipus complex, with the fundamental changes psychoanalysis initiated in the society, lost its sexual content and became less culturally coloured. It looks as if it faded away; yet confirming that would be a misleading reading of the literature. The best example of that change is Lacan's dealing with it within the tendency to liberate it from its sexual stigma. He says (1979):

> We submit that the most normalizing situation in the early experience of the modern subject, in the condensed form represented by the conjugal family, is linked to the fact that the father is representative, the incarnation, of a symbolic function which concentrates in itself those things most essential in other cultural structures: Namely, the tranquil, or rather, symbolic, enjoyment , culturally determined and established, of the mother's love, that is to say, of the pole of which the subject is linked by a bond that is irrefutably natural.
>
> (422–423)

The undeniable necessity of a structuring modality for building the individual's identity would have forced analysts to *unconsciously* search for a replacement for the Oedipus. Whether it is projective identification, defence mechanism, good mothering, accepting the lack, or defining the desire (wish) of the other, etc., there is no psychoanalysis without a replacement for the Oedipus, simply because the subject matter, at least in its clinical aspects, relates to the familial conditions that build the intrapsychic organization. Without an ontological concept of such an organizing principle we cannot do any clinical work because our work is to introduce that organizing principle to replace the disorganized intrapsychic. Hence, we have to know what and how the intrapsychical is supposed to be organized. The replacement of the Oedipus is the key to what the school of psychoanalysis tried and failed to do. Freud put his finger on a central conception in psychoanalytic work though he formalized it in a way that needed a great deal of correction. Laplanche and Pontalis say (1973):

> The Oedipus complex is not reducible to an actual situation – to actual influence exerted by the parental couple over the child. Its efficacy derives from the fact that it brings into play a proscriptive agency (the prohibition against incest) which bars the way to naturally sought satisfaction and

> forms an indissoluble link between *wish* and law (a point which Jacque Lacan has emphasized).
>
> (286)

So, it is replaceable, and was replaced.

There are three issues to mention about Freud's conception of the Oedipus complex. He discovered it through his *auto-analysis* – i.e., it has a personal stamp on it. In order to introduce it to the theory as a psychoanalytical issue he gave it the metaphorical representation derived from Sophocles' play of *Oedipus Rex*, hence the impersonal name came about. Freud's subjective experience in his own family was a starting point, but analysts were able for years to find it in their clinical work, and to explicate its meaning and demonstrate its theoretical importance (see Bion in his *Learning from Experience*, 1962). Freud's explication of the Oedipus complex is founded on an arbitrary link he created between the myth and his understanding of the interfamilial dynamics. In his conception he suggested a desire for the mother and jealousy of the father, which, if both exist, could be because it is the fate of all boys and girls in the family although in different forms. The myth became the reference to the actual experience after having been chosen by Freud to *represent* it. It was not clear at first that the Oedipus, as stated in Freud's version, will not continue – as is – to be the main formative episode in the development of the intrapsychic. Thus, he anticipated that there will be different outcomes to its dissipation and resolution, showing in the type of consolidation of events that shape the level of maturity and mental health in individual. Freud built his theory of social evolution in *Totem and Taboo* (1912–1913) on an early hypothetical social event (the murder of the father) using again the Oedipus myth in another capacity to deduce from it the social equivalent of the structuring function of Oedipus in the individual. The complex was sort of a master key to several problems, but it could not have lasted unrevised for long.

The Oedipus: penis envy and the castration complex

The Oedipus complex defined the interfamilial dynamics and led – in a natural way – to wondering about the psychological experiences of male and female children in their interaction with their parents until they resolved that complex. Better, what would dealing with the 'basically' forbidden desires result in, in deciding the resolution of the Oedipus complex? Freud's response to that query was once again confusing. He relied on a relatively sensible basis to come up with answers: *On the sexual theories of children* (1908c). Sexual issues are usually discussed with children in response to their curiosity, either to the limits of their curiosities or to limit those curiosities. Children have limited abilities to understand properly what is discussed with them. Yet, all children show that they notice the significance of sexuality in the relationship between the parents, and in the family in general. Children end up creating their own *theories* about sexuality. Freud stated that his sources for infantile sexual theories were: 1. general observations that is common in any society; 2. conscious memories of adult psychoneurotic patients about their childhood; and 3. unconscious memories translated into conscious manifestations in psychoneurotic conditions. That paper – as Strachey said in his note about it – "launched a quite remarkable quantity of new ideas for the first time on the world" (ibid., 207). One central idea in that rich revelation of infantile sexuality was the importance of the penis in the resolution of the Oedipus complex for both boys and girls.

It was inevitable for Freud to examine the resolution of that complex to give the interfamilial dynamics its proper structuring significance. The resolution was implicitly present in the sexual theories of children about the penis, which relates to the concept of narcissism in a very important way. For now, I would say that two insights emerged from Freud's effort to put together a comprehensive outlook on the Oedipus: *Castration anxiety* in the boy and what he called then *penis envy* in the girls. Those two 'fantasies' remained very central in Freud's many other conceptions, and he considered them the bedrock of the termination of any psychoanalytic process (1937c). Lacan, until the 1950s, was close to Freud's original conception of the Oedipus complex especially in regard to its reconstructive function in the family scene. But, in his seminars of 1955–1956 he went off on a tangent about the Oedipus making a basic link between it and his troika of phantasy, imaginary, and the real. The complex became the hub of an extensive system and conceptualizations like the phallus, the imaginary father, the fantasized phallus and several others that are not relevant to talk about here.

Castration anxiety was basically a speculation that came from Freud's assumption that all children, boys and girls, attach certain fantasies to the existence and non-existence of the penis in themselves and in their parents. They construct theories that pertain to how it could be there in boys and not in girls. He assumed that the preoccupation with that issue generates anxiety in the boys about the possibility of losing the penis, and in the girls the anxiety of already having lost it, and hoping to get a substitute. Those two insights, based on the intuition of the Oedipus complex, were supposed to explain the psychodynamics of complex clinical phenomena – such as neurotic competitiveness, phobias, some sexual perversions, inhibitions – and explain a number of non-clinical phenomena that relate to humiliation and pride, loss and gain, victory and defeat, etc. They stood as metaphors of castration (and of avoiding it), its actual happening and the hope for remedying its effect. The problem with this approach, which we have seen in the conception of the Oedipus complex, was using castration anxiety, on the one hand, as an ontological entity in its own right, and on the other as an explanation of other phenomena. For example, Freud explained castration anxieties as a product of the child's discovery of the anatomical difference between boys and girls. In another context he explained inhibitions as manifestation of castration anxiety. Freudian literature on the issue of castration anxiety is not clear about whether castration anxiety exists and causes other phenomena to exist, or whether it is a manifestation of other existing processes. Point in fact: Freud's indecisiveness was because, when he positioned castration anxiety within the Oedipus complex, he used it to interpret the two different ways adopted by the boy and the girl in resolving its conflict. Castration anxiety was not a discovery of an ontological entity, but an insight that explains matters that the Oedipus complex creates in the final structure of the narcissism.

Castration was an issue from the beginning: does the boy really fear an actual castration or is it, to him, a metaphor for the father's dominance? Analysts differed widely about that issue, yet aside from the early pioneers they tended to downplay its impact as a reality in the child's mind. Rangell (1991), for instance, refused considering it a metaphor and emphasized that it is – at a certain phase of development – a pathological belief operating unconsciously in the child's mind. He said that it equals separation anxiety but the wider range of the derivatives of separation anxiety overtook the attention of clinicians about the derivatives of castration anxiety. On the opposite side of the spectrum we find Lacan (1957–1958) relating the complex to the issue of the lack of, and imaginary, phallus to make it more of an issue of the different castrations of the parties involved in the Oedipus triangle.

Freud mentioned *penis envy* in the context of children's theories about anatomical genital differences between the sexes. He paid attention to the girl being possibly envious of her brother for having *that* thing that she does not have. It was a *deduction* not based on solid direct children's observations, but almost a 'sensible' assumption. This deduction marked Freud's conception of female sexuality in general. He stipulated that the female attitude towards males originates in her childhood discovery of the anatomical distinction of the male's genitals. This insight evolved into a theory of femininity that has little to say about women but only about women's relationships with men. Penis envy is a strange conception in the theory of psychoanalysis. It aroused so much debate about issues that are not relevant to psychoanalysis as such, yet put the whole theory in question regarding its biases and its validity. Even though it no longer has a place in understanding female sexuality, it still continues to set a heavy shadow on the psychoanalytic interpretation of the male–female relationship. It is odd, because since it was first suggested in 1908 and all through its course of development until 1923, and with the emergence of its derivatives such the concept of 'phallic mothers' and 'castrating females', little attention was paid to an implicit misconception of it. It came as an *insight* that was a counterpart to the male castration anxiety; it was not a discovery in its own right about female sexuality but a 'logical' speculation derived from male sexuality: *females – in early psychoanalysis – were what males were not*. Before we go any further we should keep in mind two things: Freud assumed that the girl's envy of her brother, as he put it, came as matter-of-fact, and an anticipated (hypothetical) reaction to discovering the anatomical difference between them. He considered envy a natural thing to happen to the girl when she noticed the difference. He did not have any doubt about the universality of that envy. Second, he must have listened in his clinical dealings with female patients to their complaints about their social rights and envy of men in that regard. It seems from the trend of explaining those complaints that he considered them displacement or sublimation, and referred them back to childhood envy of the penis. He did not put those complaints in the psychoneurotic context: *that some men have what could easily be called penis envy of another man.*

The concept of penis envy was refuted in a different way from the one that influenced the conception of the castration complex. It began with a strong social movement that gave women new status in society and changed the stereotypicality of women as subservient to a limited motherly function. The new female identity took a sharp deviation from the old one. Saville (1999) cautioned, even, against creating a fictitious feminine identity motivated by a sort of obligation to negate the past conception. Psychoanalysts began looking into the replacement of penis entity as a formative agent in the feminine identity (Richards, 1996). Some analysts resorted to the concept of *bisexuality* to find in it a solution (Renik, 1992; Elise, 1997). The majority of analysts opted for the notion of a Primary Femininity that proceeds from the beginning in a separate course of development, and might be secondarily affected for some time by the problems of the anatomical difference with maleness. However, penis envy as a primal condition of the female child was either totally rejected or only partially accepted – but as part of a separate feminine identity.

Revising the proposition in order to keep

The universality of the Oedipus complex is only valid if and only after being revised to relate to the structural core of the interfamilial dynamics in general. We need some theoretical guidelines to maintain the notion that the family is the natural scene of building the intrapsychical core of the individual. Otherwise, we lose our orientation in regard to the influence of childhood in creating the adult. The Oedipus was Freud's attempt to identify it would be merely a bright moment in the psychoanalytic discovery that did not last long. It is the intuitions that set up the scene for the two insights of the castration complex and the penis envy complex. Those two insights require reviewing because they do not have the attributes that reveal any pertinent aspects of the intuition of the interfamilial dynamics. When Freud mastered the art of reading meanings in forms and discovering the signified in the process of signifying he resorted to deductive thinking about some of his previous insights. He found in the primary process a concept that could bridge existing gaps between the manifest and the latent. Because it was not easy always to assume the universality of the two insights of castration and penis envy, in addition to the change made to the intuition of the Oedipus complex, Freud revised the notion of castration to make it 'stand for' separation and loss (1917c), and continued considering the girls' anxieties in that phase of development within the boys' Oedipal dilemma. Thus, he used the working of the primary process to justify his views about female sexuality. He read in the several bodily and none bodily objects the capacity to become part of the narcissistic anxiety about losing the penis as an easy way to keep male and female sexuality within one context. Moreover, some symbolic, metaphoric, and metonymical processes could express matters related similarly to castration and envy. Women's strong desire for having children was explained as sublimations of penis envy. Men's persistent competitiveness was considered a continuation of the castration anxiety of the Oedipal stage. The point to make here is that Freud's conception of castration anxiety and penis envy were slightly revised to be able to understand them outside the cultural context.[2]

Freud's intuition about the role of the interfamilial dynamics in creating the intrapsychic, exemplified in the conception of the Oedipus complex, needed revision to delineate the source and the outcome in the link between the actual family structure and the structure of the myth. It was a very important revision because on the one hand the revision was to put things in their proper order: does the interfamilial structure depict the gist of the myth or does the myth portray the essence of the interfamilial dynamics? On the other hand the simplistic notions of castration anxiety and penis envy severed their links with the Oedipus complex as it stood in its concrete mythical connotation. In other words, Freud's conceptions of castration anxiety and penis envy began as insights (an insight is deducing from the obvious what is hidden), but by expanding them to mean separation and loss and relating them to more than the *phallic organ* changed them into insights within the *structural core* of the Oedipus complex, which in turn became the basis of the male–female relationship.

Freud used his insight about penis envy to explain a formative aspect in the relationship between the sexes. His insight was that there is something fundamental in determining the relationship between males and females, which regulates the source of attractiveness and tensions between the sexes. It also implicitly avers heterosexuality as the natural condition of sexuality and explicitly considers sexuality pliable to other forms of choice. Penis envy and castration anxiety complemented each other in emphasizing the notion that the male–female relationship is not a natural or predetermined phenomenon; it is determined by the intrapsychic construct of sexuality in each. Even though penis envy was very much an insight deduced from a practice with a special population at a certain period of time, it underscored the significance of the formative factor in determining the relationship between males and females, any time and in any society. Freud's intuition was exactly that: behind his deductive insights there was an inductive process that emanated from an intuition. He *intuited* that penis envy is the means to understanding a broader issue about the nature of human relations. Even when he generalized his concept – making it the organizing factor – he opened it to become subject to displacements, and sublimations, thus amenable to both inductive and deductive thinking. One of the best (if not the best) critics of the Freudian doctrine, Politzer (1928) critcized Freud for being too concrete in his clinical formulations but being abstract in theorizing his findings. He comments on that by saying that Freud was not very sure that his intuition (inductive thinking) was suitable for building a credible science, so he gave the deductive thing a prominent place in his metapsychology. Ten years before Freud died, Politzer ended his critique with this sentence: "*Metapsychology* has lived its life, and the history of psychology [psychoanalysis] is beginning" (p.165).

Freud's penis envy insight was an insight in his female patients' sexual frustrations, which was mainly part of the bourgeoisie morality of his time. He interpreted their complaints of male domination and their strict criteria of femininity as envy of masculinity. Nonetheless, he had the intuition that ontologically speaking the social demands put on women by men, whether in Vienna or Tunisia, in the upper class or in a working class, now or a hundred years ago, are structuring factors in male–female relationships. Penis envy was a metapsychological formulation of the male–female relationship.

There is an aspect of the penis envy intuition that should be put in focus. Penis envy made sex the centrepiece of the relationship between men and women. It is a very sensible place for it. Yet, when we see what happened to sexual freedom in the Western world, and maybe soon in the whole world, we have to ask: is it still the organizing factor in male–female relationship or is it going to be displaced with something else?

Yet what comes to my mind in this context is this question: how free and far could an analyst be in reconfiguring a Freudian concept without deviating from the classical theory? My answer for now is that if we revise an intuition by getting to its structural core we would still be within the limits of the Freudian proposition, if not in a better position from that proposition. This shift would require revising all the insights that are related to that intuition in order to maintain order in that proposition.

Notes

1 We should not forget that what we are talking about at this point pertains to the European and Western middle class in general. Freud was able to deal with his conception with confidence because he did not pay any attention to that fact.

2 Penis envy was supported – to a great extent – by Freud's clinical experience in treating female Viennese bourgeoisie. They were women on the verge of liberation facing the objections of the Viennese men with a deluge of hysterical symptoms.

2

METAPSYCHOLOGY

A puzzle of a proposition

Two reasons made me choose metapsychology as one of the main propositions in Freud's doctrine. Metapsychology has always been a vague and unspecific function in the theory and was scarcely mentioned in Freud's writing. Nevertheless he insisted on its importance in the theory. Even when analysts started to be critical of it in the mid-1960s, they could not just eliminate it from the theory. They tried hard to replace it, as I will show shortly. Those attempts made metapsychology more of a puzzle. It did not look like a discovery that fitted within the theory or even just part of it, or a conception that built the theory but should be replaced, or a term used to designate some undefined clinical or theoretical entity. Not only that, but there were obvious mistakes in interpreting Freud's few vague mentions of it in his writings. Metapsychology, in a peculiar way, is not a functional concept that is useful, or a structural entity that has its own stability and consistency; it is a term that neither sustains psychoanalysis as a whole nor a particular aspect in it; it is more like faith in religion. There is no religion without faith, as when there is faith there is religion of sorts; *there is no Freudian psychoanalysis without metapsychology and when there is metapsychology there should be Freudian psychoanalysis.*

In a letter to Fliess (March 10, 1898) Freud said: "The theory of wish-fulfillment has brought only the psychological solution and not the biological, or, rather met psychological one (I am going to ask you seriously, by the way, whether I may use the name of metapsychology for my psychology that leads behind consciousness)." Clearly Freud was looking for a term for his new work, which he knew was going beyond consciousness, thus taking it out of the scope of psychology proper. Freud, by that time and after writing the 'Project for scientific psychology' (1950b), knew that what is beyond consciousness is not just unconsciousness but the whole process that creates the psychical from the endosomatic; possibly why he used the term 'biological'. He mentioned the term 'metapsychology' very few times and without clarity until he came to revising his main conceptions in 1915. He said (1915d): "I propose that when we have succeeded in describing a psychological process in its dynamic, topographic, and economic aspects we should speak of it as metapsychology" (181). This was the closest he came to defining metapsychology. It is not clear, in that sentence, if metapsychology means the transformation of the psychological process into those three attributes, or if those three ways of talking about the psychological process would mean that we are talking metapsychologically. In other words, it is not clear in this definition if Freud meant that metapsychology is a term needed to deal with the three aspects of psychical processes or a term imposed on us by virtue that psychical processes need to be considered beyond psychology. Then we come to the crust of the dilemma of metapsychology when he was about to conclude his theoretical endeavours. In 'Analysis terminable and in terminable' (1937c) he said: "Without metapsychological speculation and theorizing – I had almost said 'phantasying' – we shall not get another step forward. Unfortunately, here and elsewhere, what our Witch reveals is neither clear nor very detailed" (225). It is imperative to put this sentence in its context. Freud was trying to give a theoretical formulation of the effect of psychoanalytic therapy on the pressures of the 'instinct' on the ego, when he thought of calling on the Witch (metapsychology) to help make that formulation. On the one hand he considered metapsychology to be the way to formulate the theory, and then realized that it was not enough. Right after recognizing the limitations of metapsychology in that regard he continued to say: "We have only a single clue to start from – though it is a clue of the highest value – namely, the antithesis between the primary and the secondary processes; and that antithesis I shall at this point turn" (1937c, 225). Although, it is likely to think that I am so gripped and passionate about Freud's words, I have to remind myself that I am trying to find out what Freud had in mind when he talked about metapsychologies. In this context *Freud meant by metapsychology: the structural formulation of some informative theoretical material.*[1]

The three aspects of topography, dynamics, and economics, which Freud identified as facets of metapsychological formulations, did not sit well with psychoanalysts after Freud's passing. The reasons given were mostly concerning the relevance of metapsychologies to practising and clinical psychoanalysts. There was also a gradual change – at that time – in the area of theoretical debates. The change was associated with the effect of the Kleinian approach on the concepts of the intrapsychic and psychodynamics, and shifting the interest to the relational aspect in practice. These changes enforced the need to reconsider metapsychology and its place in the theory. Three trends emerged from the plea for reconsidering the need for 'Freud's' metapsychology.

The first trend was championed by advocates of separating metapsychology from the theory as a whole. Home (1966) and Bowlby (1981) decided that metapsychology is the scientific aspect of psychoanalysis, and thus could be dealt with separately. Mackay (1981) and Meltzer (1978) deemed metapsychology unnecessary in a psychoanalysis based on the object relations conceptions.

Ego-psychology, especially in the USA, was based on the structural theory or Freud's latest attempt at theorizing psychoanalysis. Yet, the trend was to eliminate the topographic and dynamic metapsychological aspects and just retain the structural point of view. Although Hartmann (1964) was not clearly open to such a grave elimination, he minimized the significance of Freud's metapsychology by adding two more aspects to it (the adaptive and the genetic). Few things contributed to that change: the distinction between the *Ucs*. and the *Pcs* was discarded resulting in eliminating the topographic point of view, and ridding the theory of the concept of 'instinct' eliminated the economic point of view, mainly based on the unsustainability of the concept psychic energy (Meissner, 1995). Thus the pleas to limit metapsychology to the structural point of view took hold of the theory (Brenner, 1980; Gill, 1979; Hartmann, 1948, 1964; Holt, 1965, 1981; Rappaport 1951, 1959). This trend faced very little resistance (Meissner, 1981; Waelder, 1941–1942).

The second trend was the result of tinkering with metapsychology to accommodate changing psychoanalysis from a theory of the psychodynamics of the intrapsychic into a theory of interpersonal relations, thus facing a flawed theory of psychoanalysis. Psychoanalysis without metapsychology is a defective theory because, as Freud had emphasized, metapsychology is the *structuring* of the psychological phenomena and might be the structural core[2] of the theory as a whole. Thus, there was a push to separate psychoanalysis as a clinical discipline from metapsychology as a 'theoretical' theory. Doing that was meant to develop psychoanalysis as a clinical theory and leave behind metapsychology and the rest of the theoretical issues to non-analysts to deal with. G. Klein (1976) and Rabin (1995) led a movement of trying to build a theory of the interpersonal relations as the core of a theory of psychoanalysis. Their mistake was that the theory of the interpersonal could not be the core of anything because it, in itself, needed a structural core, which it did not have and would not have had based solely on clinical material.

The third trend was characterizing Freud's metapsychology in a manner that justifies eliminating it. Metapsychology was called biological (G. Klein, 1976), neuropsychological (Rubinstein, 1997), psychology (Rosenblatt & Thickstun, 1977), dualistic (Stolorow & Atwood, 1992), and several other labels, which Ellman and Moskowitz (1980) called extratheoretical labels. Moreover, some analysts suggested replacing it with other theories or using other vocabulary for its original economic, dynamic, and topographic terminology. Most significant was the opening of the field of assessing and defining metapsychology to philosophers (Grunbaum, 1984; Hanly, 1995; Ricoeur, 1970), physicists (Swanson, 1977), psychologists, and neurologists. Those discussions were an open field (Robinson, 1993) but did not help in either clarifying what metapsychology is or finding a replacement. Brenner (1996) said:

> Metapsychology meant different things to different authors, though all use it to refer to psychoanalytic theory: some to the theory as a whole, some to those parts of analytic theory that they consider less clinical

> and more speculative, some to the specifically quantitative propositions of psychoanalytic theory, in particular to the propositions by Freud and others which deal with the flux on mental energies.
>
> (41)

As such, it would not be possible to eliminate it because for some, it was the antithesis of the clinical and preserves the speculative aspects of a theory in the making; to others, it dealt with something basic in psychoanalysis – which is the changes that happen to mental energies. However, there is something to note here: metapsychology looked like an issue that had been defined in different ways. Some liked some definitions and some didn't. However, it was not actually defined by those who liked it or those who did not. It makes one wonder: how could they like or dislike metapsychology based on a definition that did not exist? Eriksson (2012), after an extensive discussion of the philosophical foundation of metapsychology in light of some of the philosophies of the human subject, came to the conclusion that psychoanalysis is a theory of subjectivity, thus metapsychology should be treated as a priori the subjectivity in psychoanalysis.[3]

The psyche and the need for metapsychology

Ordinary people, who are not psychoanalysts, cannot run a discussion about psychological issues and end it with full agreement or specific disagreement on the issues raised. They speak about those issues without noticing that they have no prior agreement on the meaning of the terminology they use. Moreover, they do not know that there are no fixed meanings to issues pertaining to the psyche. Cognitive psychologists are not in the same position because there are more fixed meanings to most of their terminology and little room for disagreement about the vocabulary they utilize. Also, they do not need more than the spoken language with its grammar to communicate intelligibly. This is not the situation in psychoanalytic circles where discussions are about psychological issues that have unconscious elements. In the first place the meaning of the unconscious has not been agreed until recently. Its involvement in forming a psychical phenomenon is not obvious or definitive enough to be disputed or undisputed. There are several 'schools' of psychology in that regard that complicate matters even more. The link between a conscious psychical phenomenon (like an affective state) and its unconscious counterpart forms sort of an inherent grammar that should determine the proper way of speaking about it. A classical psychoanalyst's understanding of a patient's lateness in arriving at his session is different from a self-analyst's understanding of the same thing because they will relate the adjectives and adverbs of the tardiness differently. They are inclined to reverse the cause–effect relationship in such a behaviour and the adjective could understate the difference. Psychoanalysts of the same school might disagree but will not misunderstand each other because they may use a slightly different vocabulary but utilize the same grammar, which will keep them on the same page. The grammar of a psychological theory is its metapsychology. Analysts of the same psychoanalytical school, even if they differ in opinion, could still communicate because their shared metapsychology gives their speech a framework of meaning. In a critical paper, Glover (1966) exposes this issue from the interesting angle of the prevalence of using terms to signify ready-made psychical entities, like projection, without putting those terms in the context of the processes that required their use. The result is a Psychoanalytic Tower of Babel.

There are very few analysts who still adhere to the Freudian doctrine, and those analysts are more inclined to consider metapsychology an integral part of the theory. Most analysts nowadays are either less faithful to the so-called classical theory, or openly critical of it. The impact of those changes on metapsychologies is evident in the status the term has in the literature. After the 'controversies' in England, the 'splits' in France, and the collapse of ego-psychology in the USA, three major trends took over the evolution of the psychoanalytic theory (see Fayek, 2010): first, a fast disappearance of psychodynamics as the core of the psychoanalytic theory; second, the replacement of the intrapsychical, as the subject matter of psychoanalytic work, with different psychological issues like the self and subjectivity; and third, a constant effort to find a way to get rid of metapsychology or replace it. After waves of targeting those three fundamental conceptions, isolating them from their historical contexts and theoretical interconnections, judging them in peculiar ways, then finding them unviable and dismissible (Compton, 1981a–d; Fayek, 2010), the field of psychoanalysis has now become rife with theories that usurped the term 'psychoanalysis'. Yet, they are not related to it in any clear way. In better words, the contemporary schools made subtle and not so subtle changes to parts of classical theory. They were critical of a theory they disfigure. Gradually the theory became lacking and flawed, and deserving to be discredited. For instance Strachey translated Freud's *Ich* (*I*) with Ego and *Es* (*It*) with Id, thus changing the core meaning of Freud's work *The Ego and the Id* (1923b). The pronoun *I* (first person subjective) became an object, reified in the Greek term 'Ego'. *It* is a pronoun of a neutral entity, and meant in Groddeck's suggestion a counterpart of the *I*. Translating it with *Id* allowed conceiving it as a reservoir of the most basic biological urges in a person and wiped out its original attribute as the 'not-*I*'; the part of the *I* that *I* does not recognize as *me*. The reification of the pronouns in that work made them *informs* or speculative elements of a psychical system forming some sort of a psychology. It did not take much for that psychology (of the ego), to be turned into a metapsychology, which took a little longer to become a metapsychology which stifled the theory as a whole.

The effect of those distortions did not come right away but they had a domino effect that led to the final blows. It started by claiming that the topographic metapsychology had unsolvable problems in spite of Freud's insistence on integrating it in the so-called structural metapsychology. The topographic point of view generated three meanings of the unconscious; one of them – the systemic unconscious – eluded most analysts and even Freud himself (Freud, 1915e). After a while came the plea to consider ego-psychology a metapsychology and to put the topographic model of psychical functioning aside. Then the plea to do away with all metapsychologies came, yet exempting the structural metapsychology of ego-psychology as Freud's final metapsychology (Gill, 1979). It did not take long, after that, for a trend to do away with the only metapsychology left, and just concentrate on building a clinical theory (G. Klein, 1976). This theory is still confounding psychoanalysts. Within that narrow range of the problem we ended up with neither metapsychology (presumably the theoretical aspect of psychoanalysis) nor a clinical theory. We ended up with 'a nothing'. There is something about that end in the Freudian text as it is translated in the *Standard Edition*. Launching Strachey's *Standard Edition* in 1950, as *the* canonized text of psychoanalysis, had played an important part in distorting the meaning and nature of metapsychology. Strachey considered Freud's revisions of the three conceptions of *Trieben*, Repression and the Unconscious as papers on metapsychology (Freud, 1915c, d, e). Those three conceptions were depicted in the theory as ontological entities: *Trieb* as a function, repression as a mechanism, and the unconscious as an informant. As entities of specific quality they were psychical phenomena. Freud revised the psychology of the three conceptions, distinguishing two phases in each. He then called each phase, depending on its precedence, primary and primal. By assuming the existence of a gap between the two phases Freud placed psychodynamics in that gap, which is the dynamic activity that creates the connections between them. Strachey (1957b, 105), in his editor's introduction to 'Papers on metapsychology', stipulated that metapsychology was Freud's theoretical formulations. Yet, when he specified what Freud was intending to add to the three papers he mentioned topics that are clearly related to psychology and not to metapsychology, such as conversion hysteria, mental mechanisms, sublimation, etc. (ibid., 106). Those topics that Freud was supposed to have written are of psychical phenomena, and about their *theoretical formulations*.[4] Freud stated clearly that his intention regarding this group of papers was "to clarify and carry deeper the theoretical assumptions on which a psycho-analytic system could be founded" (1917d, 222, fn1). The *Standard Edition* was not taken as a translation of Freud's text but was treated as 'the word of the master', thus the resulting psychoanalysis was trapped in Strachey's translation. Metapsychology was defined by Strachey's mistranslation and misconception, and analysts followed Strachey's translation instead of Freud's unquestionable definition of the term. To begin with, those distortions were considered inconsequential mistakes. Notwithstanding the general permissiveness and dismissiveness of those mistakes, their bearing on the theory was eventually revealed.

What Freud clearly shows in what he said is that he wanted to work on the psychology and not the metapsychology of those psychical phenomena. Strachey ignored that metapsychology is to talk about those psychologics topographically, dynamically, and economically. The result was that Strachey's rendition of metapsychology turned Freud's three attributes, which together constitute metapsychology, into three separate metapsychologies. *Metapsychology is the three attributes of the topographic, dynamic, and economic put together, and not three metapsychologies, as ego-psychologists in the USA presumed.* In the USA analysts even ranked those three attributes according to their significance and eventually eliminated what they considered redundant and kept the only useful one: structural metapsychology. This distortion of the functional value of metapsychology turned it, without justification, into a structure without a function, an ontological entity without any entity. Mentioned earlier, the authors who tried to get rid of metapsychology by replacing it with a modality other than Freud's did not succeed; nevertheless, they could not just walk away from it, despite not identifying its function.

Temporarily I will make a statement and prove its correctness a little later: talking comprehensively about any psychical phenomena requires dealing with its topographic state (place in the conscious/unconscious system), its origin (the dynamics of its presence), and its economy (bound or unbound energy). Therefore, metapsychology qualifies the psychical phenomena to be examined and discussed; it is the manner that turns any psychical issues into a subject for investigation, not a system to examine the psyche. However, if this definition is acceptable there will still be an unanswered question: why do the psyche and its manifestations need metapsychology to become a subject of study?

A psychology for metapsychology

Philosophers and psychologists before Freud tried to understand *the psychical* but failed because they did not have the notion that every psychical phenomenon has an internal structure that is not visible or understandable as things appear. The core of the psychical had to be identified and included to initiate understanding. The intrapsychical was a novelty, and there was no vocabulary or grammar to talk about it. Freud improvised a system of metaphors – to be the language of the intrapsychical and the terminology of its dynamics. The new vocabulary pertained to the new unfolding details of the intrapsychical; and it progressively led to realizing the need for metapsychology that would apply to more than one of the new psychical discoveries. Metapsychology is expressive only if its psychological counterpart is clear and identifiable; thus without a psychology of the intrapsychical metapsychology it would be comparable to metaphysics without physics – nothing more than unfounded mythology. This was the basis for the dismissal of metapsychology by a large number of psychoanalysts. Freud anticipated resistance to metapsychology due to its unspecific nature and the possibility of dismissing it if we fail to see its importance. He reminded us that if metapsychology seems redundant we should not forget that "we have only a single clue to start from though it is a clue of the highest value – namely, the antithesis of the primary and the secondary processes; and to that antithesis I shall at this point turn" (1915d, 225). What is the link between the primary and secondary processes and metapsychology? There is a prevailing opinion that the primary process precedes the emergence of the secondary process; thus it is archaic, primitive, disorganizing and disorganized, and the dominant unconscious mental process. Freud stipulated that all psychical phenomena have a primary state or stage: masochism, narcissism, identification, and mental representations (processes). The *primary* state accompanies or lurks behind the secondary state and affects it in different ways; in art, the primary process has more involvement in the formation of the secondary process and its infiltrations are clearer and obvious compared to the writing a legal document, for instance. Therefore, we should expect the presence of both the primary and secondary qualities in all psychical phenomena albeit in different degrees of mixing.

There must be a psychology behind metapsychology if there must be metapsychology for every psychological 'given'. However, the psychology of metapsychology seems to have eluded analysts (even Freud) since he suggested the term in 1898. Strachey's mistaking the three papers of 1915 on *instincts*, *repression*, and the *unconscious* as metapsychological papers is at least a result of not understanding the difference between psychology and metapsychology. Psychoanalysts accepting his classification of those papers as metapsychological suggest that they are also misunderstanding that difference. It is therefore natural to encounter the confusion that has overwhelmed the researchers of metapsychology. For instance, Brenner (1980) said that Freud "meant" by metapsychology the psychology of the unconscious processes. Yet, when Freud wanted to find a term to describe his discoveries he chose the term 'metapsychology' purposefully to avoid using the term 'psychology' (Freud, March 10, 1898). Brenner corrected himself a little later by saying: "He [Freud] called the theories he elaborated metapsychology, to distinguish them from psychological theories that maintained that what is not conscious is not mental" (ibid., 212). *Obviously metapsychology meant to Freud something beyond the psychical and mental, because the latter was and still is the subject matter of academic psychology*.

Psychical phenomena, like repression or the vicissitude of the *Trieben* are psychological phenomena, and we can also talk about them metapsychologically. Repression, in the cathartic theory, meant 'turning something away from consciousness and keeping it at a distance'. It was part of the psychology of forgetting but the 'forgotten' has to be identified to have a psychological quality to talk about. In the revision Freud made to the concept (1915d) he said:

> [R]epression is not a defensive mechanism which is present from the very beginning, and it cannot arise until a sharp cleavage has occurred between conscious and unconscious activity. ... We have reason to assume that there is a *primal repression,* a primal first phase of repression. ... The second phase of repression, *repression proper* ... is actually an after-repression.
>
> (147–148)

The revised version of the three concepts bypasses the issue of the content and makes the separation of the primary from the secondary the precondition for it to function and allows describing them metapsychologically. By using economic, dynamic, and topographic terminology to describe the conditions under which we could study those phenomena we move from psychology to metapsychology without difficulty and without even changing our state of mind. Therefore, the psychology of the metapsychologies should be the psychology of entities that have two basic characteristics: first, it should be the starting point in discovering psychoanalysis and the main cause of its evolvement, and permeate all the psychical phenomena and constitute their core; and second, it must be an entity capable of generating the three known metapsychologies, but remain outside of their metapsychical *definitive* quality.

Those two characteristics are found in the concept of *affect*. Green (1999a) showed in a comprehensive work on affect how that concept is so central in the theory of psychoanalysis, yet still very ill-defined and misconceived. Quinodoz (2003) underlines that difficulty saying: "[T]hough the idea of affect is much wider in scope than the simple energy-based meaning comprised in the term 'quanta of affect', it remains relatively ill-defined even in contemporary psychoanalytic theory" (142). Confusing the two terms of 'affect' and 'feeling' (Affekt, and Gefuhl) is the basic reason for the poor definition of 'affect' and using the two terms interchangeably, thus overlooking an important distinction embedded in the difference between what is primary and what is primal. This is a fact with a peculiar origin in the history of psychoanalysis. In 'Project …' Freud (1950b) talked about psychical energy as the equivalence of neurological energy, and branded it '*affect*' – a term which would allow giving the state of excitement or the quanta of affect a quality (pleasure or pain) and assign it to two conditions: bound/unbound. One of the main issues connected with the notion of energy is the tendency to reduce the excitation or control it. The discharge of excited energy is one of those ways, and binding it to an object is another. When Freud abandoned the 'Project …' and worked instead on hysterical phenomena, he noticed the significance of the 'strangulation' of *feelings* in the process of forming symptoms. The original notion of affect took a new connotation: when an affective state takes an object, it changes to a feeling (Gefuhl). In other words, what we feel is the transformation of affective states into feelings related to 'givens' in our life. Affect is the experience of a state of pleasure or pain, but it needs to connect to subjects to be elevated to the status of feeling and emotion; or it remains a *quantum* with no quale. Therefore, we should distinguish 'affect' as a primal condition, necessary for feelings to follow as its sequel;[5] thus metapsychology is, and would have much to do with, the distinction between primary and secondary process.

The complex strangulated feelings and emotions in hysteria were uncovered in hypnosis and free associating. Freud insightfully realized that feelings and emotions subtly but significantly were different from affect, which was a pure and content-less psychical state. He also realized that the strangulated feeling in hysteria was not the originator of the neurosis, but the manifestation of that neurosis. By avoiding staying at the level of the strangulated feelings and emotions, Freud unintentionally (unconsciously!) opened the way to discovering the different ways affect presents itself in consciousness (representation), one of which is feeling. This was indeed the major leap needed to move from hypnotism to free association as the means to exploring the variety of forms affect takes in the different neuroses. He had postulated – in 'Project …' – that pleasure and pain are the universal spontaneous reactions of the protoplasm; thus they are the prototype of reaction in any form of organic life. However, in humans they take the form of affect, which in turn instigates a reaction – and much more than that, as we will see later. He was also cognizant that affect's capacity to generate representations in the mind creates a rift between consciousness and the unconscious (1894a, 1896b, 1915d) – a rift that separates the affective state from its ideational state. This discovery built a psychology that was the spool around which metapsychology was woven; a psychology of the entirety of psychoanalysis. *Affect was the condition that starts the mind on its functioning journey of creating mental equivalents of the endogenous changes in the body, and the condition that made the rudimentary consciousness in animals becomes a psychical phenomenon in humans.* In other words affect is the origin of the process that generates mental representations, which in turn engender psychological life. It meets the first qualification of a concept that could be the psychology of metapsychologies; it is the starting point in the discovery of psychoanalysis and remained its prototype all along.

In the *Interpretation of Dreams* (1900a), Freud gives the first metapsychology: the topographic conception of the psychical system. It was the metapsychology of the transformation of affect – as the state of wishing that is related to the pleasure/pain principle – into mental processes (the dream), via the mechanisms of condensation (metaphor) and displacement (metonymy). This was the first clear assertion of the need for metapsychology to deal with the antithesis of the primary process and the secondary process. According to psychology at the time, especially in Brentano's conceptions, affect was the condition that instigates change and transformation in the psychical system. Freud introduced the concept of *Trieb* (1905d) to add a new dimension to that notion. It allowed him to talk more about affect in terms of its source in the vital functions of the body (which turned into the life *Trieb* fifteen years later). It also introduced the notions of the erogenic zones and the libido theory. Once those concepts were understood properly, Freud was inclined to talk of quantities and transformations of libido and to expand his horizons to formulate his discoveries in terms of psychical processes, whether in psychopathology or normalcy. The result was the birth of a metapsychology of quantities or the economics of investing the libido and the introduction of narcissism to psychoanalytic theory. The concept of an economy of psychical energy, the two systems of *Ucs.* and *Psc./Cs.*, the aspect of conflicts within psychical events, produced the terminology of dynamic metapsychology. The dynamic point of view was a natural partner for the other two metapsychologies. The discovery of the unconscious was not enough to give psychoanalysis both its distinguished place in the humanities and its lasting significance even after it became common knowledge in the Western world.

Freud's most inspiring endeavour – and the backdrop of the pan-importance of psychoanalysis – was finding the way to explore the *subject*'s psyche despite the absence of any previous knowledge of the existence of something more than what we see of the person. Affect was his starting point in that endeavour, because by identifying it as the response to the endosomatic changes in the body, or the sign of life in the person (Fayek, 2014), he found in it the attributes of ideational psychical representations.

At this point we can return to our question earlier and answer it: why do the psyche and its manifestations need metapsychology to become a subject for study? Psychical phenomena are the merger of the primal and the primary, the originator (affect) and the representation, the conscious and the unconscious. It is important to keep in focus that psychical phenomena are fusions between elements of different qualities because, as such, they are not mere *informs* but structures that have to be deciphered and given a replacement terminology. For instance, Freud needed the term 'libido' to illustrate the topography, the dynamics and the economics the phenomena of attachments, because attachment comes at different times in different states: intense or weak, conflicting or staid, clear or confused, etc. *Affect and its representations could be contentless states, and should be talked about topographically, economically and dynamically. The psyche is a product of a natural force that changes from a quantitative condition to qualitative states that generate an endless chain of representations and set up our psychical life, to remain active from beginning to end.* Interpersonal relations, similar to other social phenomena such as marriage and democracy, are entities in their own right and could be investigated in isolation because the terminology that is ascribed to them has one and the same indication. Social phenomena are what they are, and they have no further undisclosed intent. They might have some disguised connotations but they get the same terminology used with the straightforward connotations.

Analysts engage the psychoanalytic phenomena at a later stage of its formation – i.e., the stage of the formation of the psychical phenomena. Therefore, they would not consider affect a significant part of their work, because they would be dealing with feelings instead, or other representations of affect. However, knowing the role of affect and some of its manifestations in psychoanalytic work is a basic criterion for the difference between good and not-so-good psychoanalysts. Analysts who understand the value and place of metapsychological thinking will find it easy to discern the psychology or the basis of the phenomenon from its metapsychology or its representation. We need to learn about the process of representations, its onset and development; because they are the metapsychological of what we deal with in our work. Psychoanalysis, as such, becomes the psychological theory of the transformations of psychical entities, and the possible failures this process might encounter. *The psychoanalytic act is the dealing with the process that turns the pressure of affect on the mind into psychical material that the patient comes to us with because his affect with its unusual representation baffles him.* Without being aware of dealing with the metapsychology of that process we are likely to fail in doing psychoanalysis.

The theory and revised conception of metapsychology

Revising a main proposition in psychoanalysis is problematic to say the least, because it is easy to distort the proposition in an attempt to revise it. However, Freud was the best at revising his own propositions giving a basic modality to what needed to be done. Repression was an anchor proposition in the early Freudian doctrine signifying the operation that expels the objectionable psychical material from consciousness rendering them unconscious. He said (1915d): "[T]he essence of repression lies simply in turning something away, and keeping it at a distance from the conscious" (147). This way, repression created the unconscious. After several insights into the working of the primary process and a better understanding of the intrapsychical formations – and initiating the concept of narcissism – Freud revised the concept of repression (along with *Trieb, Ucs.*, and Regression). He stated that repression is not something that just happens once to defend the ego from objectionable psychical material; it is a more elaborate operation: the representative of the instinctual has to be primally denied entrance to consciousness; thus a separation between the conscious and the unconscious has to take place first for repression to kick in. The phrase 'primal repression' is followed by 'repression proper' (which he also gave the name 'after-pressure'), and works on the mental derivative of the representative and anything that gets associated with it in the preconscious. Freud's revision of the conception of repression totally reversed it, and it became the product of the unconscious instead being the mechanism that creates it. However, the revision interconnected with necessary revisions of several other conceptions all corroborated each other's revised form, bringing out their structural core to replace their informative quality (Fayek, 2015). Revising a proposition is to make the changes needed to maintain its basic signification in a new reconfiguration of the theory. In other words, the logic or the grammar and its place in the theory are maintained but the argumentation and the signification of its vocabulary undergo the necessary changes. The theory of psychoanalysis remained the same with all the revisions Freud made and accepted from his disciples; even the revisions made by the classical analysts after his passing integrated with his.

The theory remained a theory of the intrapsychic arising from the affective response to the pressure of the endosomatic stimuli on the mind. The transformation of the affective states creates the psychical representations of the endosomatic, and the representations engender the psychical phenomena by linking with the cognitive product of the secondary process. This conception of the origin of the psychical phenomena describes the birth of the human subject. It is the theory of the ways in which the psychical phenomena will be constituted, the steps it will take and the experiences that will impact them, in the manner those steps will link together, deviate and create their particularities of which the individual transpires. Then a question arises: how do metapsychologies fit in such a theory where psychical phenomena are identified structurally and not functionally? Modell (1981) defined the functions of metapsychology as:

> [First,] a selection of psychological phenomena that could be termed universal in the sense that they are characteristic of the human species; secondly, a set of assumptions upon which a psychological system can be founded and made explicit, thirdly, metapsychology functions as a modelling device, an imaginary entity, an experiment in thinking.
>
> (399)

This functional identification of metapsychology could be a guiding plan for examining the place of metapsychology in such a theory.

In the traditional classical theory there were attempts – especially from Freud – to give functional definitions for those details, with the ambition to make psychoanalysis join the nomothetic sciences. However, because there are no simple direct observable relations between causes and effects in psychical phenomena, functional definitions did not succeed in embodying the theory of psychoanalysis. The revised conceptions did not yield to any functional definition. However, they still remained amenable to metapsychological formulations, because they maintained their psychological qualities after their revisions. Metapsychology will function as the bridge between the obsolete functional theory and awaited structural theory. Thus, metapsychology is the safeguard of the revised theory of psychoanalysis against the serious though very subtle danger of distorting it as it changes. A theory or a conception without an identifiable frame of reference or grammar produces vocabularies with no stable or clear significations. Metapsychology secures that the revisions of the basic propositions in psychoanalysis will have the same required grammar and stable vocabulary. In addition, metapsychology keeps the door open for advancing and even revising the new revisions if that is needed in the future.

Laplanche and Pontalis (1973) said: "If Freud's discovery had to be summed up in a single word, that word would without any doubt have to be 'unconscious'" (474). But which unconscious of the three that Freud envisaged (Freud, 1915e)? It is not the repressed, for sure. It is the system *Ucs.*: "[W]e find ourselves thus confronted by the necessity of postulating a third *Ucs,* which is not repressed unconscious" (1923b, 18). This unconscious (Matte-Blanco elucidated and explained it extensively in his work in 1975) is present and exists within consciousness, but because of its nature it eludes the non-properly initiated in the theory. It needs the suitable vocabulary to reveal it. Van Der Leeuw (1969) said: "[I]t [metapsychology] is a way of communicating experiences, of transforming it, and a new way of thinking in psychology is put to a test" (575). Bichi (2012), Laplanche (1981), and Glover (1966) put metapsychology to the test by expounding the psychical phenomena and substantiated its viability. This is the most significant discovery in the structural theory of psychoanalysis, because on the one hand it makes consciousness the subject matter of any psychoanalytic work (not the unconscious, as it was in the informative theory); this way it requires a new understanding of that system and the psychical processes it comprises (see Fayek, 2013). On the other hand, it makes some of the previously unnoticed psychological processes take central stage in a revised theory: the representational nature of a-consciousness, the *after-effect*, the originator of the intrapsychical and its influence in structuring it. The significance of the shift to consciousness obligates present-day psychoanalysts to know more about the formation of consciousness, the dynamics of its constituents, and what they need from the other branches of the humanities to tell them about what they do not know. Most of all, 'psychoanalysis' has to contribute to the humanities by revealing what their theory of the individual says about the human subject, from which the individual has come.

The classical theory in its informative case revealed several concepts that will ultimately change the work of the analysts. The analyst is now dealing with consciousness as his focal point and the means to uncovering the *Ucs.* He must pay attention to the constituents of consciousness, which are the representations of psychical entities and events. The representations take the form of fantasies or metaphors. The fantasies and the metaphors are out – products of psychical overlapping of primary and secondary processes. Thus, and due to that overlap, consciousness contains the after-effects of psychical events and not the events themselves. The psychoanalyst does not deal with psychical issues but deals with their substitutes, their delegates, and designates. In more expressive terms: the revised proposition of metapsychology as the grammar of the psychical phenomena suits and fits much better the structural theory of psychoanalysis, because it is unidentified yet (see Fayek, 2015) and would create with time new psychologies. The psychologies it will generate will not be of operations but of processes.

As mentioned earlier, the starting point in the complex process of creating the psychical is the affective response to the endosomatic pressure on the mind. As was also mentioned earlier, that consciousness is the special way in which the cognitive and the psychical intertwine in each individual? Thus, the structural theory of psychoanalysis would be a theory of that formation of consciousness.[6] It is not very speculative to say that the only motor ability the infant needs to deal with hunger is sucking the thumb for a while and crying if hunger reaches a certain degree. However, during those experiences, the ungratified stimulus creates several affective states, the existence of which we presume. The affective states, despite affecting the mind, are a-conscious (see Fayek, 2014) because it is too early for mentation. Moreover, those states so early in life do not have the qualification to be conscious. In a fleeting but very intuitive sentence, Freud said (1915d): "With this [denying the ideational entry to consciousness – i.e., separating the physical condition of hunger, for instance, from its affective representation] a *fixation* is established; the representative in question persists unaltered from then onwards" (148).[7] We are on firmer ground at this point because we can notice in adulthood the occurrence of a-conscious fixed individual patterns that suggest a background character formation (see Chapter 3).

The usage of metaphors, symbolism, and the specific characteristic of the individual's way of expressing himself lead us to realize that the representations of the affective states are material for fantasies. It is pertinent at this point to correct a common misconception that a distinction should be made between unconscious and conscious fantasies. Fantasies are always unconscious states of mind, contentless but formative, always bodily related, and are central in giving the individual an anchor for his personality. What are called 'conscious fantasies' should be taken as daydreams and are essentially more related to the area of wishful thinking. Freud distinguishes between those two types of fantasies in calling the a-conscious fantasies *Primal Fantasies* (Freud, 1916–1917). Sucking the thumb and using other objects for sucking in unrelated times of hunger suggest a separation between the a-conscious and the conscious. It also denotes that the mental activity that replaces the actual act of nursing has a phantasmic, if not hallucinatory, nature (Gammelgaard, 2006). This is the prototype of fantasizing. In adult phantasies it would be obvious that an individual is a-conscious of the implicit phantasy that guides his psychical life, while some of the perceptive people he is dealing with would sense its existence. A sexually frustrated acquaintance was constantly searching for sexual partners in a compulsive way. His brother described his constant preoccupation with sex as hunger. I asked him to explain, and he said: it is not sex he is looking for because minutes after having sex, he is looking for the next 'meal' before he gets hungry again.

Freud used the term 'presentation' (*Vorstellung*) to mean a metal replacement for the original physical event and its memory-trace (1915e) – i.e., the condition that could generate fantasies. The concept, as he used it in his pre-psychoanalytic writings, was suggesting the inevitability of a memory to generate its representation, at least for economic reasons, to gain a place in the topographic system. Freud made a very important distinction regarding presentations and their presence and place in the topographic system. He said (1915e): "The conscious presentation comprises the presentation of the thing plus the presentation of the word belonging to it, while the unconscious presentation is the presentation of the thing alone" (201). To put things in a practical and useful way we could say that once the affective state is separated from its physiological source it gains the mental attributes and obtains the characteristics that make it pliable to further representations – representation of presentation. The sense of lack we encounter in depressive patients takes all sorts of meanings: lack of pleasure, meaning of success, love, material things, etc., which are stemming from the lack of the oral object that should have filled the lack with satisfaction. This is important because the infant being surrounded by language (born in a language) which he would eventually unconsciously assimilate brings us to the concept of representation as it fits in the topographic system. Representation could now acquire a verbal version (with all the facilities language gives to chains of connected words). In this way the representation gains access to consciousness through the links that could be initiated by the preconscious with consciousness linguistically and thorough symbols.

Freud's distinction between thing-presentation and word presentation, his assertion that the a-conscious generates what could become a representation of the actual memory, the existence of the early representations in the preconscious, therefore find their way to link with associations of conscious material; all that leads us to consider the relationship between the primary process and the secondary process. Consciousness was presumably a function of the cognitive processes until Freud came along and proved that the cognitive aspect of our mentation is not purely cognitive but comprises unconscious content. He proposed the existence of modes of mentation based on primary and secondary processes. The primary process rules the unconscious and the secondary process deals with the cognitive aspect of mentation. Better, consciousness is a function of the dynamic interaction between the primary and the secondary processes. Thus, in order to appreciate consciousness we need to know how it could function with those coexisting and conflicting and almost-contradicting mental processes. Freud said that repression proper is not performed on the endosomatic stimulus or its presentation but on the representations or the derivatives of the original source of the process of mentation. Therefore, the human mind has to arrange configurations that would combine or condense aspects of both elements. Direct and simple examples of that process are found in Freud's *Psychopathology of Everyday Life* (1901b), and the general theory of symptom formation.

Nonetheless, without paying attention to the major effect the interplay of the primary process and the secondary process has on psychical life in general, and consciousness in particular, which is the seat of both health and sickness, we would miss the most significant process in the formation of consciousness. This process, '*Nachtraglichkeit*', was first translated by Strachey as 'deferred-action', then by the improved French version of 'after-effect'. The term was used by Freud in his pre-psychoanalytic writings (1950b) but because it is a common German word as well as connotes and denotes specific meanings "the term's ambiguity admits different interpretations which have to be checked against Freud's aetiological theory and his theory of therapy – where the latter means his understanding of those factors which bring about the therapeutic change" (Thoma & Cheshire, 1991, 410).

The main issue the after-effect conception introduces to psychoanalysis is a two-stage theory of the psychical occurrence in which, at one stage, something happens but it gets its meaning at a later stage; the two later become inseparable and interchangeable. The main notion as Laplanche and Pontalis (1973) specified is that an earlier psychical event goes without being assimilated to acquire a meaningful context (childhood sexual violation). It lurks back as a floating meaningless event until another similar event happens later in life to give it its meaning, and possibly a traumatic quality that the person couldn't understand when it happened initially. They added that not everything past undergoes this kind of revision but only, and specifically, the events that maintained an aspect of intrigue and stood out among other memories looking for a meaning. Thoma & Cheshire (1991) added a new angle to the concept of after-effect by suggesting that to be true to Freud's intended meaning of the term it should be called "the effect of the after-effect", thus giving *after-effect* a substantive quality and an operational function. In other words, after-effect could be in operation without noticing it, but when it has an effect it changes the structure of a previously dormant psychical event. For instance, there is no human relationship with another that is purely based on the current moments of the relationship; there are always aspects of previous relationships that become part of that relationship in different degrees. However, the psychoanalytic situation activates those same phenomena in a different form: transference. Transference makes after-effect the director (as in theatre) that has the ability of revising the relationship between past and present in a unique way. The past gets its meaning and the present (the analytic situation) gets structured accordingly, to reorganize the present after the effect of the after-effect. Metapsychologically, the preconscious gives the unconscious its meaning, thus changing its dynamics and the distribution of its stresses. While that is happening, consciousness is reorganized on different topographic, dynamic, and economic principles – and 'cure' happens. It is important to emphasize that both the acts of interpretation and construction (Freud, 1937d) take a different perspective within the context of the after-effect.

There are three reasons for the significant place after-effect has in both the clinical and theoretical aspects of psychoanalysis. *First* is the continuous infiltration of the past in the present making it inevitable to consider the possibility that most of what looks like cognitive material and conscious experiences are influenced by links with past experiences. We should not forget that after-effect is not recalling the past event but only the memory of the past event. At the same time, there is also the facility of the present to reach out for its meaning in the past, sometimes allowing the past to distort it, as it is clear in the transference experience, because the after-effect is not unidirectional by virtue of the domination of the primary processes (Thoma & Cheshire, 1991; Perelberg, 2006). After-effect is not a psychical entity that has its own *reason d'etre*; it is indispensable in understanding temporality, which is a big issue in psychoanalyzing (Eickhoff, 2006). Therefore, consciousness, the psychical material we deal with in psychoanalysis, is a dynamic scene of a present that is failing in staying in the now, and a past that is searching in that present for meaning that is hidden within it in the form of a psychoneurosis.

Second, the meaning of the past is implicitly embedded in the psychoneurosis by means of the engagement of primary and the secondary processes in a dynamic duality. This dynamic duality configures consciousness in a way that makes it impossible to talk about it psychologically and has to be talked about metapsychologically. The reason is the unfeasibility of distinguishing in one clear cut the line between what is primary and what is secondary. Perelberg (2006) suggests distinguishing between a descriptive after-effect and a dynamic after-effect based on the place of the non-repressed unconscious and dynamic unconscious in the phenomenon. The past that is void of meaning shows as demands of unexpressed and unfinished business. To deal with that kind of past we need to know its language (which the unconscious is deciding what is said): what is its demand? The lack of clarity of the demand and arbitrariness of causal relationships in the primary process requires demystifying the event. In childhood sexual abuse by an adult, it might be that who did it is the issue that needs restoring (*was your uncle doing something sexual with you?*). In other cases, restoring the meaning of the event is what's needed in the work (*it was wrong of your uncle to use you to do that for him*). Those two acts are an interpretation that will bring the past to the present to entertain its after-effect. *Third* is to keep in mind the metapsychology of the scene of the after-effect itself. What we do in analysis, in terms of the first and the second reasons already mentioned, is to uncover the necessity of reorganizing the link between the past and the present, the causes and the effects, needs and their aims in the best way possible to achieve better psychodynamics, a more conscious command over the past and the future, and a comfortable balance between the ordinary conflicting aspects of psychical life. It is interesting that analysts who saw metapsychology a functional concept and a process of a substantive nature were anti keeping it but as mentioned earlier, they tried to replace it. Fulgenecio (2007) showed that Winnicott rejected Freud's concept of metapsychology. Analysts who considered metapsychology from the operational point of view thought differently, as Girard (2010) underlined the Freudian metapsychological foundation of Winnicott's theorization.

There are no topographic, dynamic, economic metapsychologies but there are three ways of talking about psychological phenomenon: the topographical structure in the phenomenon, the dynamics active in it, and the economical exchanges within its constituent. Metapsychology to psychoanalysis is grammar to a language. A verb in a language allows us to talk about past, present and future, and metapsychology allows us to talk about its characteristics that distinguish it from other psychical phenomenon that seem to be alike.

Notes

1 What supports my opinion is what Freud said shortly after his well-known quote above: "It is impossible to define health except in metapsychological terms – i.e., by references to the dynamic relations between the agencies of the mental apparatus which have been recognized – or (if that is preferred) inferred on conjecture – by us" (1937c, 226, fn2). The preposition *meta* indicates the underlying definition or description of the 'given', which would be its structure. The structural formulation of 'given' information turns the details into standards, causation into determinant, and forms into notions. As an example, the structural meaning of marriage is the codification of the rules of incest. Metapsychology, thus, is the term that goes beyond the given psychical information to formulate its underlying base.

2 Elder (1994) said about metapsychology: "[It is] not a description of an empirical entity, of a *mental* apparatus, or a mechanism of some sort; rather it is or should be a description *in a mental, or psychological, idiom of conditions necessary for the possibility of interpretation.* In other words, the metapsychology describes the mind as it *must be* in order for dreams, parapraxes, symptoms, and so forth, to have meaning, that is, in order for these phenomena *to be interpretable* along the basic lines that Freud set out" (179). Metapsychology expresses, in three interrelated ways, the pressure of the endosomatic stimuli put on the mind to act; thus it is inductive in nature, not

scientific in the deductive sense. Psychoanalysts who considered it the vocabulary of empirical observables were critical and did away with it; they threw the baby out with the bath water (Klein, 1989).

3 In one of the early critiques of psychoanalysis, and still the best, the philosopher G. Politzer was critical of the psychology of his time because it was turning the discoveries of the findings of the psychical into concrete duplicates of the living experience, and eliminating the individual from the equation, influenced in that by an Aristotelian endeavour of quantifying the world as an external event. He assigned the term metapsychology to anything psychological that has been concretized, thus he rejected traditional psychology in his time and considered psychoanalysis the true psychology. His view point is that in all Freud's work the human subject – not only his psychological attributes – is the centre of attention. He turned to psychoanalysis to emphasize the difference in saying that in everything Freud talks about, the human being is there. He said that psychoanalysis is the study of the concrete human and not concretization of his duplicates. In Politzer's own words (1928): "[P]sychoanalysis is a beginning, it is only a beginning, and we must, now that light is shed on its true essence, pursue research by considering a new point of view. … *Metapsychology* [concretizing the duplicates of the individual experience] has lived its life, and the history of *psychology* is beginning" (165).

4 His papers on Narcissism, Instincts, Repression and the unconscious are papers on the psychological processes involved in those phenomena and not metapsychological papers.

5 Primal, like primal hoard or primal phantasies, are states that engender sequels, and function unconsciously as prototypes. Primary, like primary narcissism is a foundation on which a secondary form stands, and lurks in the back ground but remains functional while its secondary form is active.

6 This statement sounds a strange way to describe a psychoanalytic theory. Yet, if psychoanalysis is revealing the unconscious which is, in fact, revealing the unconscious processes rather than unconscious material, where else would we find that process if not in the consciousness of the patient, and in the style of that consciousness?

7 This process is repeated in every psychosexual phase, and what decides which fixation is going to be the prevalent in the individual. Until now, the main answer is the one that was created by traumata, which needs to be revised.

3

NARCISSISM

Identity and identification

It is impossible to 'un-know' what is already known. Therefore, we can only imagine, speculate, deduce, or reconstruct how it must have been for Freud to deal with discoveries that he did not even have the vocabulary to adequately express. This difficult situation created several psychoanalytic propositions that were later misconceived. Because after the theory matured and acquired better vocabulary to express it, those propositions looked wanting and deficient, if not right-out wrong. This is what necessitates revising them. Narcissism is one of those propositions, but in an unusual way. It is a term that Freud used as early as 1910 to 'give' a meaning to homosexual object choice, which he considered to be narcissistic in a sense similar to what is implied in the myth of Narcissus (Freud, 1910h). The tendency to borrow from something known – even in a myth – to describe something totally newly discovered was one of Freud's ways of compensating for the lack of 'better words', as we have seen with the Oedipus complex. Notwithstanding, the major problem with the psychoanalytic theory in general is Freud's need to use the term 'libido' as a theoretical solution to all his discoveries. Narcissism is one of the conceptions that has been difficult to define or explain properly because of its libidinal configuration.

Narcissism is a psychoanalytic concept that *stands in the theory as something that we should all know its connotation, when it has never had a stable denotation* that analysts could identify and agree or disagree upon. This characteristic should have caused a great deal of disagreement between analysts, yet the history of psychoanalysis reveals a different picture. Freud used the term, in its libidinal connotation, in interpreting the Schreber Case (1911c) then in *Totem and Taboo* (1912–1913) to describe a stage in psychosexual development between autoerotism and object-love. The concept went through several adjustments that could easily be considered basic revisions in order to meet Freud's burgeoning development of the theory and his usage of the revised meanings. Yet he was always dissatisfied with his adjustments. When he came to make what seemed then a final statement about it (1914c) he expressed his dissatisfaction to Abraham saying: "The Narcissism was a difficult labour and bears all the marks of a corresponding deformation. That you accept what I wrote about Narcissism touches me deeply and binds us even closer together. I have a very strong feeling of vexation at its inadequacy" (in Jones, 1955, 340–341). The reason, as will shortly be given, is that Narcissism is a proposition of a major significance while Freud and analysts after him judged it as a new concept which could be of use in explaining a few psychoanalytic issues and later to describe some pathological entities. It came across as one of the manifestations of psychopathology because as it was always seen in terms of expressing a type or a degree of libidinal investment there was always the possibility of deviations in the quantity of the investment or in the object of the investment.

The libido was a necessary evil in the theory of psychoanalysis. Freud was discovering the role of sexuality in symptom formation, infantile sexuality which introduced him to the act of representations and forced the concept of *Trieb* as the term to mean the act of transforming the endosomatic into the psychological, and required duality as the basis of any psychodynamics of the psychological phenomena. He needed a term that could be used to talk *quantitatively* about the tension within the *Triebhaft* duality of the sexual and life preservation, and to make the *qualitative* distinction between the sexual urges and its antithesis (the life urges). The term was 'libido'. It was amenable to being attached to qualitative distinct urges and being used quantitatively to express the pressure those urges exert on the mind. Moreover, it had the flavour of a metaphor. Freud defined it as "an expression taken from the theory of emotions". We could call this the energy, regarded as a quantitative magnitude (though not at present actually measurable), of those instincts [*Trieben*] which have to do with all that may be comprised under the word "love" (1921c, 90). As such, *Narcissism became a borderline concept that straddles the fence between an ontological entity and a useful usable concept, a manifestation of a libidinal condition and a libidinal state of a psychical phenomenon, also as a functional concept in psychological processes and a structural proposition that comprises all the psychical phenomena that pertain to the definition of identity.*

Narcissism was sometimes treated as an ontological entity that requires explanations in terms of the libido theory, and at some other times as an explanation of the state of libidinal cathecting manifested in a type of identity. In the first case, narcissism was seen as an initial condition where the libido is totally confined to the ego (a very vague explanation), which would be called *primary* narcissism and sometimes autoerotism. In that vein, the libido then becomes invested in the objects of the ego and changes from ego-libido to objects-libido. In this context, matters become quite confusing because the interplay of extending the libido to the objects could be reversed to be reinvested in the ego. This was not the real problem; the problem was: do we have one libido that branches out into two, or two basically different libidos where one gets activated a little later? Freud said (1914c):

> A differentiation of libido into the kind which is proper to the ego and one which is attached to objects is unavoidable corollary to an original hypothesis which distinguishes between sexual instincts and ego-instincts … The separation of the sexual instincts from the ego-instincts would simply reflect the two fold function of the individual.
>
> (77–78)

He then changed his position and said that narcissism is the withdrawal of the libido from the objects to be directed to the ego. No wonder he considered the libido theory a speculative theory (Laplanche & Pontalis, 1973).

In the second case the changes in the states of libidinal investment *needed* the concept of narcissism to solve a problem: how does the libido move from autoerotism (primary narcissism) to object-libido and undergo the necessary *qualitative* changes that allow investing in something very different from its original object – the ego? It is not possible to consider the initial state of the libidinal investment to be in the ego because Ego (analytically speaking) is an agent that has to be constructed of affective, cognitive, and behavioural elements to qualify as subject for libidinal investment in the first place. It could be regarded *as is* a primary narcissistic condition – as mentioned earlier – but not an object for libidinal narcissistic investment. More clearly expressed: in order to elucidate the process that brings the newly born out of his complete obliviousness of the world around him to awareness of its existence, Freud envisaged and called the first condition of the infant autoerotic – suggesting, thus, a *preliminary sense* of being that is separate from another awareness of the external world. This view is erroneous because the infant takes a few weeks to realize his presence by recognizing his reflection in a mirror.[1] What is important about this is the futility of inducing that recognition by external means and its happening spontaneously around the fourth month after birth. A sense of existence is a precondition to recognizing one's reflection in a mirror.

In order to bypass the flawed conception of an original state of libidinal investment in the ego, Freud inserted an intermediate phase in the model of psychosexual stages of development, between autoerotism and objects-love. These stages in the psychosexual model have erotogenic zones, conflictual nature, and result in types of resolution of the conflict, each having a timespan that is determined by the resolution of the conflict. The point of conflict then becomes either a point of progress for the ensuing stage or a point of fixation that gives the erotogenic zone of that stage control over the formation of the intrapsychical structure of the person. The narcissistic phase that Freud suggested was an effort to justify using the libido as an explanatory tool after narcissism seemed to have exposed a basic flaw. Thus Freud said (1914c):

> Let us now, taking any part of the body, describe its activity of sending sexually exciting stimuli to the mind as in "erogeneity", and let us further reflect that the consideration on which our theory of sexuality was based

> have long accustomed us to the notion that certain other parts of the body – the 'erotogenic' zones – may act as substitutes for genitals and behave analogously to them … For every such change in the erotogenicity of the organ there might then be a parallel change of the libidinal cathexis in the ego.
>
> (84)

The picture thus seems to have undergone a basic change and a major revision. The psychosexual stages of development have similar purposes and functionalities, and each stage has a narcissistic phase in it that should be part of its evolution – i.e., in each stage of psychosexual development acquired, an intermediate phase of narcissism that matches the conflict and resolution of the conflict of that stage. Both Bouvet (1959) and Grunberger (1979) 'saved the day' by appropriating narcissistic conditions to each stage of development. As such, narcissism would not be an aberrant type of love, a perversion in object choice, a state of withdrawal into the self, or a grandiose sense of significance; it would be a phase in the maturing (or immature) sense of identity, and relating to the other and to the self as another.

The reason for not being definitive in the understanding of the concept of narcissism in psychoanalysis is that there was no definitive stand on its proper place in the theory: is it a pathological condition caused by something else, or the cause of pathological conditions of different natures? This question is rare in a functional theory of psychoanalysis where the cause–effect relations are of paramount importance. For the concept of narcissism to last in the theory without getting a definitive functional place in it is telling about its nature and significance. The ones who dealt with the concept, including Freud, knew that narcissism is commonplace in psychological life and sometimes it acquires a more intrusive quality that disturbs a relationship with others. They also – without exception – knew that whether it is a pathological condition in its own right or causes pathological conditions – it is not explainable in terms of the economics of energy. *It is a proposition about identity, identification, and the differentiation of subject-object*. The reason I am saying this is that any way the analysts understood and used narcissism, they either talked about its distortions in terms of narcissism as an obstacle in the person's effort to define himself to the other (Bach, 1977; Kernberg, 1967, 1970, 1974), or a hindrance to defining the other to himself (Fosshage, 1995; Kohut, 1972; Smith, 1985), which indicated that Freud had three distinct periods in the development of the concept of narcissism. These were related mainly to moving from a simplistic view of an economic consideration of the libidinal investment to a qualitative conception of development and identification. Crockatt (2006) finds the concept applicable to the Kleinian main propositions like projective identification. Kohut (1968) elicits a whole syndrome based on narcissism – the narcissistic personality disorder – and builds his theory on the variations in that syndrome.

Yet another group of analysts were puzzled by the import of the concept on the theory despite its defectiveness. What they did was to tinker with the concept to 'correct' it enough to keep it in the theory. Kohut, by creating the syndrome of the narcissistic personality disorder created a new psychology (Self-Psychology) to replace the whole 'drive psychology' of the classical theory (1959, 1987). A concept like that would not have survived if it did not have more to it than meets the eye, especially when we realize that it survived Freud's insistence on keeping it and revising it in a libidinal framework when the theory of the libido was unable to sustain his main conception of *Trieb*.

For a while in the 1960s and 1970s there was a trend to expand the scope of psychoanalysis beyond the psychoneuroses to include what Freud previously called 'narcissistic neuroses' (in contrast with transference neuroses (1914c)). When that trend was at its peak, 'narcissism' was the main medium used to explore the possibilities and difficulties in dealing with the psychoses, hypochondria, and severe depressions, which led to the psychosomatic disorders. When it continued later in a less ambitious way there were some major attempts to introduce psychoanalysis to a new theoretical outlook with new theoretical reformulations making narcissism a main subject matter.

Towards a structural meaning of narcissism

The conception of narcissism needed a revision from the start and proved to have more to it than being a mere concept. Analysts who tried to revise the concept faced a variety of difficulties in dealing with its deceptive straightforwardness. Summarizing the literature on the subject of narcissism is a huge task. Even concentrating on any particular stretch of time would give a skewed view of the issue. However, I could say that most of the difficulties in what I was able to review were in two areas: 1. keeping the quantitative conception of narcissism but finding a substitute for the terms 'libido' and 'investment'; and 2. having a new conception of narcissism that does not dilute its substantive meaning.

The first problem stems from Freud's effort to accommodate the model of narcissism in the theory of *Trieb* because it was always conceived in dualities. So, he faced the possibility of starting with one libido (C. Younge's refused hypothesis), which divides later into two to accommodate the polarity of sex and self-preservation. Freud agonized about the libido theory at that point, because Young's conception of a singular libido seemed to be right. Another problem was deciding if the id is the source of the libido or if it is the ego that is its original container.[2] Grunberger says (1979):

> Whether the subject loves himself more or loves himself less will depend … not on the amount of object libido available to him, but on the relation between his narcissism and his instinctual libido. His narcissism may (or may not) permit him, so to speak, to accept from his id a certain quantity of

> libido, which can be measured, but narcissism per se cannot be evaluated quantitatively.
>
> (6)

Friedmann (1988) expresses that same problem even more clearly in saying:

> Correctly stated, Freud's thinking on this matter was both ambiguous and equivocal. Freud's position on whether it was the ego or id that served as this "great reservoir of libido" changed a number of times. These equivocations concerned Strachey and made him added Appendix to Freud's 1923 work *The Ego and the Id*.
>
> (499)

Greenberg said (1990):

> The significance of 'Beyond the pleasure principle' (BPP) cannot be understood by focusing solely on its manifest content. BPP is the product of theoretical displacements and compromise formations the motivation for which lies in the innovations introduced in 'On narcissism'. These innovations threatened assumptions about conflict and rationality inherent in Freud's libido theory.
>
> (282)

Most of the works that tried to adjust the basic conception of narcissism to the flawed concept of libido had to confront, and failed to deal with, narcissism as part of the system of energy. The analysts who opted to reformulate the conception of narcissism faced another difficulty. Meissner (2008a) presented a new approach to the conception of narcissism. He distinguished between *a self* that is a substantive autonomous agency (an ontological entity) that functions consciously and unconsciously. At the same time, *another self* that is an object of narcissistic investment could coexist. There is no problem with the idea of the two 'selfs' and their coexistence, but there should be – at least – a hint to the origination of each and the intrinsic internal link between them. In another work (2008b), Meissner distinguishes between *drives*, which he believes is the seat of the concept of narcissism, and *motives*, which he offers as a substitute for *drives* as the basis of a new conception of narcissism. He said (2008b):

> A theory of narcissism as motive, … may be more productive to help the patient understand that, whatever his envious or shameful or superior and entitled reactions may be, they are *motivated*, and thus have underlying reasons – and the motives for these reactions can be gleaned from an exploration of the infantile past that is being replayed in the psychoanalytic present. Furthermore, the patient can be helped to see that he does, in fact, have something to say about these motives: he can either replace them

> with other, more mature and adaptive motives, or he can bear the pain of whatever narcissistic injury or loss they entail, thereby putting them into a more adult perspective.
>
> (792)

The difficulties psychoanalysts had and still have with narcissism is also prevalent in their clinical understanding of what should be done with it. In most cases narcissism is considered a diagnostic entity or part of a diagnostic category [personality disorders]. In some other cases, like self-psychology, it is not a psychopathological condition but the core of all psychopathologies; therefore, it is seen as an interpretative theoretical tool. Green (2002) adapted narcissism to several other basic conceptions in psychoanalysis and talked about life-narcissism and death-narcissism, positive and negative narcissism, depicting it as an addendum to main issues in the theory. Abrams (1976) said: "If patients had not reached the stage of clear delineation of object and self, they could not develop a transference neurosis … a narcissistic organization never thereafter wholly abandoned even after external objects are cathected with libido in a constant way" (218). Statements like this one, and those similar which we would find in case reports on patients with narcissistic difficulties, suggest two things: a failed expectation of the patient's readiness or ability to engage in the therapeutic process of analysis; and a sense of frustration that the analyst seems to know what is happening but is helpless in effecting change. Bach described this situation saying (1977):

> Analysts who work with narcissistic patients frequently complain of the difficulty they experience in "getting through" to the patient and "making themselves heard", or, with growing irritation, they speak of "making a dent" in the patient or "cracking the narcissistic shell". They sometimes develop an intense feeling of frustration about the impermanence of even their effective interpretations and compare it with talking into the wind or writing on the sand, only to have one's words effaced moments later by the waves.
>
> (209)

I expressed the same feeling (2011) and described the analysis of a patient with narcissistic disorder as bringing *herself to the session to be analysed and then taking her back to her daily life*, as described also by Kernberg (1978).

There is no doubt that if the conception of narcissism is so difficult to grasp hold of, it is because it is an indirect casualty of the conceptions that relate to it and should not. For instance, it could be that the nature and function of the concept of the libido, which had and still has a major role in its explanation, is the main factor in distorting the connotation of narcissism. It could also be the notion that narcissism is an aberration in self-perception or in relating to others that is baffling psychoanalysts, without any of them asking: could there really be an object relation? In better terms, narcissism is an assumption of irregularity while it might be an unavoidable or inevitable psychical state. Addressing this requires turning the conception of narcissism from a piece of information that could cause things to happen or being caused to happen into a theoretical phenomenon that has a structural core that is missed, has to be identified and then defined. Although Freud's choice of the myth of Narcissus is deliberate, there is no definite proof that it was fully consciously determined.[3] We need to know what it was about the myth of narcissus that attracted Freud's attention to use it, and what was it actually meant to be used for.[4] Like the myth of Oedipus we realized that its structural core was the interfamilial dynamics and not incest and parricide; we should now look closer into the myth of narcissus to uncover its structural core. The myth goes like this:

> When Narcissus was born, his mother Leiriope asked Teirisias the seer if her newborn child would live a long life. He replied: "If he never knows himself." Narcissus grew to be a very beautiful youth who was adored by many lovers of both sexes. Among those who loved him in vain was the nymph Echo. She had previously been doomed forever, by the Goddess Hera, to repeat the last words of others' speeches. Hence, she was unable to initiate a conversation with Narcissus, and her incommunicable love for him wasted her to a mere voice, unnoticed by him.
>
> A young man who Narcissus also spurned, as he had done with Echo and the rest of his admirers, prayed that his rejecter should himself love unrequitedly. Nemesis, the goddess of retribution for evil deeds, arranged it so that Narcissus would see his reflection on the surface of a pool. He fell in love with his image and lay beside the water, helpless to touch his reflection and unable to tear himself away from it, until he faded away. His body was transformed into a flower, and thus Teiresias's prophecy was fulfilled.
>
> (Tripp, 1970)

Levi-Strauss (1955) advises that when we deal with a myth we do not read it as an event that has a sequence, but as a meaning that has a structure. The myth of Narcissus has the structure of an identity that fails to materialize resulting in fading without being, dyeing without end, and continuing but only in repetition. It happened a few thousand years ago, but happened again a few decades ago to Dorian Gray (from Oscar Wilde's great novel of the same name), and is happening to every newborn human up until now and indeed until the end. It is a myth of the meaning of acquiring an identity or a sense of being. The myth is not about self-love or choosing objects that are similar to self. However, the myth depicts the obsolete and lifelessness of Narcissism.[5] I would underline three points in the myth, which are clear in the main body of the myth and also have distinct links with the issues of narcissism in psychoanalysis. The only love mentioned in the myth was Echo's love for Narcissus; the rest was admiration and desire. Echo's love was an auditory form of his visual encounter with himself, which is one of the subtle aspects in the life of the narcissist who does not stop talking to himself. In both cases Narcissus heard only himself and saw only himself. In both the cases of failed love the outcome was death; Echo's and Narcissus's. Love in that myth was the synonym of death. The second point is Echo's love for Narcissus was doomed by the impossibility of getting him to hear something else but *his*-self, thus she did not materialize as an object. The result was vanishing in Narcissus's own voice confirming that the myth was exposing in a multi-determined manner the existence of death in the relationship with Narcissus. The objects in the narcissist's life are mute and lifeless. The third point is Narcissus's imaginary objects-of-love, whether Echo or his image, which were neither able to arouse a desire or a wish that could be satisfied or frustrated. Thus, that quasi-object was not capable of giving birth to a sense of being, which emerges with the formation of a wish and anticipation. *The myth of Narcissus is about the failure of developing a sense of being that would give birth to the external world.* It is structured around the trials and tribulation of the naissance of identity.

Psychoanalysis and the issue of identity

In 1897 Freud wrote two drafts – L and M – where he used the term 'identification' to indicate the modelling of the subject's self after someone else's. In that sense identification was used in the transitive mode of the verb 'to identify with or by'. It remained in that format as the more familiar concept of identification in psychoanalysis, even after Melanie Klein added the two mechanisms of projection and introjection, clarifying by them the function of identification in relating to others. Nevertheless, identification in its transitive format was used to explain a psychopathological process and its outcome condition. The development of the term in the Freudian doctrine was subtle. It underwent an unnoticed, though significant, change with the introduction of the Oedipus complex to the theory (1910h). It gradually moved more to the intransitive mode of the verb (identified the father and the mother as …). Another major change took place in *Totem and Taboo* (1912–1913) followed by the introduction of Narcissism to the libido theory (1914c). As mentioned earlier, Freud had to improvise an intermediate phase – in psychosexual development – between autoerotism and object love and called it narcissistic-identification. *Recognizing another aspect of identification, which in this case is identifying with the image of someone, took the concept of narcissism out of the domain of psychopathology, because it was deemed a necessary step towards normality.* It also entered the concept of identification into a sphere other than the limited scope of copying someone else. There is something to be noted here: when we use the verb to identify' in its intransitive mode it denotes defining the identified object like 'he identified me as a friend' or 'identified himself as a friend'. The concept of identification was no longer connoting a pathological mechanism but became the formative process of the *I* (Ich, translated by Strachey as Ego). The intransitive format of the verb proposes a distinction between *I* and non-*I*, which is necessary for identification to happen. Identifying the non-*I* has to precede or happen concurrently with identifying one's self. Thus, how does one identify himself? How could I say I am *Me*, if that is possible at all? If analysts were so interested in the pathological conditions that the mechanism of identification created, why were they not equally interested in the emergence and development of the subject's own identity?

It is not difficult to envisage a developmental line of the sense of being to answer this question.[6] The newborn infant spends the first four months without knowing he existed: he has no means to know that he is part of the things around him. This assumption is based on the fact that the infant does not recognize his reflection in the mirror before age four months although he could recognize his mother in the mirror holding him (Lacan, 1949). Although the infant, in that early time of his life, shows the signs of awareness of the existence of the world around him (sounds and other sensory stimulations), and people whom he deals with (recognizes the familiar and the unfamiliar), his awareness of himself needs something more than the outside world. As in the myth earlier, Narcissus was not *in-the-world* but had a world around him that catered for his needs. It would be a mistake to call that narcissism in the sense of self-centeredness or selfishness because those two conditions come after the self is acknowledged. But eventually the infant's endosomatic needs with their pressure on his mind and the caregiver's response to them would become 'experiences'; experiences of discomfort and comfort depending on how the caregiver responds to them. Two things happen when the infant *experiences* his endosomatic stimuli. The first is developing a *relationship* with the caregiver, and the second a preliminary sense of presence that comes from the caregiver's reaction to his demands. The manner in which the caregiver responds to those demands identifies the infant's presence to him: he cries at the discomfort of needing nourishment and his mother feeds him, identifying his endosomatic discomfort as 'You are hungry'. In other words, when the mother responds to the infant's need she is identifying him to himself; she is giving his sense of presence an identity, which would naturally weave in the forming relationship. The first identity is 'given' to the child; he is told who he is by his mother's reactions. We can imagine how psychical problems could emerge from such a very elementary process if the mother cannot read the infant's needs properly, or if she responds to it with feelings that become constituents of the identity she gives to her infant: "You are a bad boy for needing that now", etc.

At age six months the infant can always identify himself in the reflection in the mirror and enjoys both that and the little games he can play in front of the mirror. Lacan made an issue of the Mirror Stage (Lacan, 1949), but I will take it as Wallon originally presented it[7]: a moment when the infant starts to own an identity given to him – in the months previously – in the form of reflections from the outside world, whether from a mirror or just the mother and the others who do the mirroring. The given identity becomes a nucleus of a sense of being; it is the *Me* that the infant will build around it his speaking self or the *I*. We should stop for a moment to go back to the myth to learn something significant about the mirror stage. Narcissus spoke to Echo but his speech came back to him; he did not speak with her. He loved the man who had his image reflected on the surface of the water, but Narcissus loved only himself because there was no one to love but an image. Narcissus talked *to* Echo but unknowingly heard only himself. He saw the image of a beautiful young man who kept gazing at him without knowing that young man was himself. He knew an-other self, but as the oracle prophesized it was *his* and he had to die for doing that. In other words, if there is no other to address the individual there will be no voice (talk) and no image (recognition) of the self – i.e., there would be no narcissism. Narcissism is a psychical condition that can only be created by the existence of the other. Better, *narcissism is identifying the self in the reflection coming from another; Freud's narcissistic identification.* The evolution of the sense of *Me*-ness will be affected by the mother's potentialities such as allowing the infant to refuse her identification of him, or giving his *Me-ness* the freedom to express new needs (some psychological demands). In other words, the emergence of a sense of *I*-ness from the core *Me*-ness is a very vital and significant factor in the infant's formation of a true sense of himself (not of a self). The dynamics of that interaction with the mother regarding the consolidation of a sense of owning the *Me* leads to the emergence of an *I*; an *I* that speaks for the *Me* (the illustrious ego). Yet, it is noticeable that the infant at this stage of development still needs to be identified by name and not addressed as a pronoun: *Bill is a good boy, and not you are a good boy*.

The gradual change from a 'no presence' to a presence that acquires an identity is not a one shot deal. The identity of the early presence is related solely to a creation of the oral activity and its psychodynamics. The infant acquires an oral identity because this is the main issue of interaction between him and the mother in the first year. The demand of the oral phase and the resolution of its conflicts forms and consolidates an oral *Me*, which Erikson (1963) characterizes as a trusting/mistrusting *I*. The crucial point in the formation of the infant's oral character is whether he will be allowed to own his oral identity or whether the mother would persist and insist on keeping it for herself through nurturing the infant's dependency on her – thus continuing giving it to him. In other words, the infant might not get the chance to own his oral identity and go on relying on the existence of a mirror to offer him an identity. The significance of distinguishing between owning an identity and remaining on the receiving end is in the crust of narcissism: if the infant has to get his identity from the mother's reflection of his image he will have to be content with a narcissistic identification; identifying with an image that will always be conditional on what the other reflects back, therefore an unpredictable identity, or owning an identity that is unstable in all circumstances.

The same processes have to be relived in the next phases of development because they come with new tasks that will impact the infant's identity. In the anal phase, the toddler has to interact with his mother around his bowel movement and exercising some regularity in keeping and letting go. He will experience a new sense of presence and will be reflected in an image of that presence. As in the previous phase he eventually has to own his identity, which in this phase will be about autonomy vs. doubt and shame. Once again, the dynamics of dealing with the conflict of that phase could create the possibility of a narcissistic identification with an image reflected by the caregiver about the success and failure of developing the ability to regulate keeping and letting go. It is important to consider that the infant will enter this phase (and each new phase) and deal with its conflicts through the identity that managed to be formed in the previous phase. Thus, the *Me* (the infant) of the oral phase has to construct the *Me* of the anal phase. It will always be a matter of *who is who* in each psychosexual phase: is it the infant who is experiencing the events of the phase or the image that the mother reflects who is the real player? The phase of narcissistic-identification that separates the absence of existence from owning the identity is vital because it decides if the individual will have an identity or will be looking for one in every encounter with the other.

Around three years of age – and after the passing of the oral and anal demands – the child becomes both curious about sexual differences and able to create his own theories about those differences. The penis takes a centre place in the conflicts, and the resolution of those conflicts, for two novel and significant issues that overshadow the phallic phase of development. The first issue is the role of sexual distinction between male and female in structuring the intermediate period of narcissistic identification. The second is the Oedipus structure and its imposition on the process of identification. Preliminarily we could say that the pre-Oedipal phases are characterized by a closed relationship of mother–infant, where narcissism would have no outlet to release the infant from that bind. There is no third to free each of them from the other. Therefore the phallic phase, with its Oedipal framework, introduces a third party who could either be a source of enrichment or of complication in the resolution of phallic narcissism. The child will have two possible sources for his narcissistic identity and could modify and change his identification based on his relationship with the new parent. For the boy, the father makes the mother of the Oedipal phase a new object and, for the girl, the father is a new object. Identification becomes a three-party situation, because the father will contribute to the integrity and consolidation of the sense of *Me*-ness of the boy and would give a new meaning to the I-ness. At the same time the father's relationship with the mother would give the girl a different sense of *Me*-ness that would affect the function of her *I*.

The Oedipus structure would influence the narcissistic condition of the child in a remarkable way. Instead of the narcissistic image that the caregiver would reflect to the child and the child having to own it or to let it own him, the third party in the Oedipus triangle opens the narcissistic stage to a new possibility. The male child would find in the father a narcissistic image that he could identify himself by. The mother then does not remain the source of his narcissistic identification but the subject of the new narcissistic identification he develops with the father. The girl would also see her mother not as her source of narcissistic identification but as the subject she would identify with to gain her father's admiration. The Oedipus triangular situation moves the acquisition of an identity from owning an image reflected to the child through the caregiver's judgement of the child to identifying with an external living subject who engages the child in the interfamilial dynamics. The shift from taking in the identity given by a parent is different from identifying with by being a part of the triangular dynamics. Identifying with a parent happens when the parent ceases telling the child what he is and demands from the child to be what has to be. Better, identification in its intransitive meaning happens when the child is neither given an identity that he could accept or reject (a sense of *Me*-ness), nor agree or disagree with, but when he is left to discover the identity of his parents and start forming his own *I*-ness.

The process of identifying one's self is not based on identifying *with* or *by*. It is a process in its own right. Identifying with or by someone else happens when there is no solid narcissistic-identification established, and there is a defined identity 'out there' that is possible to copy. As in the Oedipus complex narcissistic-identification is no more acceptable by the two parents, and the child is expected to identify with the parent of the same sex. Of this conception of the emergence, Grunberger says (1979):

> Development and consolidation of an identity brings us face to face with the concept of narcissism. If we use the Myth of Narcissus and Lacan's usage of the mirror as the birth place of the imaginary I, we could say that narcissism is caught in the mirror between a Me and its I.
>
> (68)

In a more detailed way: narcissism is the relationship one has with his image. The image of the self could be reflected by the other, imposed from outside or formed and owned by the person freely; anyhow, it is identification with an image. In other words, the human being has no way to be directly himself, but only via the medium of an image. We could also make a subtle, but useful, distinction between *Me* and *I*. Narcissism is caught between *Me* (my sense of being, which is manifested in a state of awareness) and an *I* that figuratively and literally speaks for me. *Me* is the unconscious identity that is *supposed* to be the closest to my authenticity. The *I* is what is *supposed* to be the talking Me. There are two explanations for that indispensable *alienation* (the transformation of the subject into an object) from the self. The first: historically and developmentally we begin our psychical life as objects and know that before any sense of being. The second: getting a sense of being from the reflection of our image has to translate into a being observing that sense of being. Even if this process succeeded perfectly (which never happens) there will be the duality of a subject observing a subject that happens to be the same subject. There will always be a gap between the *I* and the *Me* in every human being's psychical life and it will be exactly like Narcissus's ponds. In that pond will reside a state of narcissism (not a case of narcissism). Out of that state comes our identity which will be contingent on three factors: the degree of the distortion done to the *Me* by the caregiver; the *I*'s familiarity with the nature of the *Me*; and the *I*'s admission and awareness of the existence of the gap.

Narcissism: the turning point

Between 1914 and 1923 Freud revised his main propositions and psychoanalytic conceptions in a drastic way (See Fayek, 2013). In those nine years some works like *Beyond the pleasure principle* (1920g) and *The Ego and the Id* (1923b) were considered turning points in the evolution of the psychoanalytic theory. A closer look would prove that those two works would not have been possible to think of – let alone write – without the revisions of the 1915 so-called metapsychology papers. Yet, the seeds for what are considered turning points were already in *Totem and Taboo* (1912–1913), and *On Narcissism: an introduction* (1914c). In better terms: In *Totem and Taboo* and *On Narcissism* there were what was to turn psychoanalysis around but that needed to revise four more principal propositions in the theory to make that possible: *Trieb*; Repression, the Unconscious, and Regression. That was done in 1915, but mistakenly Strachey called those revisions metapsychological.

Some analysts suggest that abandoning hypnosis was a turning point away from the catharsis theory, which is a weak suggestion because Freud still expected free association to do the same job hypnosis used to do. Others identified that moving to a purely libido theory was another turning point, but the libido theory was not axiomatic enough; the term 'libido' was better than 'catharsis' but had the same denotation. However, most theorists of psychoanalysis mean and identify the turning point in psychoanalysis as the 1920 change of the *Trieb* theory and the emergence of ego psychology in 1923. It is undeniable that in those two works there were two fundamental shifts. The first is the disappearance of sexuality as the main etiological factor in psychoneurosis – thus the libido theory had to be set aside, partially. The second, consequently, was replacing the topographic metapsychology with a new topography that was later given the name 'the structural point of view'.

The first vicissitude changed the originator of psychical life from sexuality/self-preservation to life/death, but maintaining the concept of *Trieb* as the condition of the new duality – i.e., exerting pressure on the mind to act. The duality of life and death does not qualify as an originator of psychical life because it was the bedrock of all organic life, and their pressure on the mind would not be individually identified. We have to use our familiarity with the structural core of those terms to make sense of this vicissitude. The life/death duality was still *Triebhaft*, not in terms of its behavioural expression but in its impact on affect, the originator of psychical life. It is a *Trieb* that will define the very basic in a person's identity and not just his psychical life. In other words, the dynamic exchanges between life (binding and constructing) and death (destructing decaying) would reveal a foundational level of existence which embodies the most elementary of the unconscious states of mind. Notwithstanding, it is peculiar that this vicissitude solved the problem caused by the second vicissitude of eliminating the *Ucs.* in a new conception of the subject. The life/death duality being a basic fundamental *Triebhaft* duality preserved and entrenched the concept of the unconscious in the theory and forced Freud to re-instate it in his new theory of the subject.

The second change was eliminating the topographic point of view with its cognitive systems of *Cs., Pcs.* and *Ucs.*, and replacing it with the three agencies *Ego, Id,* and *Super-Ego*. This exchange inadvertently meant the end of the psychoanalytic conception of mental and cognitive functioning. Losing the psychoanalytic modality of mentation eradicated the concept of the unconscious and its entire attributes like the working of the primary process. By opting to replace the topographic point of view with psychical agencies, Freud was unable to do without the topographic mental modality and had to insert it in the new modality of agencies; hence each agency had to have mini-topographic systems. He said (1923b): "The division of the psychical into what is conscious and what is unconscious is the fundamental premise of psychoanalysis" (13). At the same time reducing the *Trieb* to a duality of life/death revealed a very important change in the direction psychoanalysis had to take and continue on with. There was a stepping back from the psychodynamics of symptoms and the other psychical phenomena related to that, advancing instead to constructing a new psychology of psychical agencies. The three agencies of *I* (ego) the *It* (the not-me or the Id), and aspects or functions of the *I* and the *It* that are emancipated from both get into a balancing game of power and influence. There is no denying that the changes to *Trieben* and to the topographic systems move psychoanalysis to the issue of the subject's identity after being, for three decades, a theory of forces and urges. There is also no denying that ego-psychology was a desperate effort to give this new perspective a theoretical framework. It could be said that analysis was moving from the analysis and interpretation of the role of the interpersonal relationship with the caregivers to the examination of the formation of the intrapsychic as the core of a person's *character*.

Narcissism created a cleavage between preoccupation with the state of the individual and his functioning (becoming narcissistic) and the nature of the human subject and the structural nature of his identity (being narcissistic). Freud said (1912–1913): "A human being [the subject] remains to some extent narcissistic after he has found external objects for his libido. The cathexis of objects which he effects are as it were emanations of the libido that still remains in his ego and can be withdrawn back into it once more" (89). For instance, analysis moved from the act of dealing with the manifestations and indices of the *Trieb* to the structuring function of the *Trieb*. In other words, psychoanalysis moved from a theory of psychical entities, psychical mechanisms, and metapsychologies without a psychology to a theory of the human subject – a theory of the *I* that could be anything but will always be the centre of the subject's identity. Better, psychoanalysis moved towards a theory of the formation and de-formation of the *I*, its authenticity and fallacy, its flexibility and rigidity, its link with the body or emptiness of any relevance to the subject, etc., instead of a theory of causes and effects. I think it is very easy to recognize now the disastrous effect of translating *I* by Ego; it objectified and reified the most subjective, dynamically active and central in a theory of psychoanalysis. The unfortunate translation of *Trieb* by drive caused the misconception of psychoanalysis as a drive psychology, and translating *Ich* or *I* by ego returned psychoanalysis back to analysis of psychical entities instead of underlining the major turning point towards a theory of the subject.

As I mentioned earlier, the gap between *Me* and *I* is primary in the process of acquiring an identity, and it is also the seat of narcissism; the narcissism Freud considered unavoidable. But to show the nature of the relationship between *I* and *Me,* I quote an interesting statement by Freud (1923c), when discussing a person's responsibility for his impulses:

> If I seek to classify the impulses that are present in Me according to social standers into good and bad, I must assume responsibility for both sorts; and if in defense, I say that what is unknown, unconscious and repressed in Me is not my "ego" [not *I* or myself], then I shall not be basing my position upon psycho-analysis, I shall not have accepted its conclusion – and I shall perhaps be taught better by the criticism of my fellow-men, by the disturbances in my actions and the confusion of my feelings not only "is" in *Me* but sometimes "act" from out of me as well.
>
> (133)

In this statement Freud raises the two most important things introduced by the concept to the theory of psychoanalysis: 1. the gap between the *I* or the assumed and acquired identity, and the *Me*, the reflected image of the self and expected to become the core identity; and 2. that *Me* is unconscious while *I* is trying to express the *Me* consciously as authentically as it could.

This is an introduction to the main point in the concept of narcissism and how it changed psychoanalysis.

Freud was able first to realize that identification was more than a defence mechanism or a pathological process. Abraham (1924) used the term 'internalization' to describe identification, mostly in the oral phase, and Ferenczi (1912) introduced the term 'introjection' to explain identification in a different psychosexual stage. As a result, Freud regarded identification as a formative process of the *I*. In *Totem and Taboo* (1912–1913) he suggested the term 'incorporation' as the basis of three processes that lead to identification: assimilation, internalization, and introjection. The following year he introduced the concept and the term 'narcissism' as a stage in the development of the *I*. It was at first a desperate attempt at rescuing the catharsis theory from its fate. But, once he had the insight that identification is a formative process of the subject (*I*) and not a pathological mechanism, he borrowed from Greek mythology the example of Narcissus to explain the very structuring aspect in acquiring a sense of *I*-ness, separating *I* from *Me*.

It became clear that Freud had to deal with the psychology of the subject who is comprises an identity that needed a speaker to express it. Better, the being of the human subject is dual and his intriguing nature comes from the non-exact replication of the two components of his being. This is when, in 1915, he wrote the three papers that Strachey called the metapsychology papers (they were three papers on the psychology of *Trieb*, Repression, and the Unconscious). In those three papers we see the real turning point in the theory of psychoanalysis, which was instigated by the insight of narcissism. The three concepts were entities in the catharsis theory, but in their revisions (along with the concept of regression) he assigned to each of them a preliminary stage which is structurally different and topographically *Ucs*, and needed a means of expression; thus, they became processes of changing from a primary to a secondary state. This is the idea of processing an imposed unconscious identity into an assumed conscious identity.

Reading the *Ego and the Id* as the book on a new topography of *I* (Ich) and the *Id* (Es) is absolutely impossible. Strachey not only distorted the denotation of *I* by making it an object with functions, thus no longer the pronoun of the first person, but also changed *Es* which should be translated by *It.* He gave a very peculiar reason for that. He said that there was confusion about the concept of the unconscious, so he decided to make *Es* the nominator (partially) of the *Ucs*. In Freud's explanation of borrowing the term from Groddeck we notice without too much speculation that he was *impressed* by Groddeck's realization that the *I* acts as if it has a counterpart, which is undefined or something like 'a-not *I*'. The *It* has no place in the sphere of consciousness; it is out of the sense of *I*-ness. Strachey's translation took psychoanalysis back full blast to the catharsis theory when he translated *It* with *Id* and made it the container of instincts in their most elementary meaning as biological urges. This is the reason for my thinking that *The Ego and the Id* was a psychoanalytic blunder.[8]

To sum up, the period from 1913 to 1923 was one that witnessed the rebirth of a real psychoanalysis: identification became a formative process of the *I*, the formative process of the *I* forced a revision of the pressure of repression and new explorations of the vicissitudes of the *Trieb*, along with redefining the systemic unconscious *Ucs*. (the a-conscious). When those things were integrated, Freud was able to go 'Beyond the pleasure principle' and approach the subject of the *Ich* and the *Es.*; to get to the puzzling phenomena of the Narcissus-subject. We need to understand what the place of narcissism is in the total theory and grasp the insights it gives us to save present psychoanalysis from demise (Fayek, 1981).

Narcissism and the psychology of the subject

Laplanche is of the idea that Western culture is the culture of the subject (1997), and to a limited extent the Lacanian view of the subject. The main thrust towards the philosophy of the 'subject' was the German idealist metaphysics in particular.

However, this thrust reached an impasse after a valiant effort of two centuries to define (identify) the subject. The impasse came from the impossibility of defining the subject defining as an object because his consciousness is a major aspect of his identity (the *I*), and it transcends itself in perpetual consciousness of its consciousness. When the human subject talks about himself to inevitably participate in defining his identity to the other, he loses his subjectivity, which is his true identity (the *me*). The subject in the idealist philosophies was an embodiment of dualities; duality of one talking and yet he is supposed to be listening, talking when supposed to be silent. Transcendental consciousness, in a peculiar way, *is* Narcissus's reflection in the pond expecting to talk about the one looking at him. For Narcissus to talk he had to think he was talking about the image in the water, and believe that the image was listening. The subject does not exist as he is but in a duality of him and a counterpart (his otherness). In spite of the insights of some philosophers like Schopenhauer who spoke of an 'unconscious' of sorts within the subject's presence and existence, that unconscious was not of the same fabric of the subject's subjectivity. It was 'something' to contend with.

Western culture was waiting for an intuition that would unlock the riddle of a subject who is unconscious of his duality but living it fully all the time; living a duality but unable to recognize himself in that counterpart that he is not conscious of. This duality was approached by Freud first through hypnosis: he silenced the conscious-subject to listen to his counterpart. But he wanted the subject to listen to his counterpart accepting it as himself so he could tell Freud things about that dormant counterpart. The intuition, which Western culture was waiting for, came to Freud from asking the dreamer (it happened to be Freud himself) to talk to him about his dream. He discovered the method of interpreting dreams (1900a). The subject is quietly asleep, says things by dreaming them (the dream is the speech of the sleeper), wakes up, and if he could listen to what he had dreamed he could then make Narcissus talk with his reflection in the pond: silence is broken and consciousness ceases to transcend itself. The speaker is not the listener, despite both being one. Freud, then, realized that parapraxes (1901b) could do the same thing – i.e., turns the unconscious aspect of the subject's duality into a consciousness that dispels such duality. He went further, showing that in ordinary talking, especially if it is free and not guarded, we can hear that counterpart revealing himself. Mastering the attributes of the processes that bridge the conscious and the unconscious allowed the symptom of the psychoneuroses to talk to the doctor and be translated to the consciousness of the patient. *Freud opened the impasse of the separateness between the subject and his counterpart by discovering the language that the counterpart uses*: the language of the primary process. Lacan likened Freud to Champollion who used the Rosetta stone in translating an unknown language to a known language: he translated the language of the dreamer to the language of the awake.

Freud's attention to the intents of the counterpart are foreign to the subject, thus it exists in a state of unconsciousness. However, the times that Freud was able to discover those intents revealed that the unconscious is still able to be expressed in manners that are familiar to the subject. The unconscious intents were expressed, but in a disguised way and in a language that is not the language of the conscious subject. This is when he came to a very significant insight: our psychical life is made of two distinct conditions – primary and secondary. Freud found out that the primary processes have the capability of linking with the secondary processes and infiltrate them (in padded words, as Lacan called them). In the revisions of 1915 Freud gave a primary stage to each of Narcissism, Repression, *Trieb*, and the *Ucs*. Thus, those concepts, which were previously simple ontological entities, changed by being of two phases: because changing from a primary state to the final state entailed a process of transformation, those concepts have gained a structuring core. There was no longer repression but a process of repressing that deserves individual examination in every patient. The most significant aspect in that insight is understanding what happens to the primary after the subject moves to the secondary stage. Freud found that the primary stays lurking in the background and never vanishes. Primary narcissism, the systemic unconscious, primal repression and the pressure of the endosomatic on the mind – all continue exerting their pressure on the mind and linking with their secondary finding in ways to be represented. The duality of the subject was not a duality of body and mind (the Cartesian duality) as the contemporary schools claim; it is the duality of the primary and the secondary processes. Laplanche defined that duality well when he said that the interpretation of an unconscious thought does not end it because it has two inscriptions: a systemic one which is never erased; and its copy which could be interpreted and restored in another chain of ideas. The primary process relates to the originators of the psychical; it turns the endosomatic into representation that will be the nucleus of the intrapsychical. The intrapsychical structure is the *Me* (Moi, Mich, etc.), it is the true-ness of subjectivity.

We have to consider the input of the other, which is vital in the formation of the *Me*-ness of an infant and then of the child's identity. The infant has to acquire the language (not speech) of the caregiver to express his *Me*-ness so it would be understood, to learn what would please, and how being pleased would look like. The speaking *I* (Je, Ich, etc.) emerges from the *Me*, and when it peaks it uses the language of the secondary process (condensation, displacement and the pictorial form of the thing-presentation). The *I* is unable to notice or fathom the workings of the primary process, hence the *Me* creates the dream, or makes a joke, or forms a symptom. Sometimes the *Me* sneaks in the speech of the *I* and shows its face in a slip of the tongue. In other words, we have a narcissistic condition in every person: a split between an *I* and its counterpart (image), a silent *Me* and a speaking *I* (echo), and an *I* that does not know itself completely because its counterpart is silent (the reflection that we get from the other). Therefore, we should not consider narcissism an 'abnormality' because it is the human condition; *humans can only exist narcissistically because it is impossible to have only an* I *that has no origin or a* Me *that has no speaker and is not the speaker.*

However, narcissism could become abnormal or the seat of abnormality. Even though in terms of the libido theory it might sound strange to consider any kind of narcissism normal, Freud (intuitively) said: "Narcissism in this sense [having a place in the regular course of human sexual development] would not be a perversion, but the libidinal compliment of the egoism of the instinct of self-preservation, a measure of which may justifiably be attributed to every living creature" (1914c, 73–74).

The existence of a *Me* distinct from the *I* and the gap between them is the province of the psychoanalytic theory of the subject. That distinction relates to some basic attributes of the subject's dualities: authentic vs. false, true vs. lie, *Cs*. vs. *Ucs*., defined vs. diffused. There is always an implicit distinction in our minds between the two sides of the 'subject's coin'. Is *I* the honest representative of the *Me*? Is it aware of its demands or does it leave it to the disguised ways used by the *Me* to express itself? Is the *Me* the dominant partner in that duality thus the subject is more authentic but less sophisticated (hysterical)? Or is the *I* the dominant partner thus the patient is more sophisticated but less spontaneous (obsessional)? What is the place of the other in the subject's narcissistic condition? Is there what are called narcissistic personalities, narcissistic disorders, and what would they be if narcissism is the natural human condition? Without exaggeration, all the psychoanalytic issues, theoretical or clinical, individual or group, pathological and creative, etc., could be reformulated in the language of the phenomena of narcissism; they will get no speculative reactions.

Before Narcissus encountered his image he was not narcissistic. He was like children before they developed a sense of *Me*-ness. The first sense of *Me*-ness comes as a first sense of you-ness, which the caregiver identifies and projects to the infant. Gradually the infant will claim that identification and take it as his. In the hypothetical Narcissus's terms: *There is someone very beautiful there … Oh that is Me!* By taking good possession of the caregiver's definition the infant starts to give the sense of *I*-ness but it takes many experiences and months of work on the part of the infant to reach: *I* am this *Me*. Narcissism is then born and establishes the nucleus of the intrapsychic. In a normal (non-pathological) development the caregiver identifies the infant's needs properly, building a correct image of the infant, which he will adopt willingly and build his *I*-ness accordingly. A prevailing conception of narcissism is that it is a psychical condition that progresses in a continuum; it starts and continues with degrees of intensity. In the 1970s Kohut (1972) and Kernberg (1970) coined the term 'narcissistic disorder', suggesting that it is a unified condition. Fact in point: each stage of psychosexual development has its own narcissistic position, emanating from the kinds of new needs the child has to deal with. Thus, the caregiver would have to give the infant a new definition of himself in dealing with the new demands of that new phase. Each phase in development is a new stance for a new narcissism – i.e., there is oral narcissism, followed by anal narcissism, and phallic narcissism. If each narcissistic phase went well the person would establish a comprehensive narcissism where *I* would become all those *Me*-s. Erikson was quite perceptive when he extended the developmental phases to eight because in every stage in life the person's narcissism has to correspond to the psychical demands of that stage. The narcissism of an attractive young woman has to remain solid when beauty is gone and the demands (and benefits) of ageing kick in.

The core of narcissism is complex. First the mother has to identify her infant's need correctly and to be able to give him back a clear definition of those needs. This is not possible without some distortions from the mother's own character and needs. The infant then assimilates that to form a sense of *Me-ness*. Nonetheless, it is still the infant who would 'sense' if his mother has read him right or misread him. Repression of his own affects in that case is primary – i.e., is a repression of an affective reaction to the mother's potentials and limitations. The *I* that emerges from that *Me* will be false or an as-if *I*. This too is not straightforwardly done, because the infant has to trust his mother in the oral phase, or be sure of her judgement in the anal phase, etc. The *I*-ness is another hurdle because the infant has to identify his *Me-ness* comfortably. In the anal phase, for instance, a mother identifies her infant as stubborn when he might actually be just constipated, scared, or enjoying holding back. The infant is accused of stubbornness for not defecating and not out of stubbornness. In spite of the power of the mother and the helplessness of the child in terms of identifying his Me, there comes a moment when the actual Me would be primarily repressed, thus it exists in disguise. In other words, narcissistic disorders happen when the child is offered an identity that is not reflecting his true Me and he has to deal with either a false *Me* or a false *I*. This condition is further complicated by the widening circle of caregivers with the child's development. There will be more than just the mother to contribute to his identification and those caregivers might disagree with the mother's perception of the child. Therefore, others could be new sources of identification, as he would also be another *I* for them.

Freud suggested that *I* (ego) *has* two masters (I am not sure of the super-*I* as a third master). Therefore, in narcissism we have to consider the dynamics of the Me, the *I*, and the other. In the subject's relations with others he will be looking for the others' definition of himself. His *Me* would constantly be examining the other's perception, the *I* would be careful in what it is expressing, the other's own narcissistic nature would unconsciously have an input in the relationship. In any relationship of the subject with another there is a compulsion to repeat aspects of the original narcissistic situation with the caregiver of looking for feedback. In the so-called narcissistic personality disorder, or even just a narcissistic personality, the subject is absorbed in his own narcissistic endeavours, which makes him oblivious of the other and his narcissistic endeavours. Thus, he falsely seems not relating to others, while he is actually very much in a relationship with that other – but an imaginary relationship.

In a brief expansion of this point, if the *Me* or the authentic component of the subject's duality is well founded it will master the way the *I* will do in dealing with the other. The subject would be his true character, and would be receptive of the position the other takes from him. In case of a repressed Me (primary repression) it will infiltrate the *I* in the disguised ways we encounter in psychoneuroses, and the *I* will have to 'manage' the situation it is actually having with the other. However, in narcissistic disorders we encounter the reverse condition: a false *I* not allowing the true subject to be, and either submits completely to the other, or compulsively seeks his feedback to build its character, or puts the emphasis on impressing the other. It is important to remember that we are talking here about a general context of psychopathology, but the specifics come from the fixation on a phase of development. There are anally produced psychoneurosis, oral character disorders, and phallic narcissistic disorders.

A question could arise at this point: is this theoretical configuration better in any way than the original conception of the subject as an object, describing relations in libidinal terms, and looking at psychopathologies from the perspective defence mechanisms? The answer is simple: the original theory that we are familiar with is based on modalities that substitute for the subject: he is narcissistic, obsessive, aggressive, etc. The true theory of psychoanalysis is a theory of the subject's condition: how he relates to others, deals with his choices, manages his frustrations. In other terms, the psychology of the subject forms a theory of narcissus, not a theory of narcissism. Narcissus could have lived if he stopped looking infatuated at his image, and psychoanalysis could be revived and survive if we do not keep looking at the images of the subject.

Character and narcissism

One day I received in the mail a postcard showing an image of East European countryside, and what looked like a family having a pleasant meal in the back garden of a house in the countryside. The background view of the image was the view in the postcard. The picture was of an ex-patient who finished his analysis a few years prior, and a young woman looking at him with love and admiration. He indicated that he and his eldest daughter (who caused him great pain all her life) were visiting the village that the family was originally from. The picture gave me a message that has its meaning in his analysis: a change in his relationship with his daughter, and indirectly overcoming his deep hatred for his mother. He was born in Canada but his mother – the matriarch of the family – made him live in the old country by being sometimes 'ridiculously' insistent on keeping some old tradition of the old country. In his analysis he insisted that she hated him as she hated Canada, and he reciprocated by hating her and 'her' country. The picture and the implicit changes psychoanalysis might have brought about set me thinking. What did I do in his analysis?

After all is said and done what we receive in our offices is people who are made miserable by their thoughts, imagination, compulsive behaviour, helplessness regarding their failure in establishing gratifying relationships with others, including the dearest ones, and most of all helplessness towards the compulsion to repeat. They come expecting to get rid of what causes their unhappiness. We know that we do not do that – i.e., we do not treat morbid thoughts, faulty imagination, and morbid behaviour, mend relationships or teach methods to stop repetition compulsions. We psychoanalyze a person and hopefully *he* will do what he thought *we* would do for him.[9] We also know that what the patient comes with is what he will leave with: nothing he will get rid of, nothing will be added to him; only rearrangement of his intrapsychic core, or what he is as a subject. The degree of success will depend on our talents and expertise and the patient's inclination and capabilities. So, what we could honestly say that we do is bring the subject's *character* – or most of it – out of the convoluted ways narcissism distorted it. We try to change the faulty narcissistic structure of that person to give his character the chance to emerge. Character is the person, 'the subject', the human being, the one who although embodies his particular duality is still what he is. The patient comes with his character affected by his condition and hopefully will leave with his character more intact. This characterization would – no doubt – sound unacceptable or simplistic in the ears of the sophisticated psychoanalyst. Yet whatever he would say about psychoanalytic therapy will not expose something I missed in the sophisticated 'procedure' (I know, because my training was in sophisticated psychoanalysis).

What is character?

Freud published a three and a half page paper titled 'Libidinal types' (1931a). It was the only paper in his whole text on character. He acknowledged that human beings could be grouped in multiple ways based on physical as well as mental attributes. So, he suggested using the libido (the energy of *Trieb*, which straddles the physical and the mental) to setting up purely psychological types. He suggested three 'pure' types: the erotic, the obsessional, and the narcissistic. He then added three mixed types: the erotic-fascistic, the obsessional-narcissistic, and the erotic-obsessional. He stipulated that those types do not coincide with any clinical group; on the contrary "they must comprehend all the variations which according to our practical judgement fall within the limits of the normal" (217). Yet he questioned if in their extreme states they might approximate the clinical picture and bridge the gap between the normal and the pathological. Freud approached the human subject from something basic: how the psychical energy is structured around some subjective character, and how it is not pathological or able to become pathological but could get involved in psychopathology. We should note that Freud considered character a psychical construct that is independent of what might happen to it. In other words: *character is what carries the burdens of the psychoneuroses*. To avoid summarizing a paper that is a summary in its own right, I will just mention the main thoughts about a libido turned into character types. Libidinal types should fit well in the narcissistic duality model and position the subject within that proposition well.

The erotic character is dominated by fear of losing love; therefore, it is very dependent on others who may withhold love from him. According to the narcissistic duality model this character is incapable of assuming the responsibility of expressing the *Me* and is more responsive to the narcissistic expectations of the other. The *Me* has to resort to the working of the primary process to express itself indirectly, in patterns of behaviour or symbolic expressions. Yet the *Me* still aspires to seek the help of the other as a substitute for its *I*. This libidinal type is what we frequent in the crushed person, the hypocrite, the follower, and the back bencher in any gathering, not necessarily for lack of presence but for its insignificant presence.

The obsessional character is dominated by conscientiousness or, as Freud said, by his super-ego. He is more concerned about truth than relationships, is self-reliant and has a strong *I* (M. Bouvet described in 1953, the obsessional patient as one who suffers from the strength of his ego; not its weakness). Although the subject might be struggling with his true Me and its pressures, he does not yield to it or to the other – i.e., he has an orphan *I*, who suffers the pressure of the *Me* but does not yield to it. We meet that character in situations where accountability, predictability, reliability, dependability, and non-compromise are required. Although the obsessional character is not show-offish, he is not missed and is always noticed.

The narcissistic character, according to Freud, is someone who has no tension between his ego (the *Me*) and super ego (the *I*) and has no place for the other in his psychical life; thus he is seen as a 'personality'. In that type there is no obvious need (for the other) and no conflict within the intrapsychic. In terms of the narcissistic duality model I proposed, the narcissistic type is an *I* that dominates the *Me* and treats the other as another *Me* that should be dominated. This character is an *I* that is not defined as a subject but identified as an object. We see that in persons who identify with their social position, wealth, power, etc. Two examples of that character are De Gaul's famous sentence "I am France"; and Hitler's boasting about the third Reich as if "The third Reich is me [him]".

Freud's paper, curiously, fits very well in the narcissistic structural model, which could even give a better description, than the libido model, of the psychodynamics of those types and their composite derivatives. Furthermore, we can respond to Freud's speculation of the relation of those libidinal types to pathology – by asking if some of them have a special disposition to pass over into neurosis, and if so, which types lead to which forms of neurosis. Experience shows that all those types can exist without any neurosis. On the one hand Freud had hoped that he had come to a reasonable classification of psychological types that pertain purely to normality. Nonetheless, he had hoped to find a link between them and pathology. The model of narcissistic duality keeps us at the level of the normal, because it is within a framework of the developmental model that answers to both normality and psychopathology. It is also a framework that has a place for the constitutional factor, which its existence is undeniable in people but still is a mystery in psychoanalysis. Moving from the normal to the pathological in that model does not require any additional hypotheses.

Despite the defunct libidinal theory, it cannot be thrown away with the bathwater, as the saying warns. We lose a very essential element in the proposition of narcissism if we do not keep psychosexual development with its phases and its corresponding system of psychodynamic diagnosis. Bouvet's model of object relations (1959), based on the modality of psychosexual development and its system psychodiagnosis, came earlier than the contemporary object relations theories. In other words, the turning point of introducing narcissism into psychoanalysis as a possible remedy to the ills of the libido theory proved to present us – unintentionally and unplanned – with the structural foundation of the intrapsychic to replace the functional theory of the libido, confirming the contiguity of psychoanalysis.

The issue of the place of character in psychoanalysis could be demonstrated by a vignette. In a rather difficult analysis of a narcissistic-obsessive type, the patient – who was quite pretty – failed to get into a meaning relationship that would lead to a marriage. She was obsessed with her desire to get married and equally obsessed by her failure in achieving that objective. The subtle and the not-so subtle things that made those relationships fail were discovered and uncovered. The patient was entering an age group from which it was difficult to attract eager suitors. However, she was gaining more gratifications than before in her field of work as a result of recognition for significant achievements. Working through her 'unconscious' sabotaging of relationships revealed a parallel reluctance to getting married because it was in her mind (precociously) linked to curtailing her professional success. Better, she realized that her genuine aspiration was not marriage but success, and marriage was indirectly one of the signs of her success. Reaching this puzzling point proved to be difficult for her to cross because she was not able to understand that professional success and social success were together one success that characterized her psychical life – i.e., she has to be successful, period. From material that was always there in her memory about parental discrimination between her and her two brothers, her mother's passivity towards her father's womanizing, and the need to please her father by being 'the virgin daughter' were part of the whole psychodynamics (she came from an Asian-Moslem back ground where premarital sex was not permitted). Analysis approached termination when the patient had a clearer look at her character; a character that was trying to achieve in order to please. What changed is what she envisaged to be pleasing, but she continued being a pleasing and pleasant person. Analysis terminated with a sense that she can live with this orderly feeling of herself that she gained in analysis. I would not be the least surprised if I knew that she got married after all.

Counter-transference and narcissism

Previously, I located narcissistic structures in the gap between the *Me* and the *I*; where the *Me* is the unconscious aspect of the person's identity, and the *I* is the *Cs./Pcs.* aspect of the identity. I also proposed that that gap comprises all the fallacies, inaccuracies in self-images that come from assimilating the caregiver's misconception, and most of all the dynamic link between the *I* and the *Me*. It is not difficult, then, to see that anonymity, abstinence, and neutrality are meant to protect the patient from the analyst's own narcissism so that he could develop a more personal and free undistorted transference. It also keeps the analyst's response to the patient within the transference relation the patient initiates.

Yet, the analyst is constantly forced to respond to the patient's transference, which implicitly and sometimes explicitly identifies the analyst in a manner that does not agree with his own sense of identity. This paradoxical situation – the psychoanalytic situation – sets off reactions from the analyst. Thus, I would define *counter*-transference as the analyst's conscious/unconscious reaction to intruding on his identity. The reaction stems from the analyst's narcissistic structure, and his tolerance of the patient's attempts at changing his identity to being a personal identity from his childhood experiences – i.e., a change from analyst to a father figure. The analyst might precociously respond to that positively or negatively, but supposedly his auto-analysis (self-analysis) could, without little difficulty, point out to him his reaction to the patient fantasies. In the daily practice of a psychoanalyst, he should be able to notice some changes in his attitudes towards the different patients in treatment. They differ according to their transference to him, but they should be in all a preconscious sense of comfort or discomfort. This is when auto-analysis has to be activated to decipher the counter-transferences. Counter-transference would be experienced – in those incidences – as accepting or rejecting being given a new identity, and consequently a new function. The comfort/discomfort indicates that the analyst is yielding to the patient's transference's expectations. Dealing with counter-transference would then mean uncovering it in auto-analysis, discovering the patient's fantasies in his transference and uncovering them to him, interpreting the transference and reconstructing the analytic scene. This is doable if the analyst has kept his identity out of the psychoanalytic scene.

If the analyst puts his I-dentity into active participation in the analytic scene, if he puts in his narcissism as a replacement for his role as the analyst, it is likely that he will be played well by the patient. The patient would be in the position to manipulate the analyst consciously and unconsciously. The analytic scene would become a struggle between two transferences, since the analyst's identity is a product of his early experiences.

Notes

1 The mirror in this context is not the material reflective surface we call mirror but anything that reflects to the child a sense of separate existence like the mother's smile when she is happy with him or her frown when she is not.

2 This issue and some related issues make *The Ego and the Id* (1923b) a psychoanalytic blunder.

3 Levi-Strauss said (1955): "A myth always refers to events alleged to have taken place long ago. But what gives a myth an operational value is that the specific value is that

the specific pattern described is timeless; it explains the present and the past as well as the future" (139).

4 It is appropriate to ask if Freud resorted to the myth of Narcissus just to frame the issue of libidinal investments, the division of the libido, the intermediate phase between autoerotism and object love, and taking the self in its physical condition as an external object.

5 In 1981, I published a paper entitled 'Narcissism and the death instinct'. The paper has a much better explication of the myth and the interplay of life and death on one side and wish and desire on the other. I could not include those ideas in this revision because it would have interrupted its intended objective.

6 This area requires extensive and more elaborate work in the field of child observation. I have underlined the importance of psychoanalysts posing to child psychologists intelligent questions about this issue and similar other issues, in my book entitled *Future Psychoanalysis* (2015).

7 Henry Wallon is a French child psychologist who had a major role in establishing a psychological theory of cognitive and identity evolution in children. His impact on psychology and psychoanalysis in France is felt till now although he died in 1962.

8 I wonder how it reads in its original German.

9 We like to say that a patient has to want to change or be cured in order for an analysis to accomplish its objective. Patients without a doubt want to be cured but they do not know how, and we are not supposed to tell them how – that is if we knew. We only unfold the disguising wrap of the neurosis from the issue and the patient does the rest: *we analyse and the patient does the therapy*.

4

THE CLINICAL PROTOCOL

A basic proposition

Psychoanalysis is, in people's minds, a clinical method of psychotherapy. In the minds of psychoanalysts it is a profession, and has been and still is to a degree considered a different calibre of psychotherapy. The fragmentation of psychoanalysis into schools did not change much the psychoanalysts' attitude that they are different from the other specialists in the mental health field. Point in fact: psychoanalysis started from within the first recognizable psychotherapeutic endeavour. Nevertheless, there is no denying that the main discoveries that made its psychotherapeutic practice unique and distinguishable came from Freud's other discoveries, which he made outside the clinical practice. Those discoveries influenced the practice of psychoanalysis in a way that is clear in the manner that Freud chartered its protocol.

Revisiting and revising Freud's clinical protocol is justifiable by the recent debates about the declining interest in psychoanalysis (Cesio, 1995; Fayek, 2010, 2015). However, my revision of the protocol – in the present context – is for reasons that most analysts would not disagree with, although they might dispute their significance. The kind of revision I have in mind for the clinical aspect of the Freudian doctrine is based on intuitive aspects in his delineation of its characteristics, which are borne by the whole doctrine that we already have; properly documented, archived, studied, and commented on, by many thinkers. Thus we can look at the constituents of his intuition and find the meanings embedded in it. However, there are two particulars about the issue at hand that need to be underlined. First, psychotherapy as an act did not exist before Freud; it was carried out by people all the time in casual ways but not practised as a specified act. It was Freud who identified and defined it as an explicit act. As such, psychotherapy began as a specialty, and it just happened within the medical profession and was considered part of the tradition of medicine. There was no precedency to its practice beforehand. Although there were some common and shared traditions in the practice of the different specialties in medicine, they were left to the practitioner to follow. Yet, Freud created a protocol for practising this novel act, in terms of the framework of practising it, and standardized the technicalities of its practice. He outlined the framework for both the patient and the therapist. The notion of a clearly defined framework should be one of the aspects of the protocol that should be re-examined because it was never considered in the practice of any profession previously, let alone that it has become the main principle in any psychotherapeutic endeavour thereafter. All the changes and modifications made to the original Freudian protocol, even in non-psychoanalytic psychotherapies, have accepted the standardization of the conditions under which psychotherapy is practised.

The second particular is the discrepancy in the importance of the clinical aspect in the Freudian text compared with the place it occupied in psychoanalysis in general. Until now, psychoanalysts have considered psychoanalysis a clinical theory and discipline, and a profession, whereas the non-clinical aspects are considered inconsequential, or at best derivatives of the clinical function. Yet, the clinical material in Freud's text is very limited in all aspects. It is limited to three incomplete cases (Dora, 1905e; the Rat Man, 1909d; and The Wolf Man, 1918b), a supervision of a child analysis, analysis of the memoirs of a paranoid person, and casual extracts from other cases. This part of Freud's writings, limited as it was, was enough for him to derive from it the most creative, extensive, and remarkably informative theory of the individual. We need to ask a second question: which is the tail and which is the dog in relation to psychoanalysis? the theoretical body of information or the clinical body of information? This has been a ceaseless query in psychoanalysis until now (Brenner, 1981; Wallerstein, 1989, 2005).

My interest and intention in revising the Freudian clinical protocol is to set the scene right: *In a moment of exceptional intuition Freud improvised a protocol for investigating the core nature of the human being through people who went to him, his colleagues, and still come to us enquiring about their subjective nature and their particular experience of it. His protocol and the set up for investigating the human subject says many things about what distorts that investigation, and what the investigator should refrain from doing to allow the best chance for the investigation to succeed Freud's clinical protocol. This reflects the structural core of psychoanalysis as a theory of the human subject.*

The main features of the clinical protocol

Freud's actual and serious thinking of delineating the technique of psychoanalysis occupied the period from 1909 and 1912, with his first paper dedicated to that subject being 'Wild psychoanalysis' (1910k). The tone of that paper set the tone for all his other papers on technique, which was what *not to do* more than what to do. This is a very significant point to note: Freud's clinical protocol of avoiding things that could mess up the process created a situation (the session) that is unique in the life of the human subject. If the patient (the human subject) seeks psychoanalysis to find out what is causing his unhappiness and unhealthy ways, he would not get it by improving his means to find out but by changing that means. The psychoanalytic clinical protocol generated and constructed a human situation that is totally new, and ingenious in getting the subject in touch with himself without the many distortions we all have to integrate in our self-awareness.

Freud's recommendations (1912e) are obtained from his papers on technique, and various others of his writings that relate to technique. Some of the literature on the subject will also be mentioned if it has a major impact on revising the Freudian proposition. I will itemize and separate the recommendation he intended for the analyst, the ones intended for the patients, and the ones that pertain to the process.

The analyst

Freud had several recommendations for the analyst to observe, which are equally important to allow the objective of 'psychoanalysing' to be fulfilled. Like the recommendations for the patient, the ones for the analyst have the same objective: differentiate between a common relationship with the other and a relationship with the patient. We will see the difference after itemizing the recommendations.

Freud recommended in a rather strict way that the analyst should not disclose any information about himself; he should remain anonymous. This recommendation was badly misunderstood over the years by analysts. The notion of anonymity is for the analyst not to talk to the patient about himself, and not even about what the patient knows about him. We shall see later when we expound the concept of anonymity how and why it is considered a major factor in the success or failure of the analysis. A second thing to observe in the relationship with the patient is abstinence. By abstinence Freud meant that the therapeutic relationship should be defined by clear boundaries that the analyst should not cross, in regard to social contacts, gratifying any personal need or want outside the practicalities of the clinical situation, trying to enhance or discourage any of the patient's spontaneous expression of himself. Abstinence is the equivalent of anonymity in regard to impersonal matters. Some analysts, between the 1930s and 1960s, especially in the USA, took those recommendations to an extreme and acted in a more detrimental way by being too impersonal to be credible.

The third thing to observe is neutrality. Freud also pointed out the importance of not doing anything that would affect the patient's own way of advancing in his analysis. The main issue in this recommendation is refraining from encouraging a patient to do something that seems to enhance the process, like talking about a certain issue, or discouraging a certain attitude or behaviours like silence or even falling asleep during the sessions. This recommendation is underlying the importance of giving equal attention to all the material the patient brings to analysis, verbal or non-verbal, interpretable or non-interpretable, active or passive. Freud's clinical protocol and his theoretical formulations regarding the process of therapy advise giving *the process* more care than *the content* of the material. In a paper on technique (1911e) he said:

> The production of dreams is at times so copious, and the patient's progress towards comprehension of them so hesitant, that a suspicion will force itself on the analyst that the appearance of the material in this manner may be simply a manifestation of the patient's resistance taking advantage of the discovery that the method is unable to master what is so presented. (92)

Some of those recommendations, when performed properly, might affect the patient negatively if not explained and prepared for. The analyst has to make clear to the patient, from the onset, that he would not gratify any of his explicit and implicit wishes or demands, not out of insensitivity but for other consideration related to the process of psychoanalysis. The patient should understand that there will be periods of silence; the analyst will answer questions in a very limited way. What seems like the analyst being emotionally distant, and avoiding engaging in long conversation before or after the end of the sessions, is also part of the framework of a proper psychoanalysis. Adhering to the consistency and the regularity the process is a major part of the treatment. When those matters are explained and the patient expects them he would not get offended by the analyst's attitude, and his reactions to them would then be easily put in the context of the transference relationship.

Handling 'everything' in the relationship the patient develops with the analyst as transference material is a fundamental concept in psychoanalysis. Thus, responding to it in an appropriate manner that would not turn it into a real relationship would eventually give the opportune time to be interpreted.

The last unusual recommendation Freud suggested to the analysts is not to take notes during the session or to do anything to protect or enhance his memory of the patient's material such as keeping notes of sessions. However, if there are reasons to keep notes on a case for scientific or educational purposes, those notes should be written after the session and preserve the privacy of the patient's identity.

However, some analysts made a mockery of those recommendations – especially in the 1950s and 1960s – by becoming caricatures of the 'proper analyst'. There are ways and contexts for the recommendations of the three main prospects of anonymity, abstinence, and neutrality to be adhered too without making them look like restrictive rules. The analyst's barber, neighbour, or taxi driver knows if he is particularly secretive or evasive without engaging them a relationship. The main thing is that each of those recommendations has a *therapeutic objective* behind it; they are not role-playing, which will be discussed a little later.

The patient

Freud emphasized the importance of explaining to the patient *the fundamental rule* of psychoanalysis – free association – and stressing its difference from just talking about issues the ordinary way the patient might do in his daily life. The notion on which Freud built his fundamental rule was still influenced by the concepts of resistance and defence, and he wanted the patient to have the will to lower those two barriers so that the repressed would have a chance to be revealed. As we will see later when we examine the fundamental rule itself, Freud's insight in the process of talking gives free associating a different and more profound significance with regard to discovering the *Ucs.* Added to explaining the fundamental rule to the patient, the analyst should let the patient know that he does not answer questions, because if the patient tries to answer his own questions he will learn more and different things about what he asks.

Freud also added that the practical things related to the process of analysis have to be dealt with and settled before analysis starts. The most important ones are the number of sessions and the frequency of the visits,[1] the duration of the sessions, the fees, cancellations and the difference between the analyst's cancellation and the patient cancellation. The issue of the couch and vacations, and the duration of treatment, are also practical matters that have to be agreed upon before the initiation of the analysis. It is also important to let the patient know that his associations about those agreements after the start of analysis are important to mention but not with the intention of renegotiating the settled agreement. Analysts gained from experience and their better understanding of 'free associating' that they should encourage talking first, then thinking about what they have said.

The procedure

The recommendations regarding the patient and the analyst create a therapeutic set up that is very different in its nature from any interpersonal relationship in our personal life. The analyst's delineation of the psychoanalytic set up presents the patient with certain guidelines almost like rules. When he reveals his own boundaries that he should not break he is – both implicitly and explicitly – asking the patient to partake in the process of analysis on the same level of ethical, technical, professional boundaries the analyst will keep. The patient is asked and is supposed to be more authentic and forthcoming in talking and revealing his-self without worrying much about the impression he would give to his counterpart. A difficult demand that eventually becomes less of a demand. The analyst, as the counterpart, is relatively without a defined character, and thus does not impose himself on the patient, which would tempt him to respond to that character. The very limited knowledge about the analyst provides the majority of the therapeutic space for the patient to occupy. The significance of the set up becomes clearer in the context of Freud's recommendations about the practice itself. The recommendations are few, simple, very interdependent, and suggestive of the manner of practice and the aim of doing analysis. He recommended that once the patient is in analysis the analyst follows the patient's own way of unfolding his case, and not his [the analyst's] personal ideas about the neurosis. What tops all of Freud's recommendations is the brilliant metaphor of the chess-game (1913c). You could be taught how to start it (set it up) and what ends it (there would be no more objectives to gain) but nothing about the game itself (psychoanalyzing). Therefore, whenever the analyst faces something unexpected in the middle game he can rely on the recommendations to deal with. But, as Freud well pointed out: no analyst could go beyond his personal potential. Analysts do not treat the symptoms of the patient's interpersonal relationships; they treat the person who gets into trouble in the kind of relationships they create. Relationships are manifestations of the condition of the intrapsychic; they are symptoms. There is some sort of division of labour in the procedure of psychoanalyzing. The patient provides the material to be examined and processed, and the analyst does the examining and the processing. This might sound unnecessary to mention. However, if this is not done properly the *analyst could slip into formulating his interpretation as information, as well as some patients who make some advancement in their therapy start interpreting their material instead of averring them.*

The protocol in application

After Freud gave up on the catharsis theory and the hypnosis method around 1894, the birth of the modern act of psychotherapy began. There are four well-known and familiar changes that were introduced in the new era. The first is the reliance completely on the patient's speech and the language of his symptoms in uncovering the unconscious, and the second is paying attention to the therapeutic relation as the medium of doing the analysis. The first change made free association the means that replaced hypnosis, relaxation, and suggestion to working with the patient directly and in his natural conscious condition. The second change took Freud a few years to understand and articulate. He recognized that a great deal of the material that transpires in the analytic relationship is not related to the facts of the analytic situation. They show clear signs of regressive nature. The analyst is not treated as a therapist but as a representation of characters from the patient's past. The reactions to the analytic work were more or less tainted by childhood memories and childish reactions to the analyst's interventions. With time Freud paid enough attention to the 'therapeutic relation' and its role in instigating those unexpected distortions in the psychotherapeutic scene. Once he did that (1895d) he was able to give it an operational definition. It took several more years to include it properly in the procedure of psychotherapy and call it transference.[2] Transference is the foundation of the practice of psychoanalysis. Thus, the third change was concentrating on interpreting and reconstructing the material that comes to the patient's mind while free associating. This change was a major shift from revealing the unconscious or the repressed to the patient, moving instead to making the unconscious data something to understand better. The fourth change was using the interpreted material to reconstruct what was distorted and fragmented in the patient's mind due to the psychoneurotic process.

Free association

The term 'free association' was supposed to define what Freud wanted to replace hypnotism with – the patient letting his thoughts and other mental activities flow freely without censoring the objectionable ones. The notion of free association is derived from Carl Jung's Word-Association Test in 1910, which gave the subject a stimulus word and asked for an immediate free association to it. The idea was that without the interference of consciousness the subject would give the unconscious association of the stimulus word. Freud borrowed the term, but was not careful to note the difference between an immediate response to one unexpected word and to be talking for an hour (length of sessions at that time) to a psychoanalyst. The problem is in the impossibility of a complete freedom because of the transcendence of consciousness – the consciousness of consciousness.

As an example, John, a candidate in analysis, was feeling discouraged at the beginning of his analysis because he was not being able to follow the basic rule of free association, and was discouraged by his 'resistance' to freeing his associations. He worried that he might be inadequate to become an analyst. Working through his despair to free associate did not bring out any particular problems with his ease with the main things in his life, or unusual difficulties with his spontaneity, or having unusual idiosyncrasies that worried him to reveal. Yet, in a gradual way his expressed anxiety about free associating exposed several issues pertaining to his narcissistic make up. In other words, his difficulty was not relating to associating freely in the session but was about his narcissistic emphasis on becoming 'such' an excellent psychoanalyst. The way the analysand deals with the request to follow the fundamental rule of psychoanalysis is more important than following the rule.

In that regard I would like to mention something I learned from a number of supervisors whose experience I sought: each had a way of explaining the fundamental rule to his patient before the beginning of the therapy. My own experience, and also my own style of listening and interpreting the patient's association, made me say to the patients what it means: talking about what you know is not as useful as talking in order to know, because you will gradually notice that you, like everyone else, talks about two things at the same time. In therapy we need to know the other thing too. It is a fallacy to think that there is free association, because we – humans – are always conscious of our consciousness, and the best we can do is to let the things that are associated with what we are conscious of get a chance to show part of themselves within our regular talk. The analyst has to be prepared to listen to the other unconsciously said things within the consciously said.

When Frau Emmy asked Freud to stop interrupting her 'chain of ideas' in the sessions Freud abandoned hypnosis, or encouraging his patients to remember certain things, in particular helping by putting his hand on their foreheads and asking them to close their eyes. He *freed his patients to associate as they wished about what they wanted to say.* His only suggestion to them was not to judge anything before saying it. Freud's brilliance was manifested in his ability to recognize something else that was subtly and implicitly said in the associations while the patient was unmindful. Better, Freud recognized that the repressed finds ways to reveal itself in what seems to be banal thoughts, conflicts, superficial rhetoric – i.e., in associations that do not seem to be freely coming. One of the best examples to the double meaning is in *The Interpretation of Dreams* (1900a) where a woman was compulsively saying to her husband in her mind "hang yourself", but with some probing about the circumstances that accompanied this thought, it was found to mean get an erection (the May Beetle dream, 289–292). The clinical protocol – the part mentioned and the parts that will be mentioned – are to avoid influencing free association so that the entwining meanings reveal the unsaid.

At the beginning of analysis patients talk more about what they know and what they always thought to be important in regard to their difficulties. Gradually, they realize – from the work of interpretation – that what is important is not what they knew but what they say irrespective of what is said, because they could see within what they say something else that reveals itself. Step by step they realize the significance of talking in order to know. Free association gets freer and better with analysis. It is in this change that the story of each analysis resides: talk and listen to what you say. When this is well demonstrated and experienced by associating and interpretation the patient is ready to go on to auto-analysis, (wrongly called self-analysis[3]). Good analysis does not end with a split between the patient and his-self, but by a unity that needed to be achieved between him as speaker and listener in the same act.

The idea of free association came from Freud's belief that the repressed has a way of revealing itself if the patient lowers his resistance. Jung based his Word-Association Test on that idea. Yet, Freud proved to himself – and of course to us – that he was able to get to the patient's unconscious without any specific act of lowering the resistance (there is no such thing in the first place) by just listening to the patient talk. Another example of this achievement is the case of Fraulein Katherina (*Studies on Hysteria*, 1895d, 125–134). In this early case Freud interpreted the young woman's symptoms in the context of what she said, which was enough to uncover the repressed – without hypnosis or suggestion.

Free association, as the patient's simple talk – with some insinuation to him to talk and then think about what he said – reveals the real nature of the system *Ucs.* Even though Freud made a clear distinction between this system and the 'repressed' (1915e), my experience in supervision (and regular contacts with colleagues) evidenced that it is deeply ingrained in the mind of psychoanalysts that there is repressed material that the patient is unconscious of (or preconscious) that has to become conscious through the removal of resistance. This notion means the unconscious is 'something' that we need to interpret when it gains access to consciousness. My longer experience in practising psychoanalysis and discussing a wide range of cases with my colleagues makes me say with conviction that we do not retrieve in any analysis any sensational material that surprises the patient or the analyst to the extent that it could be considered a breakthrough of the unconscious or the preconscious into consciousness. Most, if not all, of what we retrieve in analysis is preconscious material that remained vague, thus preconscious, because it was isolated from the rest of the material and, when it gets an interpretation, it joins the rest of what the patient is averring. *In that sense there is no making of the unconscious conscious in analysis.* Furthermore, what preconscious we retrieve could hardly deserve more than some explaining and not even interpreting.

Clinical examples would show that. A patient who hated her father for sexually abusing her recalled – after some trepidation – her excitement when those events were taking place, although she felt badly about them after as she felt badly admitting this. When her mother was dying she had a major panic attack, which puzzled her by its pervasiveness and intensity. While in that panic she remembered her fear of her mother discovering her sexual abuse. However, those memories could not make her fathom the extent of her panic at the time of her mother's death. Although all the material until that point was preconscious there was something unconscious (the workings of the primary process) that turned the mourning and sadness about her mother's dying into a state of panic. The *Ucs.* is the working of the primary process that creates conscious and preconscious links between unrelated material.

It is imperative to make a point of this observation. The preconscious material is subject to some explaining (sexual abuse was both desirable and horrific), but it has nothing to interpret in the sense that interpretation brings out a new meaning of the event. Explaining is replacing a denotation (signifier) with another denotation (better!). When two different denotations (fear of mother and guilt for enjoying the sexual abuse) become linked due to the working of the primary process (this would kill mother if she knew, and she would kill me if she knew) share one connotation: panic attacks (signified). An unconscious link and sometimes only an unconscious aspect in a symptom is enough to create an *Ucs.* event that needs more than explaining; it needs interpretation. In this case, the patient was conscious of the two linked preconscious aspects of her symptom but was unconscious of the working of the primary process, which condensed killing and being killed, especially that the mother was dying. The intensity of the fear (panic) was due to the condensation of the two wishes in one forbidden 'desire' – sexual freedom which scared her since childhood. Her childhood experience created a wish that represented the anti-wish too. The two wishes became unconsciously linked and became a desire … a frightening desire. Free association brought to the fore the unconscious that was created by the working of the primary process and demands interpretation.

If we agree that the psychoanalytic act is an act of interpretation, we have to ask about the place of the psychoanalytic theory in that act: do we interpret the freely mentioned associations or do we apply the theory in giving the associations a meaning? The answer is deceptively simple, because the question presumes a place for the theory in interpreting the material of free association. However, we should keep in mind that the act of interpreting is not limited to psychoanalysis but is an endeavour in any approach to human phenomena. We interpret old civilizations, Sophocles' Oedipus Rex, Dali's paintings, your girlfriend's look at you after cheating on her. Interpretation is a paramount act of human thinking. Yet, as we are different in our abilities to interpret there are certain rules to apply when a serious interpretation is demanded. By passing the changes in the meaning of interpretation since Zino to where it stands now, it could be said that interpretation in psychoanalysis is an act of analysing a subject and not associations. The associations are a composite of the subject's consciousness and unconsciousness, thus we should be analysing the 'style' this composite has taken. This stand from free association requires the analyst to establish a dialectical attitude from the act of interpretation. Dialectic analysis starts from the notion that what we try to fathom is not 'a thesis' but a synthesis of a wish (thesis) and an anti-wish its antithesis. Thus, a dream is not a fulfilled wish, but an adult wish that searched for a related infantile wish creating a synthesis that is a dream. Our work towards the interpretation of the dream is to listen to the day residues (where the adult wish is) and wait for the dreamer to relate it to an infertile wish, and then we interpret the dream as the way the working of the primary process produces the synthesis. In other words, there is no place for theory in the act of interpretation because interpreting is aimed not at revealing and naming contents but to how the patient's dialectics work. If an analyst's response to free associations contained any theoretical notion in the form of a clinical concept, it should not be considered an interpretation. Furthermore, if the analyst believes that the associations he is listening to have any specific meaning and that they are not syntheses of other specific meanings he would not be able to analyse them. In addition, if the analyst believes that his interpretation is of a specific value and a final statement about a slice of association, he will miss the way the interpretation will be involved in new dialectics. His work of analysis will not be more than moving from a topic to another that maybe is a little deeper and different, but will not free the patient of most of 'his unconscious'. *Proper psychoanalysis is not done according to a theory of analysis, but according to a theory of interpretation.*

Transference

Transference is the most important discovery in Freud's clinical experience, and it fitted astonishingly well in his practical protocol of practice. Its place in the process of analysis raised heated discussions in the literature and scientific meetings, because Freud and other analysts were able to identify it but unable to define it. This topic deserves special attention because Freud, when he realized the importance of transference, was still thinking within the framework of repression and had no other theoretical means to formulate a concept like transference. For example, in his very early writing about it he said (1912b):

> The intensity and persistence of the transference [as an ontological entity] are an effect and expression of the resistance [another ontological entity]. The *mechanism* of transference is, it is true [a process and structure], dealt with when we have traced it back to the state of readiness of the libido, which remained of possession of infantile images; but the part transference plays in the treatment can only be explained if we enter its relationship with resistance.
>
> (104)

In this sentence, Freud is not absolutely clear if he meant to explain a libidinal phenomenon that influences the course of treatment, or to use the libido theory to explain a new insight about the psychoanalytic relation. However, in this early stage of considering transference as a clinical phenomenon, Freud seemed to have made a division between the regular relationship with the analyst and some distortion in that relationship caused by the psychoneurosis. He called those distortions 'transference' (ibid., 101–102). He was quite cognizant that transference is 'representation' of an unconscious root, and that it has the same attributes of symptoms (ibid., 103). Yet, he showed obvious misunderstanding of its function, as he concluded that a negative transference (relationship) is a type of resistance while positive transference (relationship) is non-resistance (ibid., 105). As such, transference was deemed a possibility that could be encountered differently at different times or in different psychoanalyses. With more and possibly longer analyses Freud came to understand the function of transference in both its positive and negative modes, and recognize that they are both the same in their nature as resistance as well as their usefulness in revealing the unconscious. In other words, Freud eventually came to realize that the relationship with analysts is fundamentally and mostly transferrential, thus whether it is positive or negative it is not a true relationship but one that is repeating a previous formative relationship with a character from the past (1923a, b). However, Freud had to give up the elementary conception of resistance in the cathartic theory and to sort out the confusion regarding defence as a neurotic process. Those confusions hindered him for some time from appreciating fully the significance of transference.

Freud's insights regarding the psychoanalytic relationship ascertain that he had discovered what proved later to be the most valuable conception in the clinical field. He discovered that the relationship with the analyst comprises representations of unconscious origin, and is not based on an actual consideration of the two characters involved in the actual and active treatment. He also discovered that everything the analyst is looking for and working on revealing to the patient is weaved in the patient's transference and is there as the non-repressed unconscious (1923b). Even dreams in the process of psychoanalysis were initiated by transferrential aims, or, as he said: "It is scarcely ever right to sacrifice [the] therapeutic aim to an interest in dream-interpretation" (1911e, 92). He also discovered that the relationship with the analyst is structured like a symptom. Thus he gradually stopped considering transference to be an ontological entity – i.e., something being there or something having its own independent presence. He started to treat it as something that happens and continues to happen in every psychoanalysis. Therefore it required exploring its dynamics and placing it as a formative operation within clinical practice. There were also indications that he became aware that any and all human relationships are transferrential in nature, because the unbound nature of affect (see Chapter 2) allows transferring memories of 'similar' events and situations to any other situation, thus the workings of the primary process open the paths between the present and the past all the time. For now, I would say that the significance of the concept of transference *always puts the human subject within his own experience – i.e., he lives himself over and over, all the time and in all his relationships, but as the pre-formed identity with its infantile wishes and ambitions. Unfailingly he approaches his relationships with the expectations of the old acquired identity, showing failure in acquiring the flexibility that comes with gaining some symbolic meaning to his experiences.*

Psychoanalyzing with the notion that we are dealing with material that is transferred from the past of the patient to the present of the psychoanalytic relationship, and that the analyst is a replacement for past characters in the patient's life, gave Freud's clinical protocol a new meaning. Freud's protocol emphasizes that the relationship between the analyst and the patient should be kept within defined boundaries (clear in the mind of the analyst but likely not that clear in the patient's mind). It should not to be tainted by social considerations to avoid interfering with the purity of the transference. The analyst's careful maintenance of the boundaries and the patient's continuous attempts at penetrating them result in a unique situation that is seldom encountered in daily life: a person with all his past experiences, his biases, psychical distortions, and helplessness in keeping things under control as he is expected to in his social life, relating to someone whom he knows very little about and who is encouraging him to be as authentic as possible and not reacting or disapproving of his transgressive desire to break the rule. The other side of the coin is an analyst who is subjected to a barrage of transferrential material, and has to refrain from reacting to it as he might have done outside of the analytic situation. Analysts have their own transferrential proclivities too and their response to their patients' transferences. They differ in the degree of tolerance of those rules, thus the relationship with their patients is not always purely neutral or not reactional. This is the vague area of counter-transference which is unsettled as yet. I could only say – for now – that there is a difference between the analyst's natural way of relating to people including his patients and the analyst's reaction to the patient's transference that is what is usually called counter-transference. As mentioned earlier, all human relationships are based on degrees and types of transferences; therefore, the analyst has his own bag of past. But if he reacts to the patient's transference because his bag of past does not agree with the patient's transference, he would be stepping out of the clinical boundaries with its restrictions. The disagreement among analysts is mostly about what is within the limits of those boundaries; but they also differ regarding counter-transference and the analyst's own transference.

The main source of the diversity in defining transference is that Freud's initial insight about it was influenced by the concept of resistance. The interesting part in that source is that transference distorts the relationship with the analyst due to the permissiveness of the psychoanalytic situation, which invites the past to distort the present. We know now that this is the desirable thing. But when Freud first discovered the distortion the past makes to the present, he tried to make the patients realize the distortion but the patients refused to consent (resisted) and recognize it, as we all know now. Thus he confused resistance and transference. But when he had the insight that those distortions are an intrinsic part of the neurotic therapeutic relationship he put the emphasis on the nature of the distortion that transference creates in the relationship with the analyst. It is difficult to agree on a typology of distortions that influences the psychoanalytic relationship, because the distortions carried by transference are usually undefinable until the analysis is close to termination. The analyst will be assessing a few technical aspects of the process such as a psychodynamic diagnosis, types of reactions to his interventions, transference as a facilitator or resistance, and its potentiality to change. The patient will be quite apprehensive about his transference, which he knows – preconciously – caused him to seek help. He would be ready to uncover it hesitantly if he is eager to change, and would be eager to test it with the analyst if he has insight about his psychoneurosis, but would not be able to admit to himself the phantasmic aspect of it. *The patient comes to analysis because he has trouble with his transference in his daily life*, which is the symptomatic reason for seeking psychoanalysis. The analyst, on the other hand, has to expect an initial period of confusion of transferences, which will eventually and hopefully settle down into the foundational transference of the patient and a stable transference from the analyst.

It should be noted that Freud's conception of transference (even before being articulated properly) made clinical practice possible because without it we would not have been able to know what we were dealing with. Now, knowing that we are dealing with relationships forged outside and before analysis started, we are able to understand what he suggested should be done in the act of analysing. But before getting to that point, we should look into a main concept that arise from transference. Freud made a very astute distinction between two categories of psychoneuroses: transference neurosis and narcissistic neuroses. The two categories are not of psychoneuroses but of transferences, because in one category there are the features of transferring something to the analytic scene and living it with quasi-conviction, while in the other there seems to be difficulty in living the analytic relationship because the patient's past resists linking with the present (Freud, 1909d, 1912b, 1914c, 1914g, 1916–1917, 1923a). As a matter of fact, the term 'transference neurosis' obscures its true meaning, and shifts the emphasis from the transference to the neurosis; while the emphasis should remain on transference. The transference neuroses are a neurotic-transference, not a transference that accompanies certain neuroses. In the narcissistic neurosis, on the other hand, the therapeutic relationship does not exist because the past seems to have formed in the absence, acquiring of any symbolic sense of being that should have been offered by the caregiver. The narcissistic neuroses – in Freud's terms – where all the psychotic and quasi-psychotic psychopathologies that have no organic cause for their symptoms. The most rampant of those narcissistic pathologies in his time were hypochondria and neurasthenia – which, in my clinical experience, still exist in what is now called neuromyalgia.[4] Those psychoneuroses, in which the unconscious aspects are not amenable to be displaced and transferred to the analytic relation, show a feature in narcissism that isolates the patient from the relationship with the analysts. Transference in those cases has no means of becoming stimulated because *relating* is locked within the undifferentiated *I–Me* structure. Hypochondria looks, clinically, like a condition formed in childhood in isolation of the rest of the child's other experiences, thus it is not unhinged from the rest of the patient's life.

The evolution of psychoanalysis to become the most important method of psychotherapy would not have been possible without the concept of transference paving the way towards the rich theoretical discoveries, which were derived by Freud from his extensive but not very successful practice. Better, if we stayed at the level of relating to our patients the way we relate to people in general, and we also ignored that there is more to what the patient is 'supposed' to be doing with us, we would not have discovered the causes of his psychoneurosis; there would not have been psychotherapy in any form, let alone psychoanalysis. Freud created a profession out of the act of listening to people and understanding what they did not say but was there in the form of making the present a copy of the past. Keeping this in mind could make us appreciate having Freud's clinical protocol to guide us in listening to the past in what is said about the present. As the therapist has no tools to practise therapy – he *is* that tool – therapy needed to structure the therapist and patients' domains to avoid the possible chaos that psychoneuroses could create. The freedom in relating to the analysts, which is encouraged, had to be formally stipulated so that acting out (enactment) would not be misconceived as part of that freedom. Psychoanalysis is practised within limitations that make acting out material for interpretation. This is the core of the tripartite recommendations of anonymity, abstinence, and neutrality as will be discussed in some detail in the next section. Freud's systematization of practice in the manner mentioned founded the profession of psychoanalyst, but it also underlines what we should be expecting to face if we have chosen it as our practice. We should expect difficulties in the course of analysis, but we should also consider that those difficulties have to be dealt with within the protocol and not outside its outline or within a diluted version of it. Although training in analysis highlights the protocol and makes it a main aspect of the process, analysts should keep training themselves in that regard, because with time and experience they could gradually become lax in observing it. A third point to observe is matching the analytic setting with the aims of therapy. The tripartite protocol is to avoid affecting transference, so it remains a beacon of guidance in every stage and crisis we face later.

Freud's clinical protocol did not come from clinical experience; it was instrumental in creating the proper clinical experience that built the theory of psychoanalysis. In other words Freud 'looks' as if he knew how to practise before he practised. This is not a strange thing because most of the important discoveries in history happened this way: knowing intuitively what needed to be known before actually articulating it. This is an idea that deserves attention because it is what happens in the practice of psychoanalysis to both the analyst and the analysand. We listen, recall previous things the patient has said, we ponder the occasion of what these associations meant to express; then we understand and interpret or reconstruct them. As we see in regard to free association, we will ask the patient to do the same thing. There are two good cases in point of that in Freud's explanation of two aspects of his set up of psychoanalysis practice. In regard to using the couch he said that it helps in "isolating the transference". We know now and understand that his justification was right to emphasize, although the explanation was incorrect. The couch changes the session from visiting with the analyst to a particular set up to working with him (doing something specific). The notion of organizing the issue of payment (paying at regular times; paying for the session, not for the time spent in therapy; paying for keeping his time whatever the circumstances that might affect the patient's attendance) changes the ordinary value of money and relates the fees to be part of the long systematic process of psychoanalysis, and associates the fees to the value of the treatment. Although Freud did not follow all his own recommendations meticulously, probably because he was not always able to deal with his counter-transference, his lack of adherence to those rules has nothing to do with the rules; they are very adequate for doing what we propose to do. Although some analysts belittled the importance of the protocol, and some even advised ignoring them (Renik, 1996, 1098a), neither did they come with the equivalent nor with a conception of psychoanalysis without a protocol.

Because transference breeds an unusual relationship with the analyst – a different relationship set up than the ordinary ones – Freud identified three stipulations that could contain the transferrential relationship and allows the analyst to manage its peculiarities.

The clinical set up

The clinical set up was based on tripartite restrictions which the analyst has to observe.

Anonymity

Anonymity is one of three clear restrictions Freud strongly advised the clinician to observe. It is *simply* the analyst not volunteering information about himself to the patient or responding to his queries with confirmation or denial. This restriction seems to be impossible to be strictly followed, and the most easily breached by the patient; it goes without saying that the patient will gather some information about the analyst whom he chooses to go to. Despite the difficulty of the analyst remaining completely anonymous, this restriction was accepted until as recently as three or four decades ago when some analysts openly rejected it and a tidal wave of intersubjectivity and the so-called '*democratizing*' of the process of psychoanalysis called not only for ignoring it but also for refuting it. The notion was that anonymity gives the analyst a different 'status' in the analytic relationship, and makes him *the one who knows*, which is undemocratic. The reasons given ranged from the impossibility of keeping anonymity, its fallacy, and ending with considering it detrimental to transference.

The excuses to eliminate anonymity misunderstand it. The analyst refrains from giving the patient any information about himself, or confirms or corrects information the patient might have already gathered. I believe that we all have some experience dealing with people whom we do not know much about and in our way of examining the kind of person we are dealing with we are guarded in revealing ourselves, because we tend to gauge our dealings with others according to what we know about them. Thus, we are more inclined to be self-conscious in those relationships. In other terms, those relationships would restrict the spontaneity of the transference, which is not a desirable thing in psychoanalysis. In addition, when the analyst refrains from reacting to the patient's curiosity it eventually sinks in that the analyst is not acting according a definite character from which the patient could predict his reaction. Anonymity is a safeguard against 'contaminating' the transference.

I will give a clinical example to expound the issue. When I first left Egypt for Canada I had a practice in psychotherapy and was quite active academically, intellectually, and politically. After my retirement in Canada, some circumstances obligated me to go back for a few years, and I opened a practice there during the time I was supposed to stay before coming back to Canada. A young aspiring actress came for analysis because of bouts of severe self-doubt and depression. One day she said that a retired actress told her that she had an affair with me before I had emigrated thirty-five years previously. She added that she did not really like me but wanted to be seen with me in the circle of friends that I had then. I did not respond so the patient left the subject and carried on. A few months later she was telling me about a new relationship she had started with a young architect who was the centre of great interest in the media for landing a contract for a major project in an Arab country. A few sessions later she averred that she did not like him but she was attracted to his lavish style of life and his connections. I made the comment that *her relationship with that man is similar to another relationship she mentioned previously.* After a moment of silence she indicated – with a little embarrassment – that she remembered. She went on to talk about her half-sister (a few years older) who was a very beautiful woman and had a successful career in the media. She wondered if her sister became that successful because she used her beauty. After a long period of silence she was in tears talking about a mother who was also very attractive but had a bad reputation, and of a passive and loving father who was humiliated because of his wife's public display of immorality. The issue of immorality, which put her, her sister, and her mother in one camp, and deceived men in another, seemed to have dictated her conflict and her childhood desire to be different and to have a respectable father. Analysis took off from that point.

Before analysis begins, I prepare the patient's for situations like that where they might learn something about me that could be embarrassing, awkward, unacceptable, etc. I also tell them that my lack of response is intended to keep them talking about it if they so wished, irrespective of my silence. Rarely, if ever, especially in didactic analysis, did an analysis go without the candidate coming up with some piece of information about me. In some cases, the need to get a reaction was so strong that it took the analysis to the brink of failure. Notwithstanding all that, and if I needed to I would remind the patient of the clarification I made before beginning the analysis, the personal issues raised by candidates about me proved to be just ways of talking about an aspect in their *own* lives that were different from the ordinary material that usually fills the sessions. Anonymity is a natural thing in human relationships and we practice it and experience it with others in our ordinary lives, in different degrees, with all the people we encounter, including ourselves. We know things about others, but not everything. We know others in different degrees – even the closest ones – and we do not know everything about ourselves either. When we enquire or ask the other about what we do not know or what we know but want to know the truth about, it is always in relation to something in us – i.e., are you honest, caring, did you do this or that? We are not really interested in others for the sake of it, but always in relation to ourselves. Our relationships with others are dependent on the degree of knowledge we have about someone, and the accuracy of what we know, and most of all on the margin of error allowed in that relationship. As a rule, the relationship between intimate people permits misconceptions more than if it is between less intimate ones. Since anonymity is the norm in relationships, then what is specific about it in psychoanalysis?

Anonymity in clinical psychoanalysis is defined as a non-optional condition: the patient is informed about it and about what to expect in that regard. It is distinct from the banal background of its permeation in interpersonal relationships by the analyst neither volunteering it nor hiding it. This way, the analyst's anonymity, and whatever it is, becomes and remains part of *the analytic setting*. It defines the relationship with the analyst as a therapeutic one and not a personal one. The significance of identifying this from the start is to make the patient ready to discover unconscious meanings in what he was accustomed to take at face value before, like power games, testing the analyst, idealizing, disliking, etc. The lopsided situation of one refusing to say anything about himself and the other asked and expected to say everything would be wrong to consider in terms of rights, status, knowledge (a senior analyst could seek the help of a less knowledgeable one), or righteousness. It puts knowing in brackets: who is here and for what? The analyst is there to help the patient become more aware of himself, and the patient is there to know more about himself, too. Therefore, the analyst's anonymity is the safeguard against fuzzing the transference, which is the means to the objective of analysis. Anonymity is very much related to narcissism. Freud's first warning about anonymity was in regard to the analyst talking about himself as a model for the patient. He even warned against showing modesty to encourage the patient because there is an implicit narcissistic appeal in that, too. Thus, anonymity – *in the clinical sense* – is an antidote to the analyst's narcissism. There is a great deal of anecdotal and biographical literature on famous analysts who caused damage, just by their narcissistic insensitivities. The analyst's narcissism, if pronounced and announced, would act as a sponge to the proper transferential relationship of analysis. Anonymity is the condition that keeps the analyst's narcissism to himself. However, this recommendation evoked objections from some analysts (Renik, 1995, 1996, 1998b).

Neutrality

Although a well-trained analyst could manage anonymity reasonably well, it could be betrayed by another aspect which Freud brought to attention: neutrality. Neutrality is more commonly misunderstood because it is a term used in different and many areas of human life. It is also understood through its reverse meaning – bias – which is not difficult to encounter in psychoanalysis, both in clinical practice and theoretical form. In Freudian psychoanalysis neutrality has one specific meaning regarding one specific aspect of clinical practice. Laplanche and Pontalis (1973) named three areas of treatment in which the analyst should carefully exercise neutrality: 1. views on issues pertaining to personal convictions (religion, social values, political events, etc.); 2. implicit (or explicit) theoretical preference; and 3. giving advice or counselling to the patient. Before we get to each of those three areas in some detail, I would like to mention two points that relate to neutrality as a whole. The three areas of neutrality are part of the same clinical stand the analyst takes from anonymity and abstinence. By refraining from giving opinions about 'issues' the analyst keeps his identity undefined and does not gratify or frustrate the patient's own leanings. Therefore, neutrality is instrumental in leaving the space of relating to the analyst available to transference alone. Neutrality encourages free associating indirectly because it holds back the analyst's views from influencing the patient's freedom to express himself. Some analysts considered neutrality detrimental, creating artificial distances from the patient (Renik, 1998a, b).

Neutrality in regard to personal convictions is significant in a subtle way. If there is neurotic involvement in the patient's system of beliefs, which is more than just possible, the analyst should work to reveal them, and without neutrality it will be impossible to deal with the contribution of the psychoneuroses in forming the patient's system of beliefs. The patient's unrestricted freedom to say what he thinks about his belief system would expose the intrapsychic structure of that system. Consequently it is possible to make changes in it – if needed. If the analyst reveals his own system of beliefs, the patient, in all likelihood, will modify the psychoanalytic relationship to an interpersonal relationship – i.e., will relate to the person who is sitting behind him and not to the analyst listening to him. Like any other relationship it will not be amenable to interpretation to effect changing to its intrapsychical core. We can envisage the kind of therapeutic atmosphere if the analyst and the analysand were of opposite (or the same) political, religious, moral camps. But as long as the analyst stays neutral one of the factors in the equation would remain undeclared and the outcome remains open.

I can talk about theoretical neutrality in psychoanalysis only, because it is the only therapeutic school that stresses it. Approaching an analysis with no theoretical preference is important, because interpretations should be of the patient's association, without any attempt at fitting the material into any theoretical modality. Theoretical neutrality affects both listening and interpreting the associations. If the analyst is not adhering to Freud's clinical protocol he will be affected by one of the metapsychologies: listening to the conflict between psychical agencies or systems or Oedipal/pre-Oedipal material – and so forth. His interpretations would be influenced by the same paradigms or *aimed* at making changes within those paradigms. Candidates in training and young psychoanalysts do that almost absentmindedly. Neutrality, in that regard, is refraining from framing, referring, or reformulating the subject's associations in anything outside the subject's life – real life. An example could help. A patient spent hours describing his sexual life with his numerous one-night stands. His material could have been listened to and interpreted in several sub-theoretical categories, in the classical sense. My remark to him was: *your associations are telling me about two things that are not necessarily or always related: your sexual prowess and women's attraction to you*. The remark was stemming from the patient's associations and the two intertwined issues in them. Those associations had to be understood first in order to be interpreted if interpretation is required. Is he doing sex or using sex for achieving something else? Is he a stud to attract women or are women attracted to him because he is a stud? Clarifying that aspect in the patient's life does not belong to the theory but to the patient; neutrality was related to his subjective experiences.

The area in neutrality that all analysts find themselves under pressure to breach, from time to time, is counselling and advising the patient. Both those activities evidently forfeit the principles of anonymity and abstinence. Daily experience shows that people, from their childhood on, seek advice and counselling that permits them to do what they *want* to do. They seldom take advice or concede to counselling that disagree with their wishes. In analysis there is an extra danger of doing that: the patient could take advantage of a counter-transference aspect in the analytic relationship to achieve something else by extracting the analyst's opinion about a situation. An example could clarify that analytic situation. A patient who had some sexual difficulties was in a passive unhappy relationship with his wife. She asked for a divorce and sought the help of a lawyer. The patient was negotiating the terms of the divorce without help. He complained in his analysis about being intimidated by his wife's presence in the meetings with her lawyer. Knowing his predicament with sexuality and his passivity when it comes to relating to his wife I suggested that having a lawyer to represent him could help avoid his presence in negotiating the terms of the divorce. The situation started to get out of hand with the involvement of another lawyer in the matter. Luckily, his wife realized that the two lawyers had an interest in complicating matters and accepted a quick settlement to avoid the accumulating legal fees. My suggested solution to his intimidation was going to be disastrous. His passivity should have remained a psychical matter and not a situational issue.

Abstinence

Abstinence is the third clinical positions the analyst has to take in dealing with and managing the transference. Clinically speaking, the patient's neurotic demands seek satisfaction and gratification in the analytic situation creating, thus, a major obstacle in the analyst's way to perform the analysis. Abstinence was suggested by Freud as a rule that both analyst and analysand should adhere to. This is the reason the analyst should mention it and remind the patient of it when he is asked to bypass it. In principle it is *abstaining from gratifying any wishes or desires in the analytic relationship*. Thus, the analyst should be careful of his own wishes of being accepted, liked, admired, or loved by the patient, and using analysis to gratify them. This rule covers a wide spectrum of wishes and desires. In regard to the patient, those same wishes and needs that the patient might have, should be dealt with differently. Although the analyst will make clear that he is not going to yield to them, he should also encourage the patient to express them and if they appear in the material in a disguised way he should 'skilfully' bring them to the analysable material. The patient is informed from the beginning that those wishes and desires will be part of the work of analysis but the analyst would strictly abstain from gratifying them by the common socially expected responses. Abstinence, clinically speaking, is meant to eliminate an aspect in the relationship with the analyst that could cloud the transference. Yet, Freud's writings about abstinence and the writings of the pioneers in the field were mainly theoretical, metapsychological, and used as a clinical manoeuvre. They suggested and recommended to the patients that they should abstain from doing certain things that could be part of the neuroses, to avoid situations that could provoke certain undesirable consequences, to avoid taking major decisions while still in analysis, and to fight against the temptation of repetition compulsion. Theoretically, the patients' abstention was meant to keep the neurotic tension at a peak to get the best results (heighten the intensity of the symptoms). Metapsychologically, it was to keep the libido frustrated outside of analysis to direct all of it to the transference, and to create by displacement a dynamic set up in the transference that is a magnification of the original set up of the neurosis. Abstinence in that conception was to *avoid* complicating the process of analysis, and it was not a technical *manoeuvre*.

Those justifications for the patients' abstinence are insupportable, and are even objectionable to present day psychoanalysts. Before I discuss the reason for that I would like to highlight a significant fact regarding Freud's intuitions. No analyst would deny or ignore the significance and importance of the rule of abstinence – if not for its organic link with the other two rules, when it would be for the impossibility of doing analysis in an atmosphere of exchanging with the patient social niceties and reacting to psychoneurotic wishes and demands. Therefore, we have to recognize something particular about Freud's intuition: *He had the intuition to emphasize abstinence without really knowing the actual significance of that rule, and even having an incorrect understanding of its foundation.* Abstinence is an attitude the analyst takes from the patient's psychoneurotic demands. It is one of the important elements of the protocol of practice. It keeps the patient aware of his status in the analytic relation as the one who is receiving a *treatment* and should not expect anything else. This attitude works indirectly on the analyst's own demands: he is there to provide treatment and should not expect more than the patient's adherence to what is expected of him: being there on time, free associating, and paying for his sessions; there should be no additional gratification to the analyst. This is not the only time Freud had an intuition years before revisiting it to make it a true theoretical proposition. Therefore, for those who criticize Freud for the mistakes he made should know the whole text well before jumping to premature conclusions. And for those who idealize Freud they should also know his text well enough to be able to reveal this feature in his thinking.

Freud's suggestion of the three analytic attitudes the analyst has to take are related to transference and free association. Two questions arise: is it possible to avoid corrupting the purity of the analytic situation by the impurities of counter-transference? The answer is definitely no. However, there is a qualitative difference between corrupting transference by counter-transference impurities and by some narcissistic gratifications that the analyst might be unconsciously seeking. It is possible to correct the former but not the latter. The second question is: if the purity of counter-transference is not guaranteed and the analyst is subject to making mistakes of that nature (Baranger & Baranger, 2008), what is the difference between counter-transference mistakes and narcissistic mistakes? The answer, temporarily, is that narcissistic flaws affect the analyst's whole practice while counter-transference affects single patients. The analyst could discover the counter-transference mistakes in his auto-analysis and correct it, but narcissistic mistakes are difficult to identify and, when recognized, the analyst should seek some professional help (De M'Uzan, 1976).

Interpretation and reconstruction

Merleau-Ponty (2003) and Paul Ricoeur (1970) stressed the difference between the search for meaning (roughly, hermeneutics) and the search for causes. The embedded issue in this distinction is a difference between an unexplainable event and a non-understandable representation of an event. Hypothetically, shop lifting by a well-to-do lady is not as it might seem and needs to be explained. Once the motives are unveiled (because it is expected to be preconscious) and pointed to a compulsion to get into exciting situations and not get arrested, the event is explained. But, the shoplifting as a representation of the desire of excitement, that desire becomes non-understandable – i.e., needs to be interpreted. Becoming better acquainted with that difference makes the act of interpretation a distinctive act of psychoanalytic psychotherapy, because we deal all the time with representations, for which motives are unconscious and remain unconscious. Interpretation, as the psychoanalytic act, puts psychoanalysis in the domain of the ideographic sciences, to which it belongs, because the main issue in homothetic science is to explain, while in the idiographic sciences it is to understand. This distinction answers the question of the place of theory in psychoanalysis: we need a theory of interpretation and not of causation. Ricoeur (1970) defined interpretation as an act of demystifying an illusion or restoring a meaning. This theory of interpretation fits psychoanalysis very well. Transference is the illusion of a true relationship when it is a relationship with an illusory person. Working through the function of displacement and the working of the primary process leads to demystifying that relationship and exposes the illusions about the character of the analyst. In the process of representing an unconscious ideation that starts early in life and undergoes a long process of transformations, it could get a distorted meaning and fixate on it. The process of interpretation would gradually restore its rightful meaning. Hence, Ricoeur's theory of interpretation (1970) is very well suited to the act of psychoanalyzing.

However, interpretation is only part of the psychoanalytic act, because interpretation is a laborious work that deals with the daily events of the patient in addition to his detailed memories of his past. Interpreting one with the other, including the interconnections between them, requires constructing the psychological life of the patient, and reconstructing all the isolated constructions and filling gaps in infantile amnesia.[5] Freud said (1937d):

> I think that "construction" is by far the more appropriate description of the psychoanalytic technique. Interpretation applies to some single element of the material, such as an association or a parapraxis. But it is "construction" when one lay before the subject of analysis a piece of his early that has been forgotten.
>
> (261)

We know now that reconstruction is mainly there to put the material in order, thus eliminating from it the distortions that caused the psychoneurosis. Greenacre (1979, 1981) considered reconstruction part of the ongoing process throughout the whole process of psychoanalysis. Therefore it could be said that the aim of psychoanalyzing is to give the patient the chance to have a correct and meaningful narrative of his life. If interpretation depends on the analyst's assimilation of a theory of meaning and founded on the nature of hermeneutics, and if reconstruction is an act that configures interpretation into the patient's narrative, does that mean the theory of psychoanalysis has no place in psychoanalysis? Is there any use for a good theory of psychoanalysis? A clinical vignette could enable the answer to this question.

A female patient came to me for analysis due to stress caused by her new job and other employment demands. She had had nine years of analysis with another analyst, then stopped for six years before she came to me. She indicated that she benefited well from her previous analysis and she understood many things about herself but the main problem remained unchanged: a compulsive, almost obsessive, need to be on top of everything and everyone all the time, and a demanding need to be praised. That need made her constantly anxious and worried – especially when she had to do something in public, which was a big part of her new job. It did not take long before she averred that as child, and until age seven, she was on top of the world. She was the most popular, rich, liked and the cutest 'of them all'. She said that two specific things happened that brought her down. The first was the sudden death of a teacher who treated her as a special child in the school, which made her become aware of death in a shock. She also started thinking of the death of members of her family and herself and had bouts of extreme anxiety about facing God and his punishment for her sins (unspecified). The second was a vague financial scandal in the company owned by the family and run by her father. Her father was removed from his position, which made her so ashamed of him and herself after being cocky and boisterous. "Two things took away all the pleasures of my life; they stopped me from enjoying what I had, and I wish that those two things had not happened and that I could be able to go back to how I felt when I was seven." I pointed out that those two things did not take away any of the things that originally put her on top of others, and there must be something else to know which had changed the *value* of those things. She reacted to that intervention angrily, because she believed that she had worked hard to find out the cause and origin of her sense of unworthiness. She believed that her fear of death and the shame from her father were the only causes of her present psychological problems.

Following that burst of anger we discovered that she was using and improvising a system of explaining everything in a manner that (to a great extent) she had learned from her previous analyst's interpretations. She believed that she was good at analysing herself and felt proud of becoming insightful and good at doing that, and expected me to admire her for that. After going through a vast number of those explanations she stopped and accused me of making her feel silly, childish, and stupid. The issue of my interfering, interrupting, and deflating her pleasure came up, but this time was unrelated to her obsessive need to go back to when she was on the top of everything. After asking if the matter was the return to age seven and having a similar situation as the one she imagined, she admitted that that wish in itself was childish. The word 'childish', after a while, became an empty word (a denotation without a connotation). However, the metaphor of the interrupted pleasure and the longing to return to that lost happiness kept dominating her associations and her social life. Then she recalled that when her father lost his position in the family business her mother became very agitated and was yelling all the time, entering rooms unexpectedly and banging doors in a manner that kept her (the patient) always on the alert. "Mother would suddenly enter my room interrupting what I was doing … mostly daydreaming." She indicated that daydreaming was so pervasive in her life that it was embarrassing her in front of her visiting friends. She believed that daydreaming was another result of her "falling from grace". A suitable event allowed me to ask her to tell me more about her unreasonable fear of God. She posed for a long time, and then said that she now remembers something from her childhood that continued until recently and always made her feel demeaned and ashamed. It was heavy masturbation and being engaged in sexual play with a girlfriend at school. She had not talked about that previously because it never came to mind in her previous analysis or this analysis.

Analysis took off after that in the direction of extensive work of *reconstruction*. The emerging awareness of a link between her early genital activity and the present sense of need to go back to when she was masturbating without anxieties brought more details. But would that be the guiding light for reconstruction? It is the core of the representational process that was in this case her childhood genital anxieties. Working through it is meant to narrow that down to a more encompassing core. In this patient more work was needed to reconstruct her previous analytic experience, which could have lasted much less than nine years if there was more reconstruction done during it. Freud said: "'Interpretation' applies to something that one does to some single element of the material, such as an association or parapraxes. But it is 'construction' when one lays before the subject of analysis a piece of his early history that have been forgotten" (1937d, 262). This point is worth a closer look. For a psychoanalysis to come to a proper conclusion there should be extensive construction and reconstruction of the vast material that was revealed in hundreds of sessions, in addition to the interpretations given to them over the time. Honing in on the main source of the disturbed representational process – in this case the genital endogenous urges – results in reorganizing the chaotic interrelations of the representations of grandiosity, guilt, punishment, and sense of entitlement; it even reveals the prototypes of future interpersonal relationships. Understanding the functions of construction and reconstruction is very important in dealing with the many scattered suggestions in the different conceptions of termination (Bergman, 1997; Blum, 2003; Fonagy, 2003). I chose auto-analysis as one aspect in the process of termination to highlight the role of reconstruction in that process. The most puzzling thing in auto-analysis is who is analysing whom? The endogenous source of psychopathology is one of the erogenic zones in the body. Its representations are in the forms of metaphors, metonymy, and phantasies. When the work of reconstruction puts the erogenic zone within its linguistic context the patient becomes more capable of sorting out what he is dealing with and even the phantasy that he is living. As the analyst restores the meanings in the detailed interpretations and removes the illusions implicit in the transference he reconstructs the patient's narrative. The patient acquires a new narrative and also the main themes that permeate it. This reconstructed *I* knows now more of the *Me*, its past, and its structure to permit continuing the process that analysis has begun; analysing the Me autonomously. Abend (2008), like many other analysts, remains stuck with Freud's clarification of transference, which negated its quality as resistance and its therapeutic usefulness. Thus, he talked about transference as an agent of therapeutic impact and differentiated between it and reconstruction as two different therapeutic agents. This point of view misunderstands both concepts: transference imparts the material for reconstruction, and without transference reconstruction will always have a hypothetical quality. Faimberg (1996) highlighted this link between the transference and reconstruction through the working of after-effect which allows the patient to try to give some meaning to old experiences from present material – i.e., reconstructing his transference.

Diagnosis and the patient's associations

In Chapters 2 and 3 I expounded the notion that formation of psychoneuroses is based on representing the endosomatic mentally, thus creating the psychical phenomena. A colleague debated that this point of view could be interesting theoretically but does not seem helpful for the practising analyst, because of the difficulty of tracing back the end result of such a complex net of representations to its endogenous source, and the limited good that it would do to the patient even if he managed to follow that analytical process.

The process of representing the endogenous stimuli in the mind forms the background of psychical life in a peculiar way. The pressure of the endosomatic need is totally unconscious but the human infant allows it to be known through the expression of pain. The external response to that need is of a linguistic nature, even if it is not verbal, because it still receives a linguistic translation from the caregiver, i.e., the message is linguistically registered. The physical relief offered to the infant translates to the infant the caregiver's understanding. Thus, the endosomatic will gradually become set within a linguistic framework. As Freud stipulated, the first representations are thing-representations which advance to word (verbal) representations. The mother's understanding of the infant's scream to be of hunger will make her give him the breast. The infant's need is translated, whether rightly or wrongly is not the issue, because the issue is the translation. The infant learns from the translation the 'meaning' of his need. The mother's response and the object she will provide will eventually be replaced with words. If the need is, for example, an oral need the object would be the breast. Waiting for the breast and the gratification of the need would generate related phantasies about the object and the gratifications. The oral physical sensations in the oral zone comprise more than the sensations of hunger; they will gradually include its meanings (love, fullness, badness, etc.). Phantasies are preverbal configurations of early representations and situations that engender rigid psychical unconscious constructs. Later in analysis they have to be made conscious if they are to lose their rigid repetitiveness – i.e., oral fantasies keep constructing situations related to deprivation and fulfilment, lack and satisfaction; they reshape the future and more complex situations. They become constituents of the person's character, neurotic type, and guiding principles in reconstruction.

The linguistic framework of the endogenous stimuli springs from such phantasies as metaphors and metonymies. Human language is characterized by an unavoidable double sense that comes from it being metaphors and metonymies of phantasies, or what Ricoeur called the equivocal nature of speech (1970). In daily exchanges misunderstandings emanate from the individual differences in comprehension of meanings of metaphors and metonymies. In artistic work, metonymies and metaphors are enriched by the artists' talents who expose new potentials in ordinary metonymies and metaphors. In psychopathology, the links between phantasies and their linguistic expressions are difficult to comprehend not because of their anomalies, but because they are complex representations of the ordinary metonymies and metaphors of the body. Nevertheless, the usage of metaphors in formulating interpretations or accepting them from the patient in place of narrative could become a means to reify the lived experience emptying it from its reality (Martela & Saarinen, 2013).

A clinical vignette deals with a sliced aspect of that difficulty but does not give the details of its analysis for brevity reasons.

A patient was talking about a disagreement between him and his wife, whom he claimed could not follow a definite way of thinking about things, and strayed away from the main topic into insignificant details of what they discussed (note what he revealed later). Talking about that, he mentioned that before coming to his session something happened that upset him and was interfering with what he planned to talk about. He wondered if he should interrupt his thoughts and talk about that *other* thing. He revealed something about his analysis (close to two years by then) that I was unaware of: he always came prepared to talk about certain things and each session was *apart* and separate from the other sessions. The subject that was interfering with what he planned for the session ran like this. He was interviewing someone to work in his department. When the patient asked him about the salary he was expecting to get, the interviewee gave a lower figure than the one the patient was willing to pay. After an "agonizing" moment, the patient offered the interviewee the job with a little more than the interviewee expected, but did not give the full amount he had in mind. He was almost panicking because of not knowing whether he was stingy or generous. For a few sessions he accepted that he would talk about that without preparation. He remembered that at age six he was collecting stamps and his father gave him, one day, a few very nice stamps. After thanking his father his father asked if the stamps made him happy. He confirmed to his father that they did, and his father smiled and said to him: "You are like your mother, stingy with your feelings." Later in his adulthood he heard the expression "constipated personality" and he immediately associated that with what his father said about him and his mother. Making this connection meant that the expression that attracted the patient's attention echoed a lived phantasy – i.e., a concern about his constipated character. Indirectly, his wife's lucid style of thinking and communication irritated him. Although most of his material after that, his metaphors and metonymies, were strongly suggestive of an anal source of his phantasy, his compulsion to find what supported that discovery became his main effort in the analysis. My interpretations were directed at the situation he was creating in the analysis by doing the same thing: separate disconnected sessions with no easy lucidity in his experience.

There is 'always' a link between the initial reason for seeking psychoanalysis, the nature of free associating, and transference. It is important to recognize that link early as a diagnostic guide to the course the analysis will take. This same diagnostic link has to be used properly in interpretation, construction, and reconstruction. The patient I am presenting in that vignette came to analysis because of premature ejaculation, which he did his best all his sexual life to hide from women. He told me about that problem in his very early sessions, but did not come back to it until I started seeing more in his transference and his relationship with his father. Classically transference is repeating an infantile relationship with a parent in the relationship with the analyst. It is disguised memories that are veiled by not putting them into words. However, for transferring an old experience or relationship from the past to the present there must be a *psychical medium* that facilitates and makes it possible. *The existence of an original phantasy is that medium*. It is the fantasy that is activated in the present, and through it the past and the present could become the same. The patient's phantasy that he was not generous with his father when he gave him the gift was reactivated and he (unconsciously) tried to be generous with the analyst by giving him neat and clear gifts of thoughts. Flugle (1953) considered that analysis of transference is the therapeutic part of the therapy. We could expand this concept a little more to say that in the transference we will encounter the original phantasy, the diagnostic link that will guide the process of interpretation and reconstruction.

The issue of diagnosis in psychoanalysis[6] could be confusing because theoretically speaking psychoanalysis has no fixed theory of psychopathology that could be the base for differential diagnoses. At the same time diagnosis should be a clinical issue, as it is in all therapeutic disciplines. But as mentioned earlier, the practice of psychoanalysis depends on a theory of interpretation and not on a theory of psychopathology; therefore, it is puzzling that diagnosis has to emanate from the same psychopathological source. When Freud embarked on his discovery of psychoanalysis the system of diagnosis at that time was Kraepelin's. Kraepelin based his nosology on separating affective disorders from thought disorders and psychoses from neuroses, and coming with his known system. It was logical that Freud and his followers should have conformed to the Kraepelinian system. Nonetheless, using the Kraepelinian framework of diagnosis proved unsuitable for psychoanalytic work. Analysts were working on the disease entities that were amenable only to their treatment method; and some literature was written to warn about the dangers of psychoanalyzing the wrong patients. Analysts excluded the psychoses (narcissistic disorders) and concentrated on certain neuroses: hysteria and obsessive compulsive neurosis. Freud and some of his bright disciples speculated about the psychopathology of the other entities and gave 'hypothetical' theoretical formulations of those conditions (Freud's Schreber Case, 1911c); they even coined a few new terms such as 'paraphrenia' and 'hypochondria'. Psychiatric diagnostic framework and its nosology were no longer appropriate in meeting the theoretical advancements in psychoanalysis. Two things changed the relationship between psychoanalysis and psychiatric nosology. Psychoanalysts encountered many difficulties in treating 'the ideal neurotics'; therefore they resorted to using their theoretical understanding to explain the analysability and unanalysability of patients. A clear example of that shift is Zetzel's (1968) revisions of the views about hysteria and psychoanalysis. The second thing was the emergence of new psychopathological conditions that were not part of psychiatry and became of interest to psychoanalysts, such as narcissistic and character disorders, psychosomatics, behavioural problems, and the opening up of the fields of adolescence and children's neuroses to psychoanalytic thought.

This is a point that will require major changes in psychoanalysis. It has to develop a system of diagnosis based on a clear *understanding* of the human subject as a phenomenon that is not subject to psychoneuroses but could suffer from its state as a human being. In better words: psychoanalysis should change from a theory of psychopathology that may have a framework of diagnosis to a theory of the human subject who could consider *his* psychological condition uncomfortable and would like to make changes to it. Psychoanalysis as a theory of the human subject could then be of help.

Notes

1 The frequency of the sessions and their duration was not a problem until Anna Freud suggested changes to her father's practice to increase the number of patients that he could see in the same period of time. Those changes were debated but when Sacha Nacht reduced the time to 45 minutes from 50, and the frequency from five sessions a week to three, it seemed that this change was accepted in general. Lacan came up with another change by doing away with the timeframe of the session as a principle, depending on the patient's degree of engagement in his session. This change did not last long and created a great deal of controversy, and analysts even in his school refused to accept that change. However, lately some insurance and third party payers insisted on dividing the hour into two equal parts and the session became 30 minutes a unit. I will discuss this matter with other issues about the practice of psychoanalysis in the next chapter.

2 Transference is one of the most controversial concepts in clinical practice despite its significance in the psychoanalytic work.

3 'Auto-analysis' is a term used to describe the subject's own work on his own psychical material and effort to do something similar to what his analyst does. The important part of auto-analysis is its happening spontaneously and not intentionally. It was wrongly translated as 'self-analysis' and became a description of a deliberate act.

4 My clinical experience covers part of the period when those two diagnoses exited and stayed until a few years ago. A new condition called neuromyalgia emerged to replace hypochondria and some hysterical conversions. It is not considered psychological in origin although there is no physical explanation for it.

5 The concept of *infantile amnesia* was once an important part of understanding the curative process, because cure was thought to come from removing repression and making the unconscious conscious. Thus the patient should be able to remember his repressed childhood experience as part of undoing the doings of repression.

6 We should consider the term 'diagnosis' on a larger scale than the scale of medicine. An engineer, an agricultural specialist, like many other experts, make diagnoses of the problem they encounter before they embark on working on it. Therefore, the term 'diagnosis' is a general term that connotes knowing before acting.

5

CLINICAL PRACTICE

The analytic situations

The notion of psychotherapy is one that could fairly be called Freudian. If there are some hints to the idea of psychotherapy before Freud, they were indistinct and faint. Freud endeavoured to treat patients whose conditions required professional attention, but there was no known medical speciality or theoretical understanding that could help them. His attempts, which began with hypnosis, were the onset of such a notion. Because he called what he was doing 'psychoanalysis' the two terms eventually became synonyms. During the few decades during which psychotherapy and psychoanalysis meant the same thing, and before some other ways of doing psychotherapy emerged, psychoanalysts derived a great deal of pride in being the only ones who did psychotherapy. However, that pride changed into a sort of protectiveness of the term 'psychoanalysis' and they insisted on making it a specific and superior type of psychotherapy, distinct from all others. For a very long time, psychoanalysis was a *trademark* while psychotherapy was a generic term.[1] The distinction psychoanalysts made with pride was due to the clear protocol of practice that was also associated with a training programme and unified standards of affiliation to an international association. Things started to change to as we now know them, and the practice of psychoanalysis has become a point of contention among psychoanalysts, both in its theoretical basis and its clinical application.

Clinical practice of psychoanalysis has become the arena where the diversities, disagreements, the emergence of the schools, and theoretical plurality have been fought. Better, for an outsider, the present situation in psychoanalysis seems to have come from conflicts around a proper way of doing psychoanalysis – just because the theoretical and, sometimes, personal disagreements are disguised. The history of the reasons for that confusion is too complex and irrelevant to what I am trying to underline. Nevertheless, it is relevant to mention three circumstances that are associated with this difficult situation. First, there were no serious discussions of how psychoanalysis is done to underline the distinctive nature of doing it till the late 1960s. Second, the issues that have arisen from clinical practice like transference, repetition compulsion, interpretation, etc., gained more theoretical attention and less technical thrashing. Thus, clinical practice was shadowing the clarity of the claim that psychoanalysis is unique psychotherapy. Third, Freud's papers on technique were not used in any convincing way (compared with his other works) to identify the practice of psychoanalysis. This could probably be for the scarcity of Freud's clinical works, his doubtful success as a practitioner, or his own uncertainty about the proper technique of psychoanalysis. Notwithstanding all those reasons, there is a very pertinent fact that should be mentioned in this regard. Freud practised his brands of psychoanalysis without any definite knowledge of what he was doing at any time in the history of psychoanalysis. Yet, he was able to originate and articulate the protocol of clinical practice and advance it. Probably he did that by virtue of being the originator of all the advancement in psychoanalysis. Alexander (2007) says:

> Observations made during the therapeutic procedure are the primary source of psychoanalytic knowledge. Most of our knowledge of psychodynamics stems from this source. Precise understanding of the therapeutic factors is significant both for improving our therapeutic techniques and also for increasing our theoretical knowledge. Between theory and therapy there is a reciprocal relationship: observations made during treatment are the main source of our theoretical knowledge, and we apply our theoretical formulations to improve our technique. This presentation is based on the premise that much in our therapeutic procedure is still empirical, and that many of the processes which take place in patients during psychoanalysis are not yet fully understood.
>
> (1073)

My objective in dealing with the practice of psychoanalysis separately from its clinical protocol is to present a few facts about its practice that have been ignored, misunderstood, and distorted by the psychoanalytic clinicians, thus ruining the unity of theory as a breakthrough in understanding the individual. The unrelenting endeavour to consider psychoanalysis a technique of therapy comes from central beliefs in the psychoanalytic circle that it was born in the Clinique, that its clinical aspect is the foundation of its theory, that its validation comes from the clinical material, and that *maybe* it has some applications outside the field of the treatment of psychoanalysis. Those convictions are blatantly wrong and unsubstantiated. Psychoanalysis did not exist before Freud's three books on dreams (1900a), parapraxes (1901b), and jokes (1905c), and their exposition of the working of the primary process was critical and fundamental in making Freud move towards listening to patients instead of hypnotizing them.

There is no trace of evidence that Freud came up with the conditions of therapy (making the unconscious conscious, etc.) from any clinical material. Those were derivative of the catharsis theory, which, despite its demise, has maintained an indelible imprint on psychoanalysis until now, revealing something psychical that has no access to consciousness, and needs analysis to become conscious. Free association and interpretations were general statements about doing therapy, but were mostly meant to be explaining and constructing the material on theoretical lines. The confusion about what is theory and what is practice, what is content and what is process, what is exploration and discovery, on the one hand, and what is therapeutic on the other, is caused by not recognizing that *Freud was applying his theoretical intuitions to the act of therapy, and not the other way around.*

Freud and clinical practice

Freud discovered quite a few astounding things (at his time) about human nature – especially in its sickness. Some were proved by him to be wrong and he corrected them to a degree. Others were found flawed and were replaced. However, Freud's lasting legacy is the way he came to those faulty conceptions and their corrections, because his way was and still is the way we do good analysis. It is not his thoughts that make him the great man that he was, but his thinking. To underline the difference I would make a distinction between *functional* concepts that he considered for a while to explain psychical phenomena such as sexuality or repression, and *structural* concepts like *Trieb* and after-effect, without which sexuality and repression would not have meant much. Functional concepts relate to specific contents, which could be replaced without harm, while structural concepts are for all types of content and are foundational. With this in mind let us see how Freud found his way in practice without having a clue about what he was embarking on.

Freud was a reluctant physician. He resisted practising it in a number of ways and for several years after graduating. But when Breuer introduced him to the 'Case of Anna O' he changed completely. It has to be mentioned here that hysteria (the nerve disease) was included earlier in medical practice and hypnosis was already well known in Europe. Thus there was nothing new in that introduction, but there was something new in 'that physician Freud'. To get to the point I will mention an event. Breuer – the more experienced physician –asked Freud his opinion about some hysterical symptoms a patient of his was displaying. He replied – very nonchalantly – they came from a pregnancy fantasy. Breuer took his hat and coat, and left without a word. Here we can see that before Freud abandoned hypnosis, and without any 'hesitation', he read what the symptoms were saying. Once again, to cut things short: Freud introduced a non-medical system of diagnosis, in dealing with non-medical psychopathology, but within the medical setting of practice. He was a medical person doing non-medical things with a new flair regarding a completely novel approach to 'handling' hysterical symptoms.

Then came the shift from hypnosis to free association. From the event I mentioned earlier and from the case of Katarina (in *Studies on Hysteria*, 1895d) we can see that Freud was able to decipher (read) the meaning of the symptoms without hypnosis. He discovered first that those symptoms – as in medicine – have meaning; however, in medicine they say something about the condition of their physiological base, but in psychoneurosis they need a psychical base from which to read their meaning. Second, repression does not delete the meaning of the symptom completely but distorts it, so it could be missed by the patient and by doctors. Third, the so-called repressed was not the cause of the symptom but the place where the missed meaning was created. Freud very perceptively realized that it is not the repressed sexual desire that caused the neurosis – as he previously supposed – but the way it got distorted and indirectly became a complaint. Better, psychopathology is a product of distorted meaning in a statement, which finally becomes a symptom. It was then very easy, sensible, and more effective to listen to the patient talking awake than talking asleep. Free association was born as the method of psychoanalysis.

We cannot define, with certainty, what Freud thought about his shift or identify concretely his thoughts about it. However, we can assume a few things from what his shift has produced in terms of practice, and presume that he became aware of such and such, but as usual in an after-the-fact manner of speaking. All we cannot say for sure is that Freud realized that free association was a better way of doing analytic therapy, but we can presume that he did. Therefore, we could presume that shifting to free association introduced Freud to a new revelation: there are no fixed relationships between causes and their symptoms, as Breuer previously envisaged. He also realized that it is not sexuality, as such, that is behind psychopathology, but that sexuality seems to be the most affected aspect in the process of the missing meaning in symptoms. He still believed that free association would reveal something repressed (for the good reason that the medical model is based on causes of diseases). But Freud was, by then, ready to move from the functional meaning of symptoms to the structural conception behind this new insight. He came to the concept of *Trieb* through accepting and exploring infantile sexuality. *Trieb, as the somatic pressure put on the mind to represent it* allowed Freud to separate direct causes (the endosomatic) from their potential representations. Whatever we could presume that Freud had discovered at that stage, one question remains unanswered: why did he put the sexual *Trieb* in a duality with self-preservation? What made Freud create a dialectic of *Triebhaft*? We will get to the answer later.

After working for a few years within this new modality provided by free association, Freud arrived at the problem of libido investments. The problem came after his work *Totem and Taboo* (1912–1913), in which the issue of identification was tackled for the first time as the 'structuring process of the sense of being'. What happens to identification and the changes to libidinal investments in the course of development introduced the concept of narcissism. The concept of narcissism presented the problems of one libido or two, object and subject, the need to restate the concepts of libidinal investments, and the limitations of the quantitative theory of the libido. This is when a second and a major shift happened in Freud's practice of psychoanalysis. It is important to underline two points in that brief and incomplete depiction of Freud's landmark shift in his practice of psychoanalysis before we go into detail about the matter. Freud had the notion that symptoms talk, so he listened without any planning as to what he was going to find or do with what he would hear. Yet, he constructed a theory of the psyche along the way. This is a very important aspect of practising psychoanalysis: an analyst should engage in every psychoanalysis without any plan, anticipation, theoretical guideline – exactly as Freud did in his successful discovery of psychoanalysis. We are supposed to be doing the same thing, listening without knowing what we will hear, and constructing each patient's own theory that created his sickness. Freud also embarked on a process in which the discoveries were in themselves the cure. Missing the meaning of symptoms created the psychical condition. Reaching the meaning, reformulating it, revealing it to the patient liberates him from his self-deception.

Freud's practice of psychoanalysis was consistent in its subject in spite of the major shifts it went through; it was interested in, and concerned with, the intrapsychic of the subject and never deviated to dealing with anything else. This point is of significant importance. Hypnotherapy was an attempt at finding out the internal cause of the external (symptoms). It was an elementary search for the intrapsychical, yet it did not try to find external reasons for the symptoms. The more Freud worked on the intrapsychical, the less functional his thinking became, and the more extensive his search for the structural core of psychopathology became. The significance of this point is its clear characterization of psychoanalysis – differentiating it from psychotherapies. Psychoanalysis is a theory of the intrapsychical and a method of treating it if it needed rearrangement. It is not an approach to adjusting or correcting a person's interpersonal relationships. Although psychoanalysis has engendered the discipline of psychotherapy, it maintained its specificity as a theory dedicated only to the intrapsychical. The main problem in the contemporary circle of psychoanalysis stems from disregarding this fact or even denying it. There could be no psychoanalytic plurality unless the field is muddled by eliminating the difference between psychotherapies with their theoretical multiplicity and psychoanalysis with its distinctive and single theory of the intrapsychic. The practice of psychoanalysis based on its distinct protocol should be a clear separator from the practice of psychotherapy – not for matters related to narcissistic or privileged status but to defining the practising psychoanalysis.

Psychoanalysis and psychotherapy

Some years ago, a former analytic patient called to ask me about the difference between psychoanalysis and psychotherapy, because her daughter insisted they were both the same (although she preferred to look for psychotherapy because it was less demanding). I discussed the matter with the mother without using any terms such as 'intrapsychic' and 'interpersonal', 'transference' and 'countertransference', 'defence mechanisms' and 'resistance' for good reasons: my ex-patient averred several times during her analysis that analysis is an intelligent way of talking about one's self. She wondered what I could have studied to make me claim that what I am doing is a specialty. She admitted, nevertheless, that every time she felt she had changed her opinion about herself in a way she felt she had not fully understood how. Her analysis terminated as she found herself becoming busy with her life beyond dwelling on herself as she used to be before analysis. The conversation led in a natural way to my saying to her: *You came because something in particular was irking you and you finished when you changed, as you suggested several times, without understanding what had changed or how*. I would answer her question this way if using technical terms: *If the patient has a definite life situation that he is not able to fathom and deal with, or a character flaw that reached the level of a need for immediate solution, and the patient showed little or no concern or insight about his input in the creation of his predicament, psychotherapy is better for him. If the patient, on the other hand, is insightful enough that he has to change if his life situation would ever change, then psychoanalysis is the therapy of choice.* In clearer and more definitive terms: *It is the patient and his objectives that would determine what therapy would be practised with him.* I am not saying that in banal terms 'diagnosis' determines the therapy; I mean what is the therapist going to practise with such patient? Practising psychoanalysis requires accurate and true following of the psychoanalytic protocol, without diluting it with psychotherapeutic interventions.

Two points are worth mentioning at this instance. In psychoanalysis the patient finds out that he is the subject of the analytic work and not the issues he brings to the sessions. He gradually and unnoticeably becomes aware that the analyst is investigating with him his place in the issue and leaving the issue uninvestigated. Whatever is revealed the patient does not feel they were discoveries, but rather matters he did not pay attention to beforehand. This happens in synchrony with free associations; the patient realizes that he said what the analyst interpreted. The new discoveries come in the analysis in two forms: the first is a new meaning (understanding) of an old aspect that was either isolated from the rest of him and is put in its proper context. The other is that matters become integrated in the rest of his self-awareness making other things become organized differently. Literally, this gradual process is analysing and reconstructing the patient's narrative. Another thing a patient includes in his self-awareness is the manner it comes together (what we call 'working through'). Psychoanalysis, in those terms, is conducive to termination – i.e., it terminates in a natural way. Termination of analysis indicates that what has to be done is done and there is nothing more to be done. Too many words for a simple idea: psychoanalysis is terminable, not as Freud suggested that it is interminable. The work of analysis takes the patient to the foundation of his character (his self) – i.e., to the part of him that is irreplaceable but could endure changes without the loss of who the person is. In the analysis of another female patient, she was disheartened at the termination work (not phase) when she realized that analysis was not meant to make her replace her spoiled childish personality with a mature responsible one. She further realized, in a sudden insight, that she did not have to change but just make distinctions between whom to reveal it to and whom to it hide from. Once the basic character is put together from working through its manifestations the patient realizes that he owns his character and it does not own him anymore, and termination – as there is nothing else to do – happens.

The other point I would like to deal with is preparing the patient for 'the day after analysis'. Patients, with few exceptions, worry about what to do if their condition returns and the analyst is not willing to offer help after termination (I emphasize that after termination the patient is not considered a patient anymore and I would not take him in analysis again – although he would be free to go to another analyst if he so wished). A male patient was very apprehensive about termination because as he said: "There is no way that I am not going to face difficulties after analysis and I am not sure how I am going to deal with them?" My reply was that he would deal with them as non-patients deal with their problems. I said that without thinking much of what that meant to him. It meant to him that difficulties would not be the same because being a non-patient makes a difference. He added, after explaining his insight, that the world is full of patients and he would be in better position because he knew the difference between being one and not being the other. In other words, he put the accent on 'not being a patient anymore', which was not the case before he came to analysis. He acknowledged that the change in him changed the world around him.

There is another difference between psychoanalysis and psychotherapy, which could have an important impact on the practice of psychoanalysis. It is customary that patients who come for psychoanalysis as the ones who seek psychotherapy present their problems in functional terms: problems for which they want know the causes, or expect that to happen. It takes months for the structural core of the problems to develop and for the patient to know the difference between causes that explain and understanding. Knowing the difference changes the patient's attitude and expectations. However, there are the rare cases that come with structural issues from the beginning, and their expectations are, from the beginning, matched to what psychoanalysis could deliver.[2] A clinical vignette could explain that difference:

Mrs. F. sought psychoanalysis although she did not suffer from any symptoms, or have a history of trauma or deprivations. She averred that people around her, family, neighbours, friends and even complete strangers, said things about themselves that used to surprise her until she realized lately that she did not have the ability to think about herself – i.e., she did not know if she could offer the equivalent of what those people talked about. There was nothing to suggest that her personal characteristics were defensive; they were puzzling and sometimes inconveniences. Her personality was not a character disorder nor leading to interpersonal failure. She thought all along that all people were alike – even in her own family. Then she realized that when others asked her things that might evoke a jealous, sad or worried response (for example), she would give an appropriate answer but did not really feel the same reactions she was relaying to others. Analysis started but did not provide the explanations to her condition. I was only putting things in perspective, such as: *you know that you should have been annoyed and showed your annoyance, but you did not feel it*. Structurally she was without a psychical life. That in itself was the beginning of her journey into 'the world of insight'. She preconciously knew the proper response to situations, but she was unconsciously treating words as the things they denote. Almost three years of going through this feature in her life instigated memories of her parents who taught her words and expected words back from her. Then there were memories of several childhood bouts of anxiety, unexplainable rage (against her dolls), and sometimes mild tendencies to self-mutilations. Her parents' reactions to those conditions were verbal.

The revival of those memories in analysis did not come as reactions to my interpretations but were casual, disconnected, and with conscious or preconscious explanations. Then, there was an episode of rage at me for failing to improve her condition, which would mean that analysis was to end with failure. This was clearly a transference response to her parents' way of bringing her up. Any interpretation of that transference reaction would have been in line with what her parents did with her, so I refrained from interpreting it. Her insistence on making me comment on her rage was the first sign of having been aware since her childhood of the strangeness of her parents and of their inability to help her. There was rage then, as there was with me, because if she had taken a different direction in her life and refused to become like her parents she would have revealed her dissatisfaction with them. If she managed to make me change her, this would have meant her analysis had failed and she had not been able to change and revolt against authority. Getting to the idea that analysis would end one day meant releasing the analyst from her grip of helplessness, as she should have released her parent from her hug of anger. The patient listened attentively to my pointing out the dilemma that she faced in her analysis and their ramifications, and in a remarkable way she did most of the work of reconstruction. *I did the analysis and she did the therapy.* This is a subtle but serious difference between psychoanalysis and psychotherapy. In psychotherapy the therapist does the therapy, and sometimes with the patient. In analysis the analyst has to be very careful not to do any psychotherapy.[3]

However, psychoanalysis takes hundreds of sessions over several months and years. It is not possible to follow its course of progress session by session and when it works it is equally difficulty to pinpoint what made it work. Therefore, we can only guess what happens in analysis in hindsight and basically accept that it works in mysterious ways. As an example:

I met Mrs. K. accidentally after twenty years of the termination of her analysis with me. She was happy to see me, as I was happy to see her. She insisted on meeting again to tell me everything that had happened in the last twenty years. I remembered her well although I did not have any specific recall of the analysis itself; yet once I looked at my notes on some of her sessions many details came to mind She was referred to me by her lawyer because she was going through a divorce and her tension and sometimes strange reaction could have had bad results if there was a court case for the settlement. She came from a middle-class family. Her father was an accountant and when she mentioned him she described him as erratic, unpredictable, gloomy; sometimes he was inappropriate, saying things that were unrelated to what he was talking about, and showing awkwardness doing that (mild dissociation!?). Her mother was the bookkeeper of the diocese of the city, and was very religious. Yet, she was constantly expressing her hate and dislikes of all kinds of people. Her younger sister was a troubled single mother, and the members of her extended family, who were living in the city, each had their own eccentricities. She was married to a man who worked in the family business, which she was also working for as a sales lady. Her husband was depressed most of the time and was on medication. He would go on drinking binges from time to time and his verbal abuse of her turned a few times into physical abuse.They had two sons.

Some months into her analysis she had the insight that she came from a 'bizarre' family, and was married into a bizarre family. This insight came as a gradual awareness as she noticed that her lawyer (and to some extent me) were stable men, considerate and 'had brains'. I remembered explaining to her that some people think about things before responding, rather than just reacting without thinking. It took her a while to realize that most people were like her lawyer, and that neither she nor her family tried to understand what was happening around them before they reacted. Although there were no particular events that she recalled in her analysis regarding her upbringing she became aware of not getting any guidance or help from 'the grown ups' in the difficult situations she faced. Her sessions were mainly about following the examples of her parents – and a dominant aunt – and never questioning their judgement. While going through the divorce her mother got her a job in town so she could leave her husband's family business. She continued her analysis for three more years before she terminated it to move to another city with her two sons.

In meeting her she shed some light on what I recalled of her analysis and I was able to remember more of it. She also talked about how she thought of her analysis for many years after its termination. As she settled down in the town she moved to with her children she paid more attention to her changes and credited them mostly to her analysis. Her insight about bizarreness and normality evolved into a process of exploring a new world of people, discovering aspects of herself she never thought she had, taking all that as 'growing up' and, most of all, as 'having her place in world'. She discovered that she loved her sons and was not just being dutiful. She experienced simple things like friendships, jealousy, and contempt. She dated a few times and discovered that she could assess the suitability of the potential partner, and could avoid those whom she considered to be bizarre. Although she did not put those changes in words

I remembered – while she was talking to me after twenty years of termination – that she was changing from being an *automat* with a disorganized intrapsychic core to becoming an alive living person with an intrapsychic that was gradually becoming organized.[4]

She said she moved to another nearby city and currently worked for a big organization. She was excited about her new stable and novel way of life. She said that she was like a teenager who had moved from home to go to university or to her own apartment. She averred that analysis removed from her way unseen obstacles: "My life was complicated for no reasons that I knew." She was still seeing her husband fleetingly whenever he came to visit his sons. She felt with time more at ease around him; and she was surprised that she began to expect his visits with happiness. Gradually she felt she wanted to restart her relationship with him. She managed to change the conditions of his visits, then suggested they get back together. He was delighted; they were remarried and had a fourteen-year-old daughter, and some grandchildren. She was full of pride and happiness telling me that. I asked her if her husband was better now. She laughed saying she discovered that her husband was not as bad as she had previously thought, and that she was part of his problems because of her erratic personality. They knew somehow that they loved each other. To my mind, remembering more of her analysis while she was talking, words like 'love', 'sympathy', even 'liking' would have meant nothing to her.

While telling me about the changes that happened in her life she mentioned then a difficult period in her analysis – which I then also remembered. About a year before she terminated the analysis she was concerned about the difference between her regular ways of relating to others and the ways others related to her. She was very agitated because she knew she should change in herself, to what she would prefer to be and the disadvantage of 'having this sick self', but did not know how to change. She expected that just doing the analysis would make the change happen. I knew that the varied and changing feelings she had for me at that stage, which were intense and sometimes very aggressive, were playing a part in obstructing some good insights that were permeating her associations. I refrained from giving any interpretations of that sort at the time, because they would only have foreclosed on something more important about her childhood situation: she was becoming preconciously aware of her memories about her parents' bad impact on her and her sister's future. She had almost vivid memories of being fated to failure in life. She remembered that during that period in analysis she felt I knew what she wanted but decided to deprive her from getting it. It was a game of who would give in first: her by changing and making me succeed, or me by giving her what she needed to make her succeed. She reminded me of something I said during that time – something like: *you want to change, as I know, but you are determined to make me do that for you and not do it yourself for yourself*. She said I also insinuated that just knowing that she has to change was an achievement but she had to know how to make the change herself, because that is what she would be doing for the rest of her life.

She said that this idea made a big difference in her attitude towards me and felt that she would finish her analysis one day. Allowing the transference to come to the boil was to bypass the preconscious dynamics of blaming her parents for what she was suffering from. I wanted to get to another preconscious mental set (unconscious) of not wanting to do something about her problems or insisting that her parents should do it for her (guilt about her parents was part of that obstinate resistance to make the change herself). I could not remember Mrs. K's analysis in detail but generally speaking it worked – albeit in a mysterious way.

The therapeutic attitude creates a *preconscious* frame of mind in both the patient and the analyst: a target, a goal, a criterion for therapy, and a hope that all things will become explainable at the end. I do not need to underline the impact of that preconscious attitude on transference and counter-transference – especially if the two attitudes are not compatible (which is often the case). Psychoanalysis would be hampered and distorted if it were influenced by a desire to cure. *Following the clinical protocol of psychoanalysis, making the subject, not his circumstances, the only psychoanalytic concern, turning the functional aspect of the complaint, helping the patient measure his success in analysis by the changes in him and in his circumstances, and doing the analysis in the manner that would allow the patient to do the therapy, is the way to practise psychoanalysis.*

Debatable issues in clinical practice

Gill (1984) identified two qualifications in the practice of psychoanalysis: *intrinsic* qualifications which he defined as the place of transference in the treatment, the neutrality of the psychoanalyst, induction of regressive transference, and resolving the whole setup by the means of interpretation alone. The *extrinsic* qualifications he gave as the frequency of the sessions,[5] using the couch, the selection of the patient. Although Freud did not include the extrinsic qualifications Gill stipulated in his suggestion of the practice, Freud developed and integrated them in his own practice. They, thus, became intrinsic in our conception of practice. The physical setting of practice: the couch and the armchair behind the patient, the time allocated for each visit, the strict observance of the time of the session; he would see the patient in the time assigned to him and stay until the whole time was taken without cutting it short or extending it beyond its time (there was no extension of its time if the patient was late for the session, and no shortening the time if there a wish from the patient to leave); to have the mental readiness and to maintain attention to everything said in the session (no taking of notes during the session); and to allow silence as part of the transferrential situation.

Freud created a profession out of the act of listening to people and understanding what they did not say. We should not forget – actually, we should keep in mind – that what he did was standardize the psychoanalytic setting for himself first, because the notion of psychoanalysis becoming an international organization was not then in the offing. Nonetheless, his parameters were what made initiating a training system possible, building the international organization conceivable, and psychoanalysis took the form that identified the notion of psychotherapy; it unified the practice of psychoanalysis all around the world. The conclusion that what Freud decided on as his way of doing analysis should be the only way is a result of not having any other guiding rules to improve it, or even no idea of why psychoanalysis needed clinical parameters of practice. What is astonishing is not only coming to that particular protocol or what it comprises, but also the way he came to it. He realized that a therapist who is going to be the tool of treatment needs to structure the patient's domain and his domain to avoid the possible chaos that psychoneuroses could create if left unchecked. In better terms, coming from our expanded knowledge of psychoanalysis, dealing with the products of the working of the primary process, require a well-defined secondary process to contain it.[6] Analysts recognized the logic behind regulating practice. Psychoanalysis is practised within limitations that make acting-out material for interpretation and not for reacting to.

Outlining the setting of practice meant that all patients would be treated within those parameters. It was a brilliant idea considering the varied and individual pressures put on the psychoanalyst by the varied emotional needs of each psychoneurotic patient. Time allocation was also a way of avoiding the different ways in which resistance and defences could be used without time structure.[7] Stipulating the aspect of paying fees has many and varied important roles in the transference and counter-transference.[8] In other words, Freud's systematization of practice in the manner mentioned established psychoanalysis as a profession. The parameters of the practice of psychoanalysis that Freud stipulated proved to have explanations. Those explanations were, in all likelihood, intuitive because analysts who followed them realized their validity despite the incorrectness of Freud's explanations. For instance, he explained using the couch as a means to 'isolate the transference'. We now know transference is not something that could be affected by any manoeuvres from the analyst. Nevertheless, lying on the couch changes the setup from visiting with the analyst to being there for working on a problem. So, the couch still has a significant place in clinical practice but not for affecting the transference, because transference is neither a means of doing analysis nor an end in its own right; it is the material of analysis, which is not used to change the patient or is what should be changed in analysis (Richards, 1984). He also divided transference into positive and negative types suggesting leaving the positive alone. We know now that transference carries within it the basic material for analysis and could not be taken as resistance or defence. Although his understanding of positive transference was flawed, however, dividing transference to negative and positive transferences is quite correct and useful. Freud's conceptions of practice are very intuitive but on some occasions they are not explained correctly, and sometimes they were explained in flawed ways but when corrected they stood the test of time.

The fact that Freud's setup for practice was imperfect did not change the fact that we needed a setup to practise. What is curious about this matter is that his flawed views about the setup did not justify dismissing them because they were very much what is needed to run a practice. However, when those two facts are not put together to guide us in utilizing Freud's parameters 'intelligently' we tend to debate their reasoning. The most serious kind of disagreement is in deciding what is intrinsic and preserves the superiority of psychoanalysis over the other psychotherapies and forget that the distinctive nature of psychoanalysis rests in its core and not its shell. The core of the frequency issue isolates the process of psychoanalysis from the ordinary daily routine of other life activities. Therefore, the frequency of the sessions is essential in the practice of analysis, because it is also clear that analysis is not an open-ended process but a specific process that requires a period of time. The number of sessions is totally a different issue. In the past, the number of sessions per week for psychoanalysis was decided arbitrarily to be between four and five sessions. This arbitrary figure did not consider anything but the analyst's own criteria of 'good' analysis.[9] The patient's need or the more suitable frequency for good work with patients was not of any regard. It is better to know now that what will make analysis work should be the main issue in deciding the number of sessions per week for each patient separately. In other words, it is the patient's need and not the analyst's need that should be the deciding factor in the number of session required.

The lack of clear understanding of the difference between a psychoanalysis performed according to a modality and analysis tailored to the patient's attributes is the reason for some existing myths about psychoanalysis, which we do not measure against the principle or their core. I will now address four of the most common misconceptions about the practice.

The issue of feelings in clinical practice

Previously I expressed my views on the rock bottom that we usually reach in clinical work and which seems to be almost unchangeable: the raw and basic identity that is formed by the caregiver's reactions to the infant's very early responses. This identity determines the modality of mental representations, which constitutes the subject's a-consciousness – i.e., the basic transformation of a stimulus into a psychical entity in the form of representation. The modality of mental representation is foundational in the phantasy life of the infant, and later plays a great part in the psychical life of the adult. The modality of mental representation and the creation of fantasy life are the two basic psychical events that define the process that gives us the concept of identification and identity. Identification is what determines how we think and what we do in our psychological interactions. However, after all that has been done in psychoanalysis until now by the thousands of analysts, some of whom have been prolific, we do not yet have theoretical explanations for most of the concepts that are traditional in psychoanalysis – like identification. As an example, an observation on a toddler: a 21-month-old child was walking beside his nanny holding her hand and seemed absorbed in his own mind. His nanny was speaking to herself in a different language, but she said something to the toddler in his language to the effect that they would do something important in the next store. The toddler, without looking at her or seeming to have been paying attention, changed his manner of walking and became more militaristic in his steps. Analytically speaking, the nanny's voice was assimilated by the toddler and he took on a new identity. All of that happened without any change in the toddler's awareness or consciousness. He identified with the nanny's change of mental set. We use the word 'identification' to describe what happened but we, somehow, use it as an explanation and not a description. Most, if not all, the vocabulary of the theory(ies) of psychoanalysis is descriptive and not explanatory, because we do not have a solid knowledge of how psychical phenomena comes into being. We do not know how repression happened or how transference changes the present and replaces it with the past. Therefore, we need, as analysts, to speculate and use what we know about those processes to approach the other scientists in the humanities to explain them to us. I will be making few comments on that in the epilogue at the end of the book.

My speculation about the infant's acquisition of his rock-bottom identity runs as follows. In the few early month of an infant's life the only source of his sense of being is the mother's view of him represented in her responses to his needs and demand (lovely, difficult, cuddly, etc.). Gradually the infant would build an a-conscious sense of being – derived from the mother's defining of him – the nucleus of a stable sense of being. The mother's apperception of the infant's biological and physical needs (the homeostatic fluctuations) will reflect her capacity and model of representing to the infant his vital needs such as hunger, rest, sleep, etc. For instance, some mothers are more anxious than others in reacting to the infant's need for nourishment or company, thus will represent that need "anxiously" in the manner they react, while other mothers would respond to those needs more assuredly. Therefore the infant would react to those needs of his in the same way the mother has "told" him what they are. The infant's modality of mental representation (the pattern of conceiving and phantasying about his own wishes) is decided then and there by the caregiver. In other words: forming an identity or identifying one's self and the reaction to one's needs are very much the nature of the psychical exchange in the dyad of infant–mother in the early interaction. What is the place of such speculation in clinical practice? The two psychical events that I mentioned above are where our psychological life is translated into *feeling*. The analyst could have an idea of what had happened to his patient when he was forming this basic identity and acquiring his modalities of mental representations from examining his patient's system of feelings. The formation of an identity and acquiring modalities of mental representation are events of significant importance in the development of a person's system of feelings, or the manner that an infant's affective life will be moulded into an emotional life.

The state of wishing generates more or less the corresponding affect depending on the continuation or cessation of the wish. Affect mirrors a raw state of pleasure or pain, which created the wish (Wunsch, Souhait). But, when it finds an object it changes into a desire. A desire is always accompanied by a feeling – a defined representation of the object of the affect. It is the mother's response to those states of wishing that would change them into feelings – i.e., preconscious and conscious desires. The affect of pain would go on but change into relief if the mother intervened by providing the infant with the object of his wish, creating a feeling of desire for what she provided. However, it takes quite a long time and many trials and experiences for wishes to find their objects. That period, with the different reactions from the mother, could be confusing until the infant, and then the child, identify them and make them his own. It is a change that makes him obtain a sense that those desires are his and not his mother's. The reason behind that is our innate or natural means to know what to feel and how to feel it. The consistency and the inconsistencies of the mother's reactions become instrumental in turning a wish into a desire, but could result in making the infant have more than one feeling for the same desire, and maybe contradictory ones.

It is not unusual to see a child reacting to what we consider something pleasing with anger and despair, or a patient feeling like doing exactly the opposite of what he believes is the appropriate thing to do. This point brings us to two issues that I raised before in my book on *Future Psychoanalysis* (2015) about future psychoanalysis, which relates to the importance of seeking and integrating knowledge of the humanities in our branch of the human sciences. Most of the research in infant observation and child psychology that are initiated by psychoanalysts were based on the desire to find in them confirmation of psychoanalytic speculations derived from some clinical psychoanalytic conceptions. They were done in the spirit of beginning the question: aren't we right?! Strangely, analysts seldom came to the other branches with a clinical problem and asked for research that would explain it for them. For instance, we know that transference is a natural way of relating to others in daily life and that there is no human relationship that is not transferrential. We also know that transference originates in childhood. Yet, we do not know why we cannot relate to others as others and that we always see into them as someone from our childhood. Better, we go with our baggage to child psychology asking for validation, but we do not look into what child psychology can offer us and try to understand those things from a clinical experience. As an example, a seven-month baby girl enjoyed very much a game of peek-a-boo with an adult. When the adult reversed the game and he blocked her view of him instead, she was not amused and lost interest. When she was the one disappearing she did not like it. When the same baby was able to move around a couple of month later and was able to hide herself behind a curtain she enjoyed the game again and developed a different sound of giggle. Do we have a psychoanalytic explanation for that development? Maybe, because we know from our experience with interpretation and the patient's own effort to interpret, that the patient feels delighted when he understands by himself. However, do we need to know what the nature of that change in the toddler was? Yes, and very much so: what is the difference between an interpretation that reveals to the patient what was unknown to him, and an interpretation of something that the patient believed – falsely – that he has known all along?

We find examples of learning from research in psychology that we should restrain the pervasive feeling among analysts that they have answers for the questions of others. Piaget's research in *The Moral Judgement of the Child* (1997) gives information and insightful meaning about the formation of the super ego that we have no idea about despite our assured usage of that concept, theoretically and clinically. Vygotsky (1962), the Russian psychologist, has a theory of thinking derived from child psychology that has very significant insights in object relations, internalization, and assimilation of culturally created tools of mentation, sign mediating tools, and their role in creating the intrapsychical framework for interactions. Those features in Vygotsky's work are of major significance in both psycho-diagnosis and the therapeutic endeavours. Going back to feelings as the main issue of this section of the chapter, feelings force us to acknowledge that, for psychoanalysts, they are affect that has been changed when its wish found its object and has become focused. The epigenesis of feelings is very obscure in psychoanalysis – thanks to the concept of libidinal attachment in the early theory – and the object relation modality of lately. We need to know how affect is transformed into feeling in the process of development for two main objectives: first, by the time a person acknowledges his feeling, the feeling could have been contaminated by so many other feelings, and becomes very misleading for the patient and the analyst alike. One of my acquaintances had difficulties with success, because he was always overtaken by a mixture of excitement, fear, and certainty of a let-down every time he was about to achieve his aim. It was very difficult to comprehend those reactions to success. I had the thought that maybe a limited change in his attitude towards success could come from discerning the mixture of contradictory feelings associated with success, by making him think that success brings to his mind a different identity from the one he is living. My attempt did not work because, as it seemed, his identity was his feelings and not the other way around.

We have been trying since the beginning of psychoanalysis to create a child psychology that emanates from clinical experience. We failed and created instead some hypotheses that are more fiction than reality. We need to go to child psychology to learn about the foundation of what we deal with in psychoanalysis. This is why I am bringing the issue of the need to learn more about child psychology and from child psychology to find in it what we think until now that we know about the nature of feelings in the human subject.

The misconception of resistance

"The concept of resistance was introduced by Freud very early on: it may be said to have played a decisive part in the foundation of psychoanalysis" (Laplanche & Pontalis, 1973, 394). In fact, the concept of resistance is very central in an indelible old conception of the unconscious, making the essence of the work of analysis to 'overcome' the patient's proclivity to resist the analytic work. This is – in my opinion – due to the comfortable belief that repression is the main problem we deal with in our work. Yet, if we remind ourselves that there is a non-repressed unconscious or, even better, that the unconscious is not repressed (Freud, 1923b; Fayek, 2005, 2010, 2014) the concept of resistance loses its special status in practice. Residence has a connotation other than the prevailing one.

An analyst in his second analysis used the word 'resistance' frequently to describe his impression of what was happening at certain times in his analysis. I always asked him to tell me what he meant by that word, and he always felt annoyed because I was supposed to know what it meant, thus did not need to explain it to an analyst like me. In due course he yielded and explained what he meant. It meant to him, 'as it has always meant to everyone' forcing back something or defying something from revealing itself. However, it took some time and a few more requests from me for him to realize that he was not resisting discovering or revealing something unpleasant, but used the term to *say to me*: *you should know* … or *you do not know* ... or *I know as much as you know* ... or *its not only you who knows*. The gradual awareness of the implicit transference meaning of resistance became clearer and he got the notion that he might be using the term to say with it something else. Instead of using resistance as an issue he used the term 'transference' instead: *I have a problem with my transference*, etc. This is when things got ahead and the narcissistic difficulties of an analyst having to be back on the couch were confronted. The short end of it was a disappointment in his first analysts who did not deal with his troubled relationship with his father; instead, he provided him with a better father substitute, which was gratifying but not the solution he was hoping for. This is a case where the term was used to mean other things. However, what Freud meant by resistance is still something we need to contend with, yet with understanding that there is nothing repressed or repressible, but only issues that are in consciousness but disguised, misrepresented, or distorted by the working of the primary process. Lacan expressed this very nature of resistance saying: *resistance is the time needed to understand* [for both analyst and patient].

Freud used the term 'resistance' – at the beginning – to describe the patient's inability to succumb to hypnosis. He soon found out, after changing the technique to free association, that there can be several ways the repressed takes to avoid being discovered. Those ways resulted in the analyst's feeling of being obstructed in doing proper psychoanalysis. He also recognized the link between the imbedded disguises in the symptom and the work of interpretation. The symptom contains the disguised, the misrepresented, and distorted psychical material. Therefore, if we call those three components resistance then we would not be able to do our work of interpretation. Our work is to deal with the working of the primary process that created the symptom and not the symptom itself. Better, our work is not to remove resistance but to interpret the forms in which it was created by the working of the primary process. This is the reason Freud said: 'informing' the patient that he was resisting or what he resisted does not engender the desirable changes, while revealing to him the disguise and distortions, changes the nature of the treatment. In the case mentioned earlier, revealing to the patient-analyst that he was using the term to disguise what he wanted to say to me without saying it, changed the analytic scene from competitiveness with the analyst to a scene of remembering that relationship with his father and working through it. Shifting the meaning of resistance from an obstacle to a tool, he enabled the phenomenon of transference to take a preconscious place in the analysis and give it the double function of revealing and resisting. Freud continued to view resistance in the context of the dynamics of the repressed and the different ways it resorts to avoid revealing the disguised. This conception put the concept of defence into focus and resistance was taken as a defensive effort from the ego against the repressed. With his insistence on that view, the theory was confusing: are defence mechanisms good as protectors of the ego or bad because they prevent undoing the repression that is causing its weakness? Freud even said that "the defensive mechanisms directed against former danger recur in the treatment as resistances against recovery. It follows from this that the ego treats recovery as a new danger" (Freud, 1937c, 238). The theory became even more confusing when, in his latest theoretical work (1926d), he posted five types of resistance which were all related to either the strength of the (sick) ego or the transformation of the content of the repressed (the unconscious) into other disguised material.

Resistance had a negative denotation in the technique of analysis. We all know that doing analysis takes time, goes through periods of no change and sometimes a reversal of progress, difficulties in the relationship with the analyst (not everything in analysis is transference), acting out (now called enactment), and the problems with transference/counter-transference interpretations. All those aspects of analysis are covered by the term 'resistance', and referred back to resistance. Seldom, if ever, are any of those analytic manifestations considered outside the notion of resistance. However, there are very few places in the Freudian text that show a lack of satisfaction with the notions of resistance, repression, and defence – places most analysts gloss over and neglect because the master himself did not give them enough importance. Freud said in *The Ego and the Id*:

> We have to recognize that the *Ucs.* does not coincide with the repressed; it is still true that all that is repressed is *Ucs.*, but not all that is *Ucs.* is repressed [we have to take note here that Freud is using italicization wrongly because he designated the italicized *Ucs.* to the systemic unconscious alone (in 1915e), which is not the descriptive or the dynamic meaning of the term]. A part of the ego too may be *Ucs.* … it could be activated without becoming *Cs.* … We find ourselves thus confronted by the necessity of postulating a third *Ucs.*, which is not repressed.
>
> (1923b, 18)

The significance of the non-repressed unconscious, which in every meaning of the word *is* the systemic unconscious and the "second kind of the unconscious" (1923b, 15) makes repression a useless mechanism. If not all the unconscious is repressed, and if some unconsciousness is created by other processes, and even when the non-repressed unconscious could be activated without any changes to it, then repression is no more than the process of forgetting or the inability to remember.

In the practice of psychoanalysis we should keep in mind that the insidious, subtle, and even unconscious modality of repression and resistance could distract us from the main issues implicitly and explicitly cited in the clinical protocol.

Deep and shallow analyses

The comparison between psychoanalysis and psychotherapy raised the issue of the depth and superficiality of the work in each. However, as mentioned earlier, the difference is actually between working with intrapsychic and working with the interpersonal. Put another way: the difference is between working with the origins and working with the outcomes, and would implicitly mean that working with the intrapsychical is working with 'deeper' layers of the psyche. Therefore, there is a question to ask in that regard: could there be superficial psychoanalyses and deeper ones? The literature is rife with notions of the depth of psychoanalysis, but very little is said about what would characterize deep analysis and distinguish it from the superficial. Some analysts describe the beginning of the analytic work to be superficial but that it becomes deeper with its progression. Some others say that depending on the patient we gauge our interpretation to the degree of psychopathology. This notion also goes well with an old idea that revealing the unconscious is disturbing to the patient, so it is recommended the analyst go easy on that matter with patients who are not capable of taking it due to the nature of the defences. A third group say that the depth we seek should be relative to the patient's ego strength. It is likely that other justifications are present in the literature and support the notion of the depth and shallowness of psychoanalytic work. However, all those justifications are a result of a prevailing conviction that we practise something called *psychoanalysis*, which we all practice, but sometimes deeply and other times superficially. I did not run into a work in the literature that stipulated the existence of superficial psychoanalyses and deep psychoanalyses from which we could choose to practise.

The metaphor of shallow and deep psychoanalyses is seriously flawed, because it is mainly based on matters that have no relationship with depth and shallowness. The claim that psychoanalysis deals with deeper psychical manifestations such as transference, phantasies, dreams, defence mechanisms, etc., does not depict the real problem. The real problem is not whether the analyst deals with those manifestations or not, but how he deals with them. The metaphor of depth and shallowness has nothing to do with the human psyche, because the patient does not select his material based on what he is undergoing whether analysis or therapy, deep or shallow treatment. The patient talks the same to whomever he goes to see, and it depends on the therapist's knowledge and training as to how to deal with the material. If this metaphor has anything to do with the field of psychological treatment it would be in regard to the depth and the shallowness of the theory the clinician is practising. In other words: the depth or shallowness in psychoanalysis and psychotherapy relate primarily and basically to theoretical distinctions between the approaches. In a nutshell: *the shallowness and depth of the treatment do not depend on the technique (analysis or therapy) or the patient (state of mind), but on the treatment professional.* The psychoanalytic theory assumes that the associations of the patient, his dreams, symptoms, or even his silence, say two things or more at the same time, and they are entwined by the working of the primary process. The analyst's task is to elicit the unsaid from the said and put that to the patient in the form of interpretations. Thus, the depth and shallowness of the good and not-so-good analyst are decided by them and not by what psychoanalysis they are applying.

Psychotherapy(ies), whatever their theoretical foundations, deal with what the patient says as the only given. They then work on modifying and changing what the given speech has indicated. Correcting symptoms or character disorders is founded on psychotherapy showing their inadequacies and shortcomings. However, with the knowledge psychoanalysis has disseminated over the years, some therapists, with the support of some analysts, invented what they call *psychoanalytic psychotherapy*. I can say with reasonable confidence (I reviewed the literature on that subject well in the 1980s) that there has been no justification in creating this category of psychotherapy except the prospect of using different vocabularies of different psychotherapeutic theories instead the vocabulary of psychoanalysis. The difference in that named psychotherapy was leniencies in adhering to the clinical protocol of psychoanalysis. The problem of psychoanalytic psychotherapy remained the same: explaining the complaint without showing its core formation has no curative effect. On the other hand, if the analyst discovers the working of the primary process in entwining something else into what the patient is saying (condensation or metaphor, displacement or metonymy, and in a limited way symbolism), the core formation of the complaint would be revealed. Interpreting those workings, the analysts restores the meaning of his symptomatic complaint. A clinical vignette could exemplify that:

A young talented engineer was promoted at a very young age to head an important department in his company. Once that happened he was invaded by an active and disturbing imagination of his subordinates secretly rebelling against his authority and undermining it. He was also disturbed by ideas that his superiors would become untrusting of his ambitions to replace them one day. In real life, he surpassed his father, an engineer, both academically and professionally and averred awkwardness informing his family about his successes. Working through the overlap of his relationship with his father and the relationships with his superiors and subordinates, the workings of displacement and condensation and the symbolic meaning of making more money than his father, restored the meaning of his imaginative concerns. Working through brought to his attention to the confusion he had about his father and the metaphor of the subordinate, the younger, and the boss. It also brought to his attention the displaced anger from the younger to the older and vice-versa. Exploring the different possible confusions that the primary process had created between his relationship with his father and the present situation seemed to have organized his mind and allowed him to drop the confusing imaginations. He was able to separate the two events, and to create a reasonable distance between his childhood anxieties and the present worries, and not to let their overlap generate active imaginations that paralyzed him. He started to be aware of his disguised childish competitiveness and guilt, and paid more attention to the function of a boss, and to the place of a colleague of his superiors. The work of analysis is meant to uncover disguised overlaps created arbitrarily by the working of the primary process to give the patient an opening to reorganizing his disorganized intrapsychic dynamics.

Psychoanalysis is a distinct theory which has a matching technique and could be done properly or improperly, but not deeply or shallowly. The analyst does not change his practising technique; but might practise the same technique differently under different circumstances. The difference does not change the depth or the intent of the work, it only takes into consideration the way the patient is going to use the discovery to initiate his therapy. If we want to be judicious and correct we should say that psychoanalysis – compared with psychotherapy – is different but not deeper, because when it is practised badly it would be deep (wild) but useless, which is worse than shallow psychotherapy, done well!

The length of analysis

Termination of anything means that it has a beginning, so it also has an end. Freud's view that analysis is *interminable* (1937c) was a blow to the idea that it has a therapeutic power, because if it does not come to a termination there must be unresolved aspects of the neurosis that have not been dealt with. The papers on the subject of termination are scarce because of a lack of agreement on what termination implies (Firestein, 1978; Laplanche, 1997; Novick, 1997). Sandler's attempt to bring the subject to some conclusion in (1988) revealed that the issue is still far from being agreed on. However, there is something important about Freud's paper that could lead us to a new approach to the problem of termination: does Freud believe that there are some rock-bottom psychical issues that are unanalysable, or that something is missing in the clinical method that stops it from dealing properly with those rock-bottom issues? In other terms: is the problem of termination related to the nature of the psyche or to limitations in the clinical method? The most significant aspect of Freud's paper is its timelessness because if we decide that Freud was wrong in considering those two complexes unanalysable and we succeeded in replacing them with different ones, psychoanalysis would still remain interminable. The problem of terminability of psychoanalysis is not related to the nature of the psyche or the limitations of the therapeutic method; it is inherent in psychoanalysis itself.

Let us first highlight a preliminary point: Freud, in his paper, stated clearly and categorically that analysis is interminable because there is a bedrock that all analyses reach, and when reached we find out that it is impenetrable. The bedrock he mentioned is penis envy in women and castration anxiety in men. Those two issues (see Chapter 1) are not acceptable now after the major changes in the interfamilial dynamic and the emancipation of women. There is also common agreement among analysts that analysis could come to good conclusions: achieve reasonable relief of the neurotic structure, release the patient from his fixations, etc., yet does not come to an end because the end is not objectively definable but is always subjectively judged. Analysts know that they do not complete the journey to a final destination, because they do not have a criterion of health. Analysts can only talk metapsychologically about psychopathology, about psychical health, the work of analysis, but have no actual psychological modality about those issues. Therefore, analysis begins from a point that is not defined, and naturally will end at a destination that will be equally arbitrary.

Freud's paper on termination has a background that is particularly useful in continuing our exploration of the length of analysis. Freud wrote that paper at a time (the 1920s and 1930s) when Ferenczi and Rank called for, and claimed that it was possible, to shorten the analysis by resorting to certain modifications in the technique – mainly using some of the theoretical formulations as a targeted objective of the treatment. This meant using a metapsychological formulation to solve the psychological problems, thus concluding analysis more directly and not through waiting for the patient's readiness to understand. Freud's response bypassed that trend and stated that by modifying the technique to reach out metapsychological ideals would amount to imposing on the patient our conception of health and cure. He thus warned against entertaining the idea of getting rid of *all* the neurotic symptoms or inhibition in a patient because that would not happen anyway. This conclusion is remarkable because I know for sure that this idea about the difficulties of termination could not be found in any other of Freud's writing and is mentioned only in this paper on termination. We know now after decades of experience how right he was; we cannot manipulate the analytic process by any artificial means. However, making the eradication of symptoms (a metapsychological conception of sorts) a target contravenes his objection to setting an objective for treatment. This point of view reveals that what Freud had in mind about analysis was the patient and not his symptoms, hence the objective of treatment was to change the patient to enable him to deal with his own neurosis. In light of this attitude towards the time-consuming work of analysis we have to assume that termination of analysis is a problem if we try to find a theoretical framework for it. Metapsychologically we could talk 'methodologically' about termination, but we cannot talk about it operationally, because we are not able to envisage a concrete and final statement about what cure is: a statement that would become the guiding map and the criterion for termination. Although Freud's paper is flawed because he used traditional metapsychology to explain the difficulties we face in terminating an analysis, metapsychology was – in its own right – instrumental in finding out that analysis is interminable.

Freud mentioned a few other things beside penis envy and castration anxiety that stand between the analyst and successful analysis. He mentioned the strength of the 'instinctual drive' as a factor in the time needed to conclude an analysis, which is a rudimentary idea from the early theory of the repressed instinctual drive. I doubt that presently we could call acting-out uncontrollable instinctual drives. He suggested that sometimes analysis collapses after termination if the patient faces unexpected circumstances. We tend to explain such things as the result of incomplete psychoanalyses. Although this is not a factor in the length of analysis he mentioned something relevant about that point which deserves attention. He said that the impact of those circumstances are not analysable, when they happen, because they are not expressed within a transference relationship (they need a new analysis). Thus, the length of analysis is very much a function of the proper or the improper dealing with transference in the original analysis, more than being a problem of completed or uncompleted analyses. That is why he considered it a gamble to suggest fixing a time for termination. He tried that and it did not work well (1918b).

In order to pave the way to thinking metapsychologically about termination let me pose a question: *How could we judge a connection between the length of an analysis and its success if we know that psychoanalysis is interminable?* If I take a trip to a destination that does not exist, how could adding more mileage to my trip make sense? I mentioned earlier that the interminability of psychoanalysis is a problem with psychoanalysis and I can add an explanation to that statement: it might be a problem (an issue) in the nature of the human subject. Analysis could be done properly but it still has to be used well by the subject and continued after it finishes (auto-analysis). In other words, psychoanalysis is not an act of 'curing' a patient but an act of treating an individual who has human qualities that we know little about, which could use or not use the rewards of psychoanalysis. Mrs. K. is an example of a treated patient who had in her more human qualities than the patient she was had. If analysis is done badly any extension of its time would be useless of course.

Nonetheless, there are two important elements in doing proper psychoanalysis: *first,* restricting our work to showing the patient that the working of the primary process is allowing other unintended material to infiltrate his conscious intentions, thus creating his neurotic puzzlement and the rest of his discomforts; and *second* working through those phenomena in their various forms as they permeate his psychical life, resulting in their negative impact on him. When we do those two things and also indirectly underline the absence of that phenomenon in other aspects of his psychical life we give the patient a grasp of his subjectivity (his identity as his personal nature). Adhering to those two factors of psychoanalysis the patient would gradually be able to construct a new conception of 'his' self and we would be able to reconstruct his construction for further consolidation of his discoveries. The end result is allowing the patient to have a consistent narrative of his life, which was in a state of fragmentation before the analysis, and to initiate order in his narrative after stopping seeing the analyst; to get into the endlessness of auto-analysis.[10] Analysis is interminable – in that sense – but only if it is done properly so the patient would be able to continue it. Once it is done properly, extending it beyond its time to finish[11] causes what Laplanche called a window of opportunity to close, and analysis fails (1997). Extending it beyond its time is like adding miles to a trip that has no destination.

Concluding remarks

I think Freud discovered the *Ucs.* but did not understand its complete and true value and meaning, exactly as the other great discoveries which had latent, further, and more to them than anyone ever thought of at their beginning. That particular meaning of the unconscious was worked out well outside of psychoanalysis, in three ideographic sciences: linguistics (F. de Saussure), Anthropology (C. Levi-Strauss), and Philosophy (phenomenology and existentialism). The systemic unconscious is the fabric of the psychological phenomena of the human subject. It is the structural core of that human subject, and has no particular content like the repressed, because the subject himself is that content. We talk without being aware that we follow a grammar; we form families without knowing that we are adhering to laws of incest; and we present ourselves to each other not realizing that we turn ourselves into social metaphors. The unconscious fabric of the subject is subject to a great deal of malformation, deformations, misunderstanding, and misconception. Our psychical life is the continuous aspiration to present ourselves correctly and to be understood equally correctly. We can define the psychoanalytic situation as a patient who does not understand important aspects of his life, so he tries to get them from the analyst's understanding of him. The analyst in turn tries to figure out from the 'misrepresentations' of the patient the fabric of his *Ucs.* He endeavours to give the patient his conclusions in a way that the patient could utilize to make changes in in himself. The analytic task is to understand, and understanding is the only aspect of revelation in psychoanalysis. Lacan's famous dictum of where *it* has been *I* should be is deceptively the same as making the unconscious conscious. What this simple note says is that the main change in analysis comes from freeing the *I* from the self-deception of speaking as someone else, or being an *It*. Thus, analysis frees the subject to speak for itself and not for a self forced on him. The *I* should be the speaker who introduces *Me* to the other. Thus, practising psychoanalysis would no longer be an act of recovering, discovering or uncovering some hidden material that creates the neurosis, and achieves cures by reporting the discoveries to the patient. Analysis becomes the act of understanding something that exists in the open but is not noticeable or fathomable. The cure is to make the patient own the process of noticing and comprehending. So, analysis is not judged by the level of its depth or completeness, but by the degree of its advancement.

Notes

1 Lately, with the proliferation of schools of psychoanalysis and the official acceptance of the IPA of the plurality of psychoanalysis (Wallerstein, 1989), 'psychoanalysis' has become a generic term.
2 Even psychoanalytic candidates in training analysis expect some functional explanations for their conditions, which are hypothetically milder than those of patients. Their analysis should be didactic in the first place – to learn how psychoanalysis is done – and if there would be some therapeutic benefit from that it should be considered a bonus. Therefore, the analysis of candidates should make the shift from functional complaints to structural understanding the focus of their psychoanalysis.
3 Freud said about construction (1937d, 259): "The time and manner in which he [the analyst] conveys his constructions to the person who is being analysed, as well as the explanations with which he accompanies them, constitute the link between the two portions of work of analysis, between his own part and that of the patient."
4 This reminded me of another female patient whose changed intrapsychical dynamics showed physically in making her more feminine: changed from a female to a woman.
5 The length of the session is another extrinsic qualification of psychotherapy in general.
6 One way of looking at psychoses is that there is no barrier between the primary and secondary process and they reciprocate in their acts of expression. Therefore, we cannot follow the psychotic way of expression because the two processes get fused in those psychopathologies.
7 Lacan tried to remove the principle of the fixed time of the session by giving himself the right to decide if the patient was talking empty words or full words. This attempt failed to get the approval of other analysts and even the members of his group. Many reasons were given but most relevant to what we are dealing with here is that he influenced, manipulated, and changed the principle of transference by taking himself out of the analytic scene by becoming its judge.
8 A rich young man paid for his analysis from a big inheritance fund. He gradually became less regular in attending his sessions, and tried a few times to leave the sessions before their allotted ending. After a few notifications of his unacceptable ways of approaching analysis I discontinued his sessions. His guardian called several times asking for his treatment to be resumed, but I refused. The patient asked by himself for an appointment and I gave him a time for a meeting. He was prompt and very apologetic regarding his previous behaviour. He asked if he could return to analysis. I raised his fees five times and he accepted. Relative to his wealth, the increase in the fees would not have caused any financial strain on him. However, his attitude towards analysis changed after that.
9 In my experience, one session a week is a waste of time, with any kind of patients. It invites very undesirable derivative transference reactions. I cannot judge its effectiveness in other kinds of psychotherapy. Because didactic analysis has been replaced with personal analysis for the candidates, I personally recommend four sessions a week for the first period of personal analysis (two years maybe!), then reducing it to three sessions a week. My logic (though I never did it and retired before thinking about it) is that the intensity of four times on both the candidate and the analyst could reveal a more didactic aspect of the process of psychoanalyzing, and the candidate (and the analyst) could learn a few things while therapy was taking its course. This could also be advisable at the beginning of the analysis of patients with mild states of decompensation until they gain or regain their equilibrium. After that the sessions could be reduced to three times a week for a few more years as a sensible way of conducting psychoanalysis. In the average cases of psychoneurotic personalities, whether symptomatic or non-symptomatic, starting

with three times a week is wiser. The regular patient who seeks psychoanalysis needs proper reconstruction of his unconscious material, based on some good analytic interpretative work. The twice-a-week regime works sometimes but in rare cases that are psychologically endowed and their circumstances do not allow them more than that.

10 Once I asked a psychoanalyst friend – who was in his seventeenth year of analysis – if he still expected to discover something new. He answered: "You say you do self-analysis (auto-analysis) all the time; I hire someone to do that for me!!!"

11 It is important to underline the fact that we have no historical, clinical, or theoretical basis to support the prototype of a 'standard' psychoanalysis of four to five sessions a week that should last for a few years (more than four in the best conditions). Moreover, there is no evidence (in research or experience) that longer analyses give better results. The slandered prototype has become an unsubstantiated dogma; thus it stands now as an obstacle in the way experience should improve what is old. Psychoanalysts have gathered a great reservoir of experience and it is time for them to discuss and revise the way psychoanalysis should be practised.

It took me more than three decades to question the prototype of the five sessions and five years analyses. My doubt came from a few analyses where I felt they had come to a stage where they should be terminated but were shorter relative to the slandered model. I also thought – in *my* experience – that fewer sessions per week (three) is more productive and occupies a natural place in the patients' daily lives. Additionally, I became aware that after three years of analysis there is very little that could be called 'discoveries', and the main work changes to mostly reconstruction and filling some gaps in the new narrative of the patients. The process of termination could be started then and should not take more than very few months to complete. If there are some residual difficulties, they should be properly assessed so that both analyst and analysand should know if they are just reactions to termination or they need further analysis, which should, in this case, be done by another analyst.

6

APPLIED PSYCHOANALYSIS

'Applied psychoanalysis' is a term created by clinical analysts to distinguish their therapeutic or psychopathological conceptions, which are considered by them to be 'psychoanalysis', from non-clinical people applying some of those conceptions to their fields of interest. Even clinical psychoanalysts, who try to use their expertise in psychoanalysis to work on non-clinical issues like novels, movies, biographies, etc., consider that to be part of applied psychoanalysis. Applied psychoanalysis in that perspective and definition is not thought to be on par with real professional psychoanalysis. It looks rather amateurish.[1] This stand from applied psychoanalysis is flawed, if not totally wrong. Freud, in the midst of his preoccupation with building psychoanalysis as a theory of psychopathology and psychotherapy, did almost as much work on non-clinical issues as on clinical ones. Among his more than 250 works, one-third of his papers were unrelated to the clinical side of psychoanalysis. His non-clinical works ranged from *The Interpretation of Dreams* (1900a), *The Psychopathology of Everyday Life* (1901b) to *Totem and Taboo* (1912–1913), 'Delusions and dreams in Jensen's Gradiva' (1907a), 'Leonardo da Vinci and a memory of his childhood' (1910c), 'Acquisition and control of fire' (1932a) and 'Moses and monotheism' (1939a). They dealt with mythology, anthropology, religion, literature, and biographies of famous persons. Therefore, we have to acknowledge that Freud's concerns and attentiveness to non-clinical issues were not casual or capricious; they were a major part of his endeavour to build psychoanalysis. He did not treat them merely as interesting or useful to the non-clinicians; he dealt with those issues as different aspects of psychoanalysis proper. *There is another unnoticed characteristic in his non-clinical work that deserves revision.*

Freud *analysed* phenomena like the *Taboo of Virginity* (1918a) and 'A seventeen-century demonological neurosis' (1923d) to explain and validate psychoanalysis.

He derived from those and similar socio-historical phenomena psychical subtleties that were not possible to notice directly in clinical work. We should therefore consider correcting the definition of applied psychoanalysis: *the theory of psychoanalysis needed the analysis of issues that pertain to the human subject in his other non-clinical, or in his individual capacities.* However, Freud's application of non-clinical issues to psychoanalysis is not uniform – i.e., some issues such as literary and autobiographical characters agreed with clinical psychoanalysis in clear ways, but other issues had the function of discovering aspects of the psyche that clinical work was insufficient to reveal. Thus, what is important to revise in the proposition of applied psychoanalysis is the prevailing belief that clinical psychoanalysis could be applied to other phenomena to show that the analysis of non-clinical phenomena could be applied and also serve the clinical theory very well. Therefore, I will name some works that had the capability and the prerogative of enriching the theory of psychoanalysis in its clinical form, whether in health or in sickness.

There are three very early works that could have easily been called applied psychoanalysis, although they are *undeniably* the origin of psychoanalysis. I do not need to say that *The Interpretation of Dreams* (1900a), *Psychopathology of Everyday Life* (1901b) and *Jokes* (1905c) came five years before the birth of proper psychoanalysis. They were the precursors of the early clinical formulations of psychoanalysis. Freud, initially a neurophysiologist and a physician treating hysterical patients and concentrating on the repression of sexual life of the neurotics, changed direction to write about dreams, parapraxes, and jokes. Those topics were, and still are, unrelated to medicine from near or far. Pursuant to those three works he wrote the *Three Essays on the Theory of Sexuality* (1905d), which removed sex from medicine and morality, and placed it with psychology and sociology. Obviously, when he started listening to his patients, instead of hypnotizing them he began to understand their speech differently and *intuitively* grasped things that were implicit in their talk. This was starting to show in his chapters in *Studies on Hysteria* (1895d). The common denominator in the main three works I am suggesting provides a different insight in the linguistic process. The insight was the equivocality of speech; the interweaving of different meanings in the intended spoken narrative. He called it 'primary' because it seemed to be lurking behind the other sophisticated usual way of speaking. It was less complex, more primitive by virtue of seeing it more in children and uneducated people, and as part of the 'speech' of symptoms. He considered the usual way of speaking a product of a secondary process that hides a more elementary speech. He insightfully realized that dreams could be a better way of looking for the working of the primary process, because they are supposed to say something but while the person is asleep and his consciousness is dormant the primary process could be the main language used. He honed in on the three basic elements in the primary process: condensation, displacement, and the potentiality of non-verbal measures to express ideas such as pictorial depiction and the use of symbols.

Moving to parapraxes was the next insightful gesture, where he saw how the primary process works unconsciously to reveal something that is consciously worked out by the secondary process. The third book on jokes reveals their similar structure to dreams and parapraxes. He took the working of the primary process back to childhood and the learning of proper speech. In childhood children confuse the rules of speaking properly, disregarding the secondary process and mixing the two processes. But what is the place of sexuality in this phase in the preparation for the first major leap into psychoanalysis proper?

Freud wrote to Fliess in October 1899 saying that the theory of sexuality would be the next work after his book of dreams. However, as he said, it would need a spark to set it ablaze. The spark arrived five or more years later, but they were not spent in vain. I believe his attention to children's early handling of the oddities of the secondary process was that spark that set the book ablaze. He realized that as the child goes through stages of maturity to reach the adult's mastering of the secondary process way of thinking and talking. Why not that sexuality is one of the things that the child has to mature into? Freud's theory of sexuality was a theory of infantile sexuality and its coexistence with adult sexuality in the psychoneuroses, exactly in the same manner the primary and secondary processes interweave in the psychoneuroses. Freud's so-called applied psychoanalysis in the three books on dreams, parapraxes, and jokes were the required preparation for infantile sexuality to emerge. Analysing infantile sexuality revealed that sexuality is not a simple thing but a number of simple things that integrated with maturity into an adult's sexuality. Therefore, there are a great many possibilities in the process of integrating those separate components of adult sexuality. He named those components as the source, the object, and the aim, and combined them in the conception of *Trieb*, and eventually the psychology of representation. It is obvious that "proper" psychoanalysis came out of non-clinical Freudian insights. A question arises: is this the case with the other major – so-called applied – psychoanalyses where something important followed them?

After using *Trieb* as the adjective of sexuality, Freud found better usage for the indefinable term of 'libido'. 'Libido' became an explanatory term of the working of the *Trieb* (though when Freud tried to give it a final definition (1921c), he still called it a speculative concept). 'Libido' was a term that was used to explain the *tie* within relationships: a relationship is an investment of libido in another person, or it is the energy that links two persons, etc. Nevertheless, there were aspects of the 'libido' that required explaining. Not all relationships are alike, meaning that 'libido' is too general a term to be an explanatory concept. It fluctuates in strength, reverses its charge from positive or negative (and visa-versa easily), and its obvious submission to the working of the working of the primary process thus makes it a manifestation of something else. With the advancement in clinical practice the libido theory faced two problems: if the libido is the measure of the activity of the sexual *Trieb*, then what is the measure of the activity of the self-preservation *Trieb*? This concern forced *narcissism* on the theory as a non-clinical concept. Freud had to face the long-avoided problem of one libido or two. The second problem was the insight that libidinal investment and libidinal cathecting were manifestations of the process of identification; even later he conceded that libido manifestations should be displaced by the conception of identification (1924d). Moreover, Freud embarked, around the same time (1912), on specifying the clinical protocol and the conditions of practising psychoanalysis. He needed to underline the phenomena of transference and its meaning, because they could not be rationalized in terms of the libido theory. *Freud had to move from the simple notion of libidinal attachment to the phenomenon of identity*. Psychoanalysis was no longer a theory that depended on the allegories or the terminologies of other sciences such as hydraulics, mechanics, and physics; it was a theory that was reaching for its own content.

The issue of identity, identification, and transformation in the psychic phenomena was not something totally new to Freud, though he needed more insightful observations to delve into it. Jones (1957) emphasized – in discussing Freud's interest in anthropology – his steady and unrelenting fascination with how the human subject came to be what it is now. This curiosity for someone whose job was working with human subjects and knew the importance of the past of the individual to his present, would naturally make him think and become interested in the past of the human subject as a phenomenon. Freud tried his hand a few times before in matters of non-clinical significance and became familiar with the concepts of primary and secondary processes – a good introduction to some more explorations. Thus, he was inclined to hypothesize and speculate about the past of the human subject more than his future.[2] The fall of the libido theory and the replacement of libidinal attachments and investment with the process of identification were good reasons to pay attention to the evolution of man's sense of identity. He needed to examine the link between the past of the species and the past of the individual in the context of the transformation of the primary to the secondary processes. In *Totem and Taboo* (1912–1913) Freud did a very impressive job in comparing the working of the primary process in the primitive mind and the child's mind. He managed well showing parallels between the Oedipus complex in the individual and a speculative primitive relation between children and the head of the primitive family, in which action in the past became the phantasies of the present. He envisaged that the individual Oedipus complex could have a phylogenetic origin emanating from the history of the human family, and a genetic source in present family dynamics. The notion of a genetic and a phylogenetic origin of psychical phenomenon, which came from *Totem and Taboo*, were linked with another significant and pioneering understanding of *identification*. He, Abraham, and Ferenczi specified three mechanisms – introjection, assimilation, and internalization – that make the process of identification take place, Thus, identification changed from a psychical mechanism into a psychical process that befits the new understanding of narcissism and linked well with the psychosexual line of development.

Totem and Taboo comprised the notion of the phylogenetic-genetic, the primal and the primary, and the inherent two-stage structure of most psychical phenomena. It started with narcissism. Freud found a solution to the problem of a singular or a double libido in the new conception of primary narcissism and secondary narcissism. This two-stage solution, a result of accepting the double source of psychical phenomenon in the *Totem and Taboo*, was the basis for Freud's revision – in 1915 – of four more fundamental concepts in his theory (*Trieb*, Repression, the Unconscious, and Regression).[3] The link between the *Totem and Taboo* and narcissism is demonstrated by Freud saying (1912–1913): "Primitive men and neurotics, as we have seen, attach a high valuation-in our eyes an *over*-valuation to psychical acts. This attitude may plausibly be brought into relation with narcissism and regarded as an essential" (89). The revision of the concept of the unconscious (1915e) was the most important acknowledgment of the shift from a simplistic conception of repression to an unconscious that is systemic (1923b). This new view of unconsciousness had a clear origin in *Totem and Taboo.* Freud said (1912–1913): "[I]t is expedient and indeed indispensable to insert a stage between these two [Auto-erotism and object-chosen], or, putting it in another way, to divide the first stage, that of auto-erotism, into two" (88).

The *Three Essays on the Theory of Sexuality* (1905d) was an exploration and application of sexuality, and *Totem and Taboo* was an application of anthropology to validate psychoanalysis, but it was *also* the forerunner of a new theoretical breakthrough of which 'Beyond the pleasure principle' (1920g) stands out as a unique applied psychoanalytic work.

'Beyond the pleasure principle' is considered by most analysts, but for different reasons, a turning point in Freud's thinking. The most common is founded on the notion that Freud replaced the pleasure–unpleasure principle as the framework of the working of the mind by the conflict between life and death. This shift was a natural response to the failure of the pleasure principle in explaining the proclivity to painful experiences, which the patients and the healthy are unable to ward off, but even invited or initiated. Pain was a challenge to pleasure. For instance, Freud explained the patient's effort to resist treatment by assuming the presence of a *compulsion to repeat* that overrides the pleasure principle. He admitted that he could only say that the tendency to repeat the painful was more primitive and elementary than the pleasure principle (1920g, 23). After explaining several other unpleasurable phenomena in the same way he posted the compulsion to repeat as a primal principle – i.e., the original of a sequel[4] that precedes the pleasure principle. He identified that as an instinctual proclivity of the organic matter to go back to its original state, and called it the death instinct (ibid., 36). He then averred that if we accept that everything living eventually has to die and return to its inorganic past, then it is sensible to say that death is the pressures of life and the pleasure principle. The importance of this hypothetical (though convincing) application of biology to psychoanalysis is that it developed and advanced the notion of the two conditions of the psychical phenomena and their transformative nature (genetic-phylogeny, primary-secondary) to a higher theoretical level. The level of Freud's works after the 'Beyond the pleasure principle' is much more sophisticated. A simple comparison between the *Introductory Lectures on Psychoanalysis* (1916–1917) and *The New Introductory Lectures* (1933a) show his command of the subject. His papers between 1921 and 1925 are less tentative and vastly definitive. His major works like 'Inhibition, symptoms and anxiety' (1926d) have the same genuine insights but were firmly based on grounded theory. The works of so-called applied psychoanalysis such as 'Group psychology and the analysis of the ego' (1921c), 'The future of an illusion' (1927c), and 'Moses and monotheism' (1939a) did not show the signs of strain of trying to elicit psychoanalytic conception from them. They were simply books written by a psychoanalyst who had a command of sociology, religion, and history, and was able to uncover implicit points in his subject.

Psychoanalysis is a theory of the human subject in his multiple capacities, and that is founded on one theory of the infrastructure of the phenomena he initiates. Therefore, there is no psychoanalysis and an applied form of it; there are only different professionals using it in their fields of work.

Notes

1 Jones (1955) had a different way of looking at it. He said: "He [Freud] was from the very beginning aware that the conclusions he had reached in this way [investigating psychoneuroses] had far wider validity. Moreover, it was that wider bearing of his work that he was primarily interested. … The proof that Freud's interest in normal, non-medical is [his first two books on Dreams and Parapraxes]" (273). Jones selected thirty of Freud's works and assigned them to the applied side of psychoanalysis, though in my estimate close to one-third of his more than 250 works may be called applied psychoanalysis.

2 'The future of an illusion' (1927c) reflects Freud's interest in the past of the human subject, and its reading shows, in a convincing way, Freud's interest, clarity of mind, ability to move from the present to the past, and, most of all, his understanding of the place of the primary process in human thinking and its possible historical evolution, likening the early times of humanity with the early time of the human subject. We do not see that same Freudian genius in his 'Civilization and its discontents' (1930a). This later book was almost a regression to the theory of catharsis with its main concepts of repression of the reprehensible.

3 See chapter two.

4 Primal is the first state of something that has or can generate sequels of itself. Freud used this adjective with subjects like fantasies, hordes, repression, father, narcissism (sixteen subjects). The primal evolves into less primitive forms, and replaces it. Primary is a different adjective used by Freud with four subjects: identification, sadism, masochism, and mental processes. The primary is the state of the condition that is followed by its secondary state, but it stays lurking behind its secondary form or gets integrated into it.

EPILOGUE

The measure of success of any theory, whether in the nomothetic field or the idiographic one, is its ability to lead to where it has to be revised. A good theory advances knowledge to a point where the specialist can understand their subject matter better and see promising horizons beyond what they already know. Furthermore, successful theories undergo minor expansions and adjustments during their lifespan, which are preliminaries of pending revisions. Hence, revising them happens to come in a natural and welcomed way to the followers of the theory. Psychoanalysis has those features of success. It started from the modest yet surprising intuition of the gifted Freud. It gave us a better understanding of the human subject. Freud continued to expand and adjust it for over half a century. Although his disciples contributed well to his work, his revisions were the most prominent. He made three major revisions to the theory: in 1905, 1915, and another attempt in 1920, but the latter needed several corrections (1923b, 1926, and a final adjustment in 1937d).

The theory proved to be successful in the sense mentioned earlier – i.e., it invited serious and better understanding of its subject matter. Some gifted and scholarly psychoanalysts tried their hand at making revisions to some aspects of the theory: the works of Bion in reformulating the primary and secondary processes (1962, 1963), Green's explorations in the concept of affect (1999a), Hartmann's reconfiguring the ego (1948), Klein's understanding of the early formations of the intrapsychical (1948), Lacan's usage of the Freudian doctrine to support his psychoanalytic view (1977), Laplanche's proposed elaboration of the life and death instincts (1976), and Matte-Blanco extensive examination of the concept of the systemic unconscious (1975) are major and substantial revisions of the basic doctrine. But, because they were individual efforts and in regard to single aspects in a comprehensive theory they were partial and disconnected, they thus aroused temporary and limited attention. Although we do not have another Freud to make a fourth revision from within the theory, and because revising separate conceptions do not take the theory where it should be as *the* theory of the human subject, revising the theory has to be a collaborative work of a number of analysts, and a cooperative work of several branches of the humanities.

Freud left a theory that was admired by so many and was rich in concepts and novel ideas. He was also fortunate because no competing theory came close to its comprehensiveness. It maintained its status as the unique theory of the psyche for a long time after Freud's death, and was able to keep hundreds of analysts, thinkers, and intellectuals working on its implicit potentials. In a way this was an attribute of potentials and survivability, but it was also ominous to its future. The theory had to evolve and develop, whether it looked adequate enough or not. To some extent some analysts, around the 1970s, realized that the theory is reaching its limits and is not providing anything new. Instead of working on revising the theory they ventured to create their own theories, and chose to improvise new psychoanalyses. To avoid misunderstanding of my views on the outcome of the discontentment with psychoanalysis that started around the 1970s, I would like to underscore what I consider an incontrovertible fact: *psychoanalysis is the theory of the psychodynamics of intrapsychical, and not a theory applicable to any psychodynamics, such as the psychodynamics of intrapsychical*. Reversing that relationship by considering psychoanalysis a theory that is applicable to other psychodynamic phenomena allowed the claim that it could be applied to explain object relations, interpersonal relations, psychology of the ego or the self, intersubjectivity, etc. In other words, considering psychoanalysis a *theory* without a definite subject matter opened the gate for plurality in psychoanalysis – a mistake that is almost destroying its foundation. The first discontented psychoanalysts tried tentatively to apply it to the psychodynamics of object relations, which was an offshoot of the Kleinian camp in Great Britain. This was followed by a faint interest in interpersonal relationships (Arieti, 1973; Chrzanowski, 1973). For a while Kohut's self-psychology offered another form of intrapsychical psychodynamics, thus curtailing – but not for long – the quiet revolution against the Freudian intrapsychical. However, once the idea that psychoanalysis can be an applicable theory and could be applied to other fields, because it was not restricted to the intrapsychic, a strong movement towards the interpersonal was revived (Aron, 1990; Mitchell, 1995). The schools of intersubjectivity followed (Stolorow & Atwood, 1992, 2002). As things look now, the initiatives to create new psychoanalyses, reshape the classical theory to apply it to different subject matters, claiming that the changes made to the theory are merely cosmetic and advancing it to modern times have failed – either in catching the attention of analysts and sustaining their interest, or outdoing the classical theory. They had their time and withered fast, or usurped the term 'psychoanalysis' to name their endeavours and maintain some vague hope for a revival of their claims. Anyway, if we look at those attempts, the passing ones and the still-struggling ones, we can say that they did not constitute any danger of demising the classical theory or replacing it. It is ethically improper of those schools of analysis to appropriate the term 'psychoanalysis', except that most of those who took that way to justify their claims were psychoanalysts who got their training in traditional institutes.

The remainder of the analysts chose to continue accepting the theory (as is), stayed loyal and devoted to the recognized associations of the IPA, and putatively adhered to the Freudian doctrine. They satisfied themselves by believing that they are 'true adherents' to the classical theory. *The adherents to the classical theory are doing it a great disservice, and are the real danger to psychoanalysis.* As mentioned in Chapter 1, a successful theory has to evolve, and if its advocates do not work on developing it, it will become useless. Herbert Spencer said (1850) "progress is not an accident but a necessity; it is part of nature". I also mentioned earlier that developing the theory is a process that starts with identifying its most central and encompassing proposals, which are the questions that the theory answered and as a result widened and expanded knowledge. With the new and expanded knowledge, new answers to the same questions would revise the theory and advance it. If this is not done under the guise of loyalty to the classical theory, then the only logical conclusion is that they are the cause of the crisis in psychoanalysis today. Proper revisions are the lifeline of the theory as its history proves. Since today's analysts are the ones who administer the local, regional, and international associations of psychoanalysis, run and supervise training programmes, and are directly responsible for publications in the field, they should be held responsible for the status of psychoanalysis now and the stagnation of the theory and its dilution to accommodate most of the current points of view. From my personal experience and some observations, I would say that classical analysts – i.e., the ones who follow the IPA line – have a spontaneous negative response to any attempt to revise the theory, to move their concerns from the organization to the status of 'psychoanalysis', to rethink the purpose and philosophy of training, or to evaluate their own proficiencies. If the theory has reached, by now, its state of perfection and does not need any changes, and if patients and candidates are discouraged by some failings in the structure of the organization, thus they are no longer interested in psychoanalysis. If the plurality of psychoanalysis has strengthened it, why is psychoanalysis in a crisis that is continuing to erode it? Recycling the theory's basics in the current publications, and using typical psychoanalytical templates as the contribution to the theory are evidence enough that there should be something wrong with *the classical analysts*. The crisis in psychoanalysis is the making of today's analyst mostly by omission. They are reorganizing the organization instead of revising the theory and evading looking at the theory they are endorsing.

When the crisis of psychoanalysis emerged (Cesio, 1995) analysts began looking for solutions, but in a peculiar way. They entertained the idea that what is needed to have concrete proof of the credibility of psychoanalysis, so 'research' became the buzzword, and still is to an extent.[1] But analysts, in general, are not experienced in research methodology; thus they gave thought to finding others to do the research for them. They missed three things in that call: they have to know what to ask the researcher to research, which they have no idea how to do; they do not know who might be interested in doing their research for them (scientists have their own research to do); there is no psychoanalytic outcome or topic that is amenable to the strict experimental parameters (the core of any research). Thus, whatever needs to be researched requires reformulation that should make it subject to experimentation. Psychoanalysis is in itself the method of researching the intrapsychical; to research a tool of research is a double-fault. Another buzzword emerged with reviving Windelband's classification of sciences into nomothetic (sciences of the laws of phenomena) and idiographic (sciences of interpreting phenomena). Analysts argued the place of psychoanalysis in those two groups without any satisfying or conclusive end, because they are not knowledgeable enough about the basis of Windelband's classification. He based it on two types of epistemological data: causality, which is the attribute of physical sciences (nomothetic); and meaning, which is the attribute of the human sciences (idiographic). This distinction, which favours placing psychoanalysis among the sciences of meanings, confronted the analysts with a deeper and more complex issue: hermeneutics and interpretation. Do psychoanalytic interpretations reveal causes or meanings? Is it science or hermeneutics? Within the maze of interconnected links between causes, meaning, interpretation, validity, science and the place of psychoanalysis in that maze, classical analysts showed features of stubbornness: they would never admit that something is wrong with the theory of today that they are using and are devoted to. The only thought that they came up with was that some other disciplines could save psychoanalysis from foreboding oblivion. Using two psychoanalytic templates to describe this stubbornness I would say: analysts are *denying* that the crisis could be of their making, and *negating* that the solution is their responsibility and has to come from within the theory, and not from some external source.

The helplessness, almost paralysis, behind negation and denial stems from an inability to envisage a change to the theory without questioning the viability of the organizational structure of the IPA and its associations. The emergence of psychoanalysis necessitated building an organization that would overlook its expansion. The reason is the nature of the psychoanalytic discovery. Freud had the intuition that neurotic symptoms are unconsciously created by the patient himself and not by physical, physiological, or sociological causes. This intuition opened the way for him to pursue the intrapsychical conditions of patients and develop his discovery beyond any previous notion of the existence of intrapsychical dynamics, at least in medical circles. His discoveries gathered around him a group of physicians who aspired to make changes to the field of psychoneuroses. Psychoanalysis was born as a movement to modernize traditional thinking about the individual. Freud was encouraged by the response of some eminent people and with the spread of his thought. After a short while he realized he had started a movement which needed establishing on defined rules. The result was the birth of the IPA in 1910. Further down the line the movement required establishing training measures to legitimize belonging to the IPA. The evolution of the movement was guided – all along – by Freud, and logically and commonsensically he was the sole owner and undisputed leader of the movement. By the time he died, psychoanalysis was no longer a movement but a well-established organization that took charge of all the needs of maintaining the Freudian discovery: the selection of members, training and teaching the theory, protecting the theory from deviations, setting the proper standards for practice, and – most of all – keeping alive the original sense of purpose and distinction. Thus, the IPA practised measures of exclusion and inclusion in regard to membership that were, on many occasions, unrelated to psychoanalysis and its purpose but were politically self-serving. Those measures were required when psychoanalysis was still a movement that was expanding and in need of protection, or a guild that needed definition. But psychoanalysis is no longer a movement or a guild. It is now a theory that has palpable existence in society as whole, and has a clear impact on the daily lives of ordinary people. It also has a noticeable presence in all other types of psychotherapy. Moreover, it has an undeniable impact, directly or indirectly, on other branches of the humanities. Accordingly, it is finding its way into academia as it becomes assimilated in several related academic specialties.

Ignoring those facts and keeping the idea of an international organization that is the single source of legitimacy to belonging to psychoanalysis reversed the logical justification for its existence. The international organization was meant to protect and nourish a budding movement. When psychoanalysis was established as a main theory in the humanities, the organization, if there were a reason for it to continue, derived its raison-d'etre from the existence of psychoanalysis. However, its existence stifled the progress of the theory indirectly. Officially, any changes to the theory had to be initiated and canonized by the IPA. The irony is that the IPA condoned plurality in psychoanalysis as parallel movements (Wallerstein, 1989), but had nothing to say about the changes those schools have made to the theory. More blatantly, the IPA was more concerned with preserving itself as an organization as long as it could contain the other quasi-psychoanalytic movements within its domain of influence (Wallerstein, 2005). Therefore, revising the classical theory is neither entertained as a possible solution to the crisis, nor is revising the system of training considered necessary to improve the quality of the psychoanalysts which seems lately to be a serious concern. There is a determined resistance to changing an attitude that has been taken from psychoanalysis from its beginnings: it is an exclusive club of initiated members who have been chosen in the same way and meeting the same particular standards of efficiency. This attitude is engraved in the notion of training, supporting a sense of exclusivity, thus securing the continuance of the inherited organizational structure, which was established at the formation of the 'secret committee' (1917). The organization keeps repairing and mending the traditional tripartite system of the IPA, in addition to the concept of an umbrella that covers all the other societies and associations of psychoanalysis worldwide. The people who were in charge of the organization from the beginning never considered that there would come a time when the movement would be established and its status as a recognized branch of the humanities acknowledged, therefore the IPA should be dissolved.[2]

Eisold discussed the gloomy future of psychoanalysis and recommended three potential solutions by saying (2003):

> I am suggesting three pathways for a reconsidered psychoanalytic project: (1) The path of partner in the psychotherapies, offering the benefits of insight and inquiry in the treatment of psychiatric disorders; (2) A comparable partnership in the "applied" fields of organizational, family, and group work, allied with other disciplines and professions; (3) The path of inquiry into false adaptations, social identities that block authentic and full human experience. There may well be other paths to be chartered, but I believe that we are already on these paths now and can take steps to clarify our goals.
>
> (579)

In other words, the keenness to keep the organization as it has always been is the secret reason for resisting revision of the theory, or letting go of the notion that psychoanalysis does not have adversaries that need to be warded off. This idea could legitimately raise a question: what is the harm in keeping the IPA even though psychoanalysis does not need it anymore? The IPA explicitly and implicitly indicates that we have one cohesive psychoanalysis, or that psychoanalysis is the same professional entity all over the world. This is not only misleading, it is also detrimental because it is affecting the necessary revision of the theory. *Revising the theory – as a fresh look at its main proposals and addressing them anew – will show that psychoanalysts have many new questions to ask other human scientists, thinkers, and neurologists, thus those other scientists have to be included in psychoanalysis and the IPA has to cease to exist in order that each convening group of interested people could form their own 'psychoanalytic society'.* This would not happen unless the IPA organization and its associations embark on changing the present attitude of supremacy of the professional psychoanalysts (the clinical analyst). This protectionist attitude, rationalized by an untrue conviction that analysis is a clinical discipline, was a cause of exiting psychoanalysis from academia due to an incorrect sense of the exclusivity of the psychoanalysts. After several decades of occupying prominent positions in the departments of psychiatry (and university hospitals), departments of psychology, and a few other prominent teaching institutions, analysts did not accept that their colleagues who are not members of the IPA had an equal right to be analysts too. Kernberg, in a very thorough and well-vetted two-part paper, examined details of the status of psychoanalysis in its present condition which lead to the conclusion that the prevailing IPA model, with whatever flexibility it allowed, is no longer sustainable. He said (2006):

> The self-destructive isolationism of psychoanalytic institutions in the USA, leading to the separation of psychoanalysis from most psychiatric university settings in the 1970s and 1980s (similar developments took place later in Germany and Scandinavian countries), was largely a consequence of the monolithic assertion of psychoanalysis by psychoanalytic institutes, and their rejection of the scientific, educational, and research requirements of university settings to explore critically all developing areas in the broad field of the mental sciences … [T]he psychoanalytic institutes, in turn, exploited this situation by marginalizing further academicians who could only maintain a limited psychoanalytic practice. This isolation, retreat or expulsion from university settings reinforced the narrowing of intellectual pursuits in psychoanalytic institutions, and was a setback to the impressive developments of psychoanalytic knowledge that had taken place in the 1940s and 1950s, particularly in Great Britain. During this period, radically divergent theories and techniques within the British Psychoanalytic Society generated a period of intense scientific and creative inquiry. Then the cultural impact of French psychoanalysis – in significant part motivated by Lacan's dissidence and its impact on French culture – led, in turn, to a cultural interchange with their environment on the part of French psychoanalytic institutions that had maintained their identity within the IPA. This development provided French psychoanalysis with an opening to cultural and political currents that compensated for the relative isolation of psychoanalysis from university settings in a strict sense. The British case illustrates the positive effects of a break-up of ideological monopolies, and the French case the positive effects of an open interchange with the surrounding culture.
> (1665)

There are two glaring facts that could only be evaded by denial and negation: first, the IPA is neither an educational facility to officially give certificates nor a training service to authorize competence, nor a professional body to licence for practice. Those three functions were performed in different degrees of nuisance and prickliness in all the IPA associated societies. However, the result in some areas was very destructive. The special status that was granted to the USA in 1938 in order to maintain the APsaA's link with it created from those three functions an unusually confused and confusing conflict in the organizations of psychoanalysis in the USA (still an active confused scene in 2016). Now, the three functions of education, training, and professional licensing are either done by social and professional legalized institutions or could be undertaken independently if the candidate so wishes. In other words, psychoanalysis does not need the IPA. Denying that fact sustains and continues a false narcissistic value to the title 'psychoanalyst'. The expansion and then the shrinking of the psychoanalytic movement were unrelated and completely independent of any particular efforts of the IPA. The expansion of psychoanalysis was due to its new and creative conceptions of the intrapsychic. Its shrinking was due to the eventual and natural outdating of its informative theory and its need for revision.

Kernberg (2007) continued examining the status of psychoanalysis and the influence of framing it in the old model of the IPA. He concluded by saying:

> This administrative structure, corresponding to the concept of psychoanalytic education as a central responsibility of a psychoanalytic society, has always been the model theoretically pursued by the IPA in developing of societies. Historically, however, this intended structure has been subtly subverted, as institutes consolidated the training analysis system in the hands of a stable powerful elite that evolved along the lines mentioned above. ... Some affiliate societies of APsaA have undertaken initiatives to change the structural arrangements between their psychoanalytic institute and the society to integrate the institute and society's efforts to assure and strengthen the local position of psychoanalysis.
>
> (168)

The IPA and its affiliate associations continued to claim to be the legitimate authority to select, train, and certify psychoanalysts, which is based on a veritable fallacy. A genuinely interested person seeking training in analysis could do that on his own and away from The American Psychoanalytic Association (APsaA) hegemony: he can find a competent analyst and have the desired personal analysis with, see patients, and seek supervision from any number of experienced analysts around, form a dedicated group of candidates like himself, and invite qualified scholars to discuss with them the literature that is well known to all people and not a monopoly of the institutes. That person could also call himself a psychoanalyst because the title is not protected by law for IPA-accredited members only. If anyone thinks this is not easy to achieve he should think that gaining a place in a training programme requires personal recommendation that are not always available to most young aspiring candidates more than just desire and determination. The difference between the two trainings would be – at the end of the day – getting a membership in the IPA or just being a true analyst, as good as any graduate of a recognized institute, without that membership.

A second point that puts IPA in question relates to professional standards. Kernberg, as well as many training analysts from different psychoanalytic associations, questioned the efficacy of the present system of training. It is very common that when a candidate meets the *minimum* required expectations for graduation, he would be anticipating accreditation, elections, and membership. The standards for graduation are decided by formalities like years or number of sessions of personal analysis, and similar criteria regarding supervision, plus attendance of the seminars. The issue of the reporting and non-reporting analyst is another factor that makes training a matter of mere formality; if properly met, the desired result of graduating is guaranteed. From my experience and the experience of several other colleagues whom I met at international meetings, and supported by Kernberg's own experience as a long-standing training and supervising analyst plus having been a president of the IPA, those standards are also negatively affected by the dynamics of transference and counter-transference in relation to the training analysts. The result is, in general, discouraging. The stipulations of standards change them from a means to an end to an end in their own right, and the desire to train is confused and muddled with the aspiration to acquire the title.

Proof of that are the changes that have happened over the years to the function of the three components of didactic analysis, supervision, and the seminars. They are no longer serving their original functions. Originally, the requirement to undergo a period of analysis was to experience the process of being analysed to know how it is done; thus it was called didactic analysis – i.e., learnt from a more experienced analyst. Some therapy could naturally happen in the process, but it was not its objective (selecting the 'normal' candidates is the responsibility of the selection committee).

Ignoring the two facts mentioned above changed the main purpose of didactic analysis; the unintended and casual purpose of therapy became the main objective and personal analysis became a therapeutic endeavour. This is evidently wrong because learning to undertake analysis would be contaminated by transference issues and idealizations, to the extent that the new function of 'identifying with your analyst' has changed from being a transference neurosis to becoming the function of the process. Supervision, which was meant to help the newcomer with observing the clinical protocol and the rules of conducting analysis, has taken the meaning of evaluating the candidate's ability to undertake analysis. Another ruined aspect of training, coaching doing analysis, changed to a process of evaluating the candidate's psychoanalytic ability.[3] The gist of Kernberg's remarks on the seminars (2007) offers several other modalities for teaching the theoretical part of psychoanalysis. The most important is suggesting linking the seminars to the local departments of psychology and psychiatry whereby the faculty of those departments become part of the teaching potentials of the psychoanalytic society. He was critical of separating academia from psychoanalysis because that would constrict the pool of talent from which the teachers of the seminars should come. The expansion of the seminar leaders would naturally expand the seminars series and would give the candidates and the actual members of the society and the institute a chance to choose what would complement their knowledge. Breaking the artificial shell that we became so accustomed to live with is one of few disadvantages of staying with a system that came about at a time when only psychoanalysts knew psychoanalysis, and thus were doing the teaching.[4]

The suggestion of breaking away from the IPA model of qualifying psychoanalysts is going to face more than objections and rejections; it will, in all likelihood, arouse doubts about the intention behind it. The IPA model is so engrained in the minds of analysts to the extent of not questioning that they are following a modality which had a legitimate reason to exist decades ago and which maybe is no longer legitimate. They do not realize that it is imposing on people to learn and practise psychoanalysis in the way it was learnt decades ago. They do not envisage that training could be done now in different and much better ways. The passive acceding to the IPA modality made analysts forget that it is their responsibility to revise the theory periodically. Worse, disregarding revising the theory caused the theory to deteriorate, and for psychoanalysis to lose its status and become obstinately problematic. I am convinced that if psychoanalysis is left to continue in its present trajectory it will disappear without any remorseful supporters. I am also sensibly envisaging other branches of the humanities 'adopting' psychoanalysis and giving it life. It seems that academia is lately more open to integrate psychoanalysis in its curricula and even teaching it as an independent subject.[5] The young people who are genuinely interested in psychoanalysis, not just in the title, can probably receive better training if they look for it independently – especially in the areas where universities are offering some psychoanalytic teaching. The new organization of the psychoanalytically inclined people will gradually emerge locally, but eventually it will find its way to a more expanded format, and maybe this trend will become a new international movement. This is going to happen despite the expected strong resistance of the psychoanalysts who are in charge now. They do not want to admit that they are espousing an already-spent and used-up version of a great theory of man, and not doing the right thing by revising it.

The last thing I would like say is that revising the theory is a must, and it needs the cooperation of the scholarly psychoanalysts who should exchange ideas about the important propositions of the original theory that would need revising. It will also need collaboration from psychologists, especially child psychologists, philosophers, anthropologists, sociologists, and linguists. I have some solid reasons to think that psychoanalysis is needed now as it was needed before, though in a different form. The need for it will force its revision. Herbert Spencer said (1862) "Evolution … is a change from indefinite, incoherent homogeneity to definite coherent heterogeneity" (138).

Notes

1 I have to wonder: how could research solve the problem of the declining interest in psychoanalysis? Is the loss of interest in psychoanalysis a result of lack of evidence of its validity? Were there any proofs of validity of psychoanalysis in its heyday? Would the IPA publish the results of those researches to convince the public that psychoanalysis is still valid? Psychoanalysis is not a theory about facts but a theory of meanings. It is enough to prove the validity of psychoanalysis by getting to a coherent link between a psychical event and its meaning.

2 Eisold (2003) envisaged a change in the profession of psychoanalysis as it stands now and seeing it becoming part of two wider circles: the human sciences and psychotherapy. He said: "But such a new 'professional project' would be significantly enhanced if we were able to develop means of self-governance that were inclusive and cooperative, despite differences and disagreements … Eventually, we might be able to put to rest the accusation that we are sectarian zealots engaged in self-perpetuating delusions" (579).

3 Psychoanalysis is not a requirement for the mental health practitioner to practice in order to impose on him 'passing' its test; it is the practitioner's desire to learn how to do it well, and he should always remain the one to decide when he is ready to do it on his own. The need for input from the training analysts in taking that decision comes from the practitioner's wish to join a group of peers who share with him the desire to learn psychoanalysis. Therefore, the nature and the function of a psychoanalytic society decide for all what is the criterion for membership. The societies affiliated with the IPA still serve the old function of excluding the non-informed persons in psychoanalysis, despite Freud's accepting non-members as equals and rich resources for his theory, like Binswanger. (Binswanger was a Swiss Psychiatrist who was influenced by Husserl's phenomenology. He was formulating psychopathology in existential terminology and he found in psychoanalysis a great source of intuitions and Freud was mutually open to his conception of psychodynamics.) Having that in mind, future psychoanalytic societies should include those who could prove their knowledge of psychoanalysis, *not by means of certification but by the evidence of their versatility in psychoanalytic thinking*. The society, not the institute, should set up the criteria for accepting a person's membership. The society would then be free to set up more than one criterion based on the qualifications of the applicant.

4 In 2010 I suggested that the future organization of psychoanalysis should emulate the Socratic symposia. The idea is the advantage of having several and different thinkers exchanging ideas about the same subject. I will give an example: a psychoanalyst might ask that, if a four-month old infant can laugh, and, at age seven months, respond to teasing by giggling, and, at age two years, differentiate between serious games and teasing games, this would indicate that the infant performs the basic conception of language before he acquires it? We can imagine the interest of the linguist in enquiring about the difference the analyst is making between the basic conceptions of language and acquiring it (Chomsky, 2006). The child psychologist could also pitch in with remarks on parental linguistic communication and action communication with the infant. But in the end they will both ask the analysts: what does all this have to do with clinical work? The answer would be: I want to know how (and what) interpretation reaches my patients.

5 In England there are two universities at least (that I know of) that offer degrees in psychoanalysis. The University of Paris V has two institutes, thanks to Laplanche, which have serious and rich education in psychoanalysis. I do not have confirmed specific knowledge of other countries that have universities offering teachings in psychoanalysis, but all indications suggest there must be some in the two Americas and the rest of Europe. In 1962 I was appointed associate professor of psychoanalysis in the department of psychology of Ein-Shams University in Cairo, Egypt. I was teaching psychoanalysis to undergraduate students. For first year students I taught Freud's Five lectures (1910a); for second year the Introductory lectures (first two parts, 1916–1917); in the third year for the course on Personality Theories I integrated several papers that had relevance to the course, e.g., Libidinal types (1931a). In forth year the professor and the chairman taught the *Ego and the Id* and a brief version of *Inhibitions, Symptoms and Anxiety* in the course on psychopathology. This programme was so popular we had to open the lectures to students from other departments. After I left and the chairman retired the programme stopped.

REFERENCES

Abend, S. (2008). Freud, transference, and therapeutic action, *Psychoanalytic Quarterly*, 78, 871–892.

Abraham, K. (1924). A short study of the development of the libido viewed in the light of mental disorders (418–501), in: *Selected Papers on Psycho-analysis*, Hogarth Press, London.

Abrams, E.K. (1976). The anarchistic transference as a resistance, *Modern Psychoanalysis*, 1, 218–230.

Alexander, F. (2007). Analysis and the therapeutic factors in psychoanalytic treatment, *Psychoanalytic Quarterly*, 78, 1065–1083.

Arieti, S. (1973). The interpersonal and the intrapsychic in severe psychopathology, in: *Interpersonal Explorations in Psychoanalysis*, ed. E. Witenberg, Basic Books, New York.

Aron, L. (1990). Free associations and changing models of mind, *Journal of the American Academy of Psychoanalysis*, 18, 439–459.

Bach, S. (1977). On the narcissistic state of consciousness, *International Journal of Psychoanalysis*, 58, 209–233.

Baranger, M. and Baranger, W. (2008). The analytic situation as dynamic field, *International Journal of Psychoanalysis*, 89, 795–826.

Bergmann, M.S. (1997). Termination: the Achilles heel of psychoanalysis, *Psychoanalytic Psychology*, 14, 163–174.

Bichi, E. (2012). Countertransference: a contemporary metapsychological view on its intrapsychic, interspychic, intersubjective and objective aspects, *International Forum of Psychoanalysis*, 21, 146–149.

Bion, W. (1962). *Learning from Experience*, Maresfield Reprints, London.

Bion, W. (1963). *Elements of Psycho-Analysis*, Maresfield Reprints, London.

Bion, W. (1970). *Attention and Interpretation*, Maresfield Reprints, London.

Blass, R.B. (1994). Dora had an Oedipus complex?: a review of the theoretical context of Freud's 'fragment of a hysteria analysis', *Yearbook of Psychoanalysis*, 32, 74–111.

Blum, H. (2003). Repression, transference and reconstruction, *International Journal of Psychoanalysis*, 84, 479–503.

Bouvet, M. (1953). Le Moi dans la nevreuse obsessionelle, *La Revue Francause de pesychoanalyse*, 17, 111–161.
Bouvet, M. (1959). Clinical psychoanalysis: the object relations, in: *Psychoanalysis Today*, ed. S. Nacht, Grun & Stratton, New York.
Bowlby, J. (1981). Psychoanalysis as a natural science, *The International Review of Psychoanalysis*, 8, 3–20.
Brenner, C. (1980). Metapsychology and the psychoanalytic theory, *The Psychoanalytic Quarterly*, 49, 189–214.
Brenner, C. (1981). *The Mind in Conflict*, International Universities Press, New York.
Brenner, C. (1996). Discussion, *Journal of the American Psychoanalytic Association*, 17, 41–53.
Cesio, F. (1995). Report to the House of Delegates Committee on 'The actual crisis of psychoanalysis: challenges and perspectives', *International Psychoanalytic Association Publications*.
Chrzanowski, G. (1973). Implications of interpersonal theory, in: *Interpersonal Explorations in Psychoanalysis*, ed. E. Witenberg, Basic Books, New York.
Chomsky, N. (2006). *Language and Mind*, Cambridge, UK.
Clark, M. (2009). Suppose Freud had chosen Orestes, *J. Analytic Psychology*, 54, 233–252.
Compton, A. (1981a). On the psychoanalytic theory of instinctual drives, *The Psychoanalytic Quarterly*, 50, 190–218.
Compton, A. (1981b). On the psychoanalytic theory of instinctual drives, *The Psychoanalytic Quarterly*, 50, 219–237.
Compton, A. (1981c). On the psychoanalytic theory of instinctual drives, *The Psychoanalytic Quarterly*, 50, 345–362.
Compton, A. (1981d). On the psychoanalytic theory of instinctual drives, *The Psychoanalytic Quarterly*, 50, 363–392.
Crockatt, P. (2006). Freud's on narcissism: an introduction, *Journal of Child Psychotherapy*, 32, 2–20.
Crownfield, D. (1992). *Body text in Julia Kristeva: Religion, Women, and Psychoanalysis*, State University of New York, New York.
Eickhoff, F.-W. (2006). On Nachtraglichkeit: the modernity of an old concept, *International Journal of Psychoanalysis*, 87, 1453–1469.
Eisold, K. (2003). The profession of psychoanalysis: past failures and future possibilities, *Contemporary Psychoanalysis*, 39, 557–582.
Eisold, K. (2008). Succeeding in succession: the myth of Orestes, *Journal of Analytic Psychology*, 53, 619–632.
Elder, C. (1994). *The Grammar of the Unconscious: A Conceptual Foundation for Psychoanalysis*, Pennsylvania University Press, Philadelphia, PA.
Elise, D. (1997). Primary femininity, bisexuality and female ego ideal: a reexamination of female developmental theory, *Psychoanalytic Quarterly*, 66, 489–517.
Ellman, S. and Moskowitz, M. (1980). An Examination of some recent criticisms of psychoanalytic "metapsychology", *Psychoanalytic Quarterly*, 49, 631–662.
Erikson, E. (1950). *Childhood and Society*, Norton, New York.
Erikson, E. (1963). The identity and the life cycle, *Psychoanalytical Issues 1*, International Universities Press, New York.
Eriksson, J. (2012). Metapsychology – the formal a priori of psychoanalytic experience, *The Scandinavian Psychoanalytic Review*, 35, 21–34.
Everett, D. (2012). *Language: The Cultural Tool*, Pantheon Books, New York.
Faimberg, H. (1996). Listening to listening, *International Journal of Psychoanalysis*, 71, 776–677.
Fayek, A. (1981). Narcissism and the death instinct, *International Review of Psycho-Analysis*, 7, 447–457.

Fayek, A. (2005). The centrality of the system Ucs. in psychoanalysis, *Psychoanalytic Psychology*, 22, 524–543.
Fayek, A. (2010). *The Crisis in Psychoanalysis: In Search of a Lost Doctrine*, Bridgeway Books, Austin, TX.
Fayek, A. (2011). *The Clinical Applications of the Theory of Psychoanalysis*, Karnac, London.
Fayek, A. (2013). *Freud's Other Theory of Psychoanalysis: The Replacement of the Indelible Theory of Catharsis*, Jason Aronson, New York.
Fayek, A. (2014). *Consciousness and the Aconscious*, Rowman & Littlefield, New York.
Fayek, A. (2015). *Future Psychoanalysis: Toward a Theory of the human Subject,* Rowman & Littlefield, New York.
Ferenczi, S. (1912). On the definition of introjection, in: *Final Contributions to the problems and Methods of Psycho-Analysis*, Hogarth Press, London.
Firestein, S. (1978). *Termination in Psychoanalysis,* International Universities Press, New York.
Fosshage, J.L. (1995). Self-psychology and its contributions to psychoanalysis, *International Forum of Psychoanalysis*, 4, 238–245.
Flugle, J.C. (1953). The death instinct, homeostasis, and allied concepts, *International Journal of Psychoanalysis*, 34, 43–71.
Fonagy, P. (2003). Rejoinder to Harold Blum, *International Journal of Psychoanalysis*, 84, 503–509.
Frazer, J.G. (2012). *The Golden Bough: A Study in Comparative Religion.* A public domain book, Kindle edition (first published 1894).
Freedman, R. and Downey, J. (1995). Biology and the Oedipus complex, *Psychoanalytic Quarterly,* 64, 234–264.
Freud, S. (1894a). The neuro-psychosis of defense, *Standard Edition*, 3, 41–61, Hogarth Press and the Institute of Psychoanalysis, London.
Freud, S. (1895). Letter, May 25, *The Complete Letters of Sigmund Freud to Wilhelm Fliess* (1887–1904), trans. and ed. J. Masson, The Belknap Press of Harvard University Press, Cambridge, MA & London.
Freud, S. (1895d). *Studies on Hysteria* (Breuer. J. & Freud, S.), *Standard Edition*, 2, Hogarth Press and the Institute of Psychoanalysis, London.
Freud, S. (1896b). Further remarks on the neuropsychosis of defense, *Standard Edition*, 3, 157–186, Hogarth Press and the Institute of Psychoanalysis, London.
Freud, S. (1896c). The aetiology of hysteria, *Standard Edition*, 3, 189–222, Hogarth Press and the Institute of Psychoanalysis, London.
Freud, S. (1897a). Draft L (May 2), *The Complete Letters of Sigmund Freud to Wilhelm Fliess* (1887–1904), trans. and ed. J. Masson, The Belknap Press of Harvard University Press, Cambridge, MA & London.
Freud, S. (1897b). Draft M (May 25), *The Complete Letters of Sigmund Freud to Wilhelm Fliess* (1887–1904), trans. and ed. J. Masson, The Belknap Press of Harvard University Press, Cambridge, MA & London.
Freud, S. (1897c). Letter, October 15, *The Complete Letters of Sigmund Freud to Wilhelm Fliess* (1887–1904), trans. and ed. J. Masson, The Belknap Press of Harvard University Press, Cambridge, MA & London.
Freud, S. (1898). Letter, March 10, *The Complete Letters of Sigmund Freud to Wilhelm Fliess* (1887–1904), trans. and ed. J. Masson, The Belknap Press of Harvard University Press, Cambridge, MA & London.
Freud, S. (1899). Letter, January 3–4, *The Complete Letters of Sigmund Freud to Wilhelm Fliess* (1887–1904), trans. and ed. J. Masson, The Belknap Press of Harvard University Press, Cambridge, MA & London.

Freud, S. (1899). Letter, October 11, *The Complete Letters of Sigmund Freud to Wilhelm Fliess* (1887–1904), trans. and ed. J. Masson, The Belknap Press of Harvard University Press, Cambridge, MA & London.
Freud, S. (1899a). Screen Memories, *Standard Edition*, 3, 301–321, Hogarth Press and the Institute of Psychoanalysis, London.
Freud, S. (1900). Letter, January 26, *The Complete Letters of Sigmund Freud to Wilhelm Fliess* (1887–1904), trans. and ed. J. Masson, The Belknap Press of Harvard University Press, Cambridge, MA & London.
Freud, S. (1900a). *The Interpretation of Dreams, Standard Edition*, 4–5, Hogarth Press and the Institute of Psychoanalysis, London.
Freud, S. (1901b). *The Psychopathology of Everyday Life, Standard Edition*, 6, Hogarth Press and the Institute of Psychoanalysis, London.
Freud, S. (1905c). *Jokes and their Relations to the Unconscious, Standard Edition*, 8, Hogarth Press and the Institute of Psychoanalysis, London.
Freud, S. (1905d). *Three Essays on the Theory of Sexuality, Standard Edition*, 7, Hogarth Press and the Institute of Psychoanalysis, London.
Freud, S. (1905e). Fragment of an analysis of case of hysteria, *Standard Edition*, 7, 3–331, Hogarth Press and the Institute of Psychoanalysis, London.
Freud, S. (1907a). *Delusions and dreams in Jenesen's Gradiva, Standard Edition*, 9, 1–96, Hogarth Press and the Institute of Psychoanalysis, London.
Freud, S. (1908c). On the sexual theories of children, *Standard Edition*, 9, 205–226, Hogarth Press and the Institute of Psychoanalysis, London.
Freud, S. (1909d). Notes upon a case of obsessional neurosis, *Standard Edition*, 10, 151–250, Hogarth Press and the Institute of Psychoanalysis London.
Freud, S. (1910a). *Five lectures on psychoanalysis, Standard Edition*, 11, 3–54, Hogarth Press and the Institute of Psychoanalysis, London.
Freud, S. (1910c). *Leonardo da Vinci and a memory of his childhood, Standard Edition*, 11, 59–237, Hogarth Press and the Institute of Psychoanalysis, London.
Freud, S. (1910h). A special type of choice of object made by men, *Standard Edition*, 11, 163–176, Hogarth Press and the Institute of Psychoanalysis, London.
Freud, S. (1910k). Wild psychoanalysis, *Standard Edition*, 11, 221, Hogarth Press and the Institute of Psychoanalysis, London.
Freud. S. (1911c). Psycho-analytic notes on an autobiographical account of a case of paranoia (dementia paranoids). *Standard Edition*, 12, 1–83, Hogarth Press and the Institute of Psychoanalysis, London.
Freud, S. (1911e). The handling of dream-interpretation in psychoanalysis, *Standard Edition*, 12, 91, Hogarth Press and the Institute of Psychoanalysis, London.
Freud, S. (1912b). The dynamics of transference, *Standard Edition*, 12, 321, Hogarth Press and the Institute of Psychoanalysis, London.
Freud, S. (1912e), Recommendations to physicians practicing psycho-analysis, *Standard Edition*, 12, 111, Hogarth Press and the Institute of Psychoanalysis, London.
Freud, S. (1912–1913). *Totem and Taboo, Standard Edition*, 13, Hogarth Press and the Institute of Psychoanalysis, London.
Freud, S. (1913c). On beginning treatment, *Standard Edition*, 12, 123, Hogarth Press and the Institute of Psychoanalysis, London.
Freud, S. (1914c). On Narcissism: an introduction, *Standard Edition*, 14, 67–104, Hogarth Press and the Institute of Psychoanalysis, London.
Freud, S. (1914g). Remembering, repeating, and working-through (Further recommendations on the technique of psycho-analysis), *Standard Edition*, 12, 147, Hogarth Press and the Institute of Psychoanalysis, London.

Freud, S. (1915c). Instincts and their vicissitudes, *Standard Edition*, 14, 109–141, Hogarth Press and the Institute of Psychoanalysis, London.

Freud, S. (1915d). Repression, *Standard Edition*, 14, 141–158, Hogarth Press and the Institute of Psychoanalysis, London.

Freud, S. (1915e). The unconscious, *Standard Edition*, 14, 195–204, Hogarth Press and the Institute of Psychoanalysis, London.

Freud, S. (1916–1917). *Introductory Lectures on Psychoanalysis*, *Standard Edition*, 15–16, Hogarth Press and the Institute of Psychoanalysis, London.

Freud, S. (1917c). On the transformation of instinct as exemplified in anal erotism, *Standard Edition*, 17, 125–134, Hogarth Press and the Institute of Psychoanalysis, London.

Freud, S. (1917d). A metapsychological supplement to the theory of dreams, *Standard Edition*, 14, 217–236, Hogarth Press and the Institute of Psychoanalysis, London.

Freud, S. (1918a). *The Taboo of Virginity*, Vol 11, 193–207.

Freud, S. (1918b). From the history of an infantile neurosis, *Standard Edition*, 17, 3, Hogarth Press and the Institute of Psychoanalysis, London.

Freud, S. (1919h). The uncanny, *Standard Edition*, 17, 217–252, Hogarth Press and the Institute of Psychoanalysis, London.

Freud, S. (1920g). *Beyond the pleasure principle*, *Standard Edition*, 18, 1–64, Hogarth Press and the Institute of Psychoanalysis, London.

Freud, S. (1921c). *Group psychology and the analysis of the ego*, *Standard Edition*, 18, 65–144, Hogarth Press and the Institute of Psychoanalysis, London.

Freud, S. (1923a). Two encyclopedia articles: (A) Psycho-analysis; (B) Libido theory, *Standard Edition*, 18, 235 & 255, Hogarth Press and the Institute of Psychoanalysis, London.

Freud, S. (1923b). *The Ego and the Id*, *Standard Edition*, 19, 3–66, Hogarth Press and the Institute of Psychoanalysis, London.

Freud, S. (1923c). Remarks on the theory and practice of dream interpretation, *Standard Edition*, 19, 109–122, Hogarth Press and the Institute of Psychoanalysis, London.

Freud, S. (1923d). A seventeenth-century demonological neurosis, *Standard Edition*, 19, 69–108, Hogarth Press and the Institute of Psychoanalysis, London.

Freud, S. (1924d). The dissolution of the Oedipus complex, *Standard Edition*, 19, 173–182, Hogarth Press and the Institute of Psychoanalysis, London.

Freud, S. (1925h). Negation, *Standard Edition*, 19, 235–240, Hogarth Press and the Institute of Psychoanalysis, London.

Freud, S. (1926d). *Inhibition, symptoms, and anxiety*, *Standard Edition*, 20, 75–176, Hogarth Press and the Institute of Psychoanalysis, London.

Freud, S. (1927c). *The future of an illusion*, *Standard Edition*, 21, 3–55, Hogarth Press and the Institute of Psychoanalysis, London.

Freud, S. (1930a). *Civilization and its discontents*, *Standard Edition*, 21, 75–155, Hogarth Press and the Institute of Psychoanalysis, London.

Freud, S. (1931a). Libidinal types, *Standard Edition*, 21, 215–220, Hogarth Press and the Institute of Psychoanalysis, London.

Freud, S. (1932a). The acquisition and control of fire, *Standard Edition*, 22, 185–194, Hogarth Press and the Institute of Psychoanalysis, London.

Freud, S. (1933a). New introductory lectures on psychoanalysis, *Standard Edition*, 22, Hogarth Press and the Institute of Psychoanalysis, London.

Freud, S. (1937c). Analysis terminable and in terminable, *Standard Edition*, 23, 209–254, Hogarth Press and the Institute of Psychoanalysis, London.

Freud, S. (1937d). Construction in analysis, *Standard Edition*, 23, 255–270, Hogarth Press and the Institute of Psychoanalysis, London.

Freud, S. (1939a). *Moses and monotheism: three essays, Standard Edition*, 23, 1–137, Hogarth Press and the Institute of Psychoanalysis, London.

Freud, S. (1950b). Project for a scientific psychology, *Standard Edition*, 1, 281–392, Hogarth Press and the Institute of Psychoanalysis, London.

Friedmann, J.A. (1988). The idea of narcissism in Freud's psychoanalysis, *International Review of Psychoanalysis*, 15, 499–514.

Fulgenecio, L. (2007). Winnicott rejection of the basic concepts of Freud's metapsychology, *International Journal of Psychoanalysis*, 88, 443–461.

Gammelgaard, J. (2006). Primary process in metapsychology and cognitive psychology, *The Scandinavian Psychoanalytic Review*, 29, 93–105.

Gill, M. (1979). Topography and systems in psychoanalysis, *Psychological Issues, Monograph 10,* International Universities Press, New York.

Gill, M. (1984). Psychoanalysis and psychotherapy, *Psychoanalytic Review*, 11, 161–179.

Girard, M. (2010). Wnnicott's foundation for the basic concepts of Freud's metapsychology, *International Journal of Psychoanalysis*, 91, 305–324.

Glover, E. (1966). Metapsychology or metaphysics a psychoanalytic essay, *The Psychoanalytic Quarterly*, 35, 173–190.

Green, A. (1993). The dead mother (*Die tote Mutter*), *Psyche – Z Psychoanal*, 47, 205–240.

Green, A. (1999a). *The Fabric of Affect in the Psychoanalytic Discourse*, trans. A. Sheridan, Routledge, London.

Green, A. (1999b). *The Work of the Negative*, Free Association Books, New York.

Green, A. (2002). A dual conception of narcissism: positive and negative organizations, *The Psychoanalytic Quarterly*, 71, 831–849.

Greenacre, P. (1979). Reconstruction and the process of individuation, *The Psychoanalytic Study of the Child*, 34, 121–144.

Greenacre, P. (1981). Reconstruction: its nature and therapeutic value, *Journal of the American Psychoanalytic Association*, 29, 27–46.

Greenberg, D. (1990). Instinct and primary narcissism in Freud's later theory: an interpretation and reformulation of: 'Beyond the pleasure principle', *The International Journal of Psychoanalysis*, 71, 271–283.

Grunbaum, A. (1984). *The Foundation of Psychoanalysis*, University of California Press, Berkley, CA.

Grunberger, B. (1979). *Narcissism: Psychoanalytic Essay*, trans. Joyce S. Diamanti, International Universities Press, New York.

Hanly, C. (1995). On facts and idea in psychoanalysis, *International Journal of Psychoanalysis,* 67, 901–908.

Hartmann, H. (1948). Comments on the psychoanalytic theory of instinctual drives, in: *Essays on Ego Psychology: Selected Problems in Psychoanalytic Theory*, International Universities Press, New York.

Hartmann. H. (1964). *Essays on Ego Psychology: Selected Problems in Psychoanalytic Theory.* International Universities Press, New York.

Holt, R. (1965). A review of some of Freud's biological assumptions and their influence on his theories, in: *Psychoanalysis and current biological Thought*, eds N.S. Greenfield & W.C. Lewis, University of Wisconsin Press, Madison, WI.

Holt, R. (1981). The death and transfiguration of metapsychology, *The International Review of Psychoanalysis*, 8, 129–143.

Home, J. (1966). The concept of the mind, *International Journal of psychoanalysis*, 47, 42–49.

Jones, E. (1954). *Sigmund Freud: Life and Work* (Vol. I), The Hogarth Press, London.

Jones, E. (1955). *Sigmund Freud: Life and Work* (Vol. II), The Hogarth Press, London.

Jones, E. (1957). *Sigmund Freud: Life and Work* (Vol. II), The Hogarth Press, London.

Kancyper, L. (2006). The role of pre-Oedipal and Oedipal factors in psychic life, *International Journal of Psychoanalysis,* 87, 219–236.
Kernberg, O. (1967). Borderline personality organization, *Journal of the American Psychoanalytic Association*, 15, 641–685.
Kernberg, O. (1970). Factors in the psychoanalytic treatment of narcissistic personalities, *Journal of the American Psychoanalytic Associations*, 18, 51–85.
Kernberg, O. (1974). Contesting viewpoints regarding the nature of psychoanalytic treatment of narcissistic personalities: a preliminary communication, *Journal of the American psychoanalytic Association*, 22, 355–267.
Kernberg, O. (1978). The treatment of patients with borderline personality organization, *International Journal of Psychoanalysis,* 49, 600–619.
Kernberg, O. (2006). The coming changes in psychoanalytic education: Part I, *International Journal of Psychoanalysis*, 87, 1649–1673.
Kernberg, O. (2007). The coming changes in psychoanalytic education: Part II, *International Journal of Psychoanalysis*, 88, 183–202.
Klein, G. (1976). *The Psychoanalytic Theory: An Exploration of Essentials*, International Universities Press, New York.
Klein, M. (1948). *Contribution to Psychoanalysis* (1921–1945), Hogarth Press, London.
Klein, M.H. (1989). Throwing out the baby with bath water: a historical analysis of the antimetapsychology movement, *Psychoanalysis and Contemporary Thought*, 12, 565–598.
Kohut, H. (1959). Introspection, empathy, and psychoanalysis: an examination of the rationality, mode of observation, and theory, *Journal of the American Psychoanalytic Association*, 71, 459–485.
Kohut, H. (1968). The psychoanalytic treatment of narcissistic personality disorders: outline of a systematic approach, *The Psychoanalytic Study of the Child*, 23, 86–113.
Kohut, H. (1972) Thoughts on narcissistic rage, *The Psychoanalytic Study of the Child*, 27, 360–400.
Kohut, H. (1987). *Analysis of the Self: An Approach to the psychoanalytic Treatment of Narcissistic disorders,* Chicago University Press, Chicago, IL.
Kohut, H. and Wolf, E.S. (1978). Disorders of self and their treatment: an outline, *International Journal of Psychoanalysis*, 59, 413–425.
Lacan, J. (1949). The mirror stage as formative of the function of the I as revealed in psychoanalysis, in: *Ecrits*, trans. A. Sheridan, W.W. Norton & Company, New York.
Lacan, J. (1957–1958). Desire and its interpretation, *Lacan's Seminars*. Lacan in Ireland Collected Translations, trans. C. Gallager.
Lacan, J. (1977). The agency of the letter in the unconscious or reason since Freud, in: *Ecrits*, trans. A. Sheridan, W.W. Norton & Company, New York.
Lacan, J. (1979). The neurotic's personal myth, *The Psychoanalytic Quarterly*, 68, 405–425.
Lago, C. and Thompson, J. (1996). *Race, Culture, and Counselling*, Open University Press, Buckingham.
Laplanche, J. (1976). *Life and Death in Psychoanalysis*, The Johns Hopkins University Press, Baltimore, MA.
Laplanche, J. (1981). A metapsychology put to the test of anxiety, *International Journal of Psychoanalysis*, 62, 81–89.
Laplanche, J. (1997). The theory of seduction and the problem of the other, *International Journal of Psychoanalysis*, 79, 653–666.
Laplanche, J. and Pontalis, J.-B. (1973). *The Language of Psychoanalysis*, trans. D. Nicholson-Smith, Norton, New York.
Levi-Strauss, C. (1955). The structural study of the myth, *Journal of the American Folklore*, 68, 113–144.

Levi-Strauss, C. (1963). *Structural Anthropology*, Basic Books, New York.

Levi-Strauss, C. (1971). *The Elementary Structure of Kinship*, trans. C. Jacobson & B.G. Schoepf, Beacon Press, New York.

Levi-Strauss, C. (1978). *Myth and Meaning; Cracking the Code of Culture*, Schocken Books, New York.

M'Uzan, De, M. (1976). Countertransference and the paradoxical system, in: *Psychoanalysis in France*, eds S. Lebovici & D. Widlocher, International Universities Press, New York.

Mackay, N. (1981). Melanie Klein's metapsychology: phenomenological and mechanistic perspectives, *International Journal of Psychoanalysis*, 62, 177–186.

Malinowski, B. (1955). *Sex and Repression in Savage Society*, Meridian Books, New York.

Martela, F. and Saarinen, E. (2013). The system metaphor in therapy discourse: introducing system intelligence, *Psychoanalytic Dialogue*, 23, 80–101.

Masling, J., Bornstein, R.F., Fishman, I., and Davila, J. (2002). Can Freud explain women as well as men? A meta-analytic review of gender differences in psychoanalytic research, *Psychoanalytic Psychology*, 19, 328–347.

Matte-Blanco, I. (1975). *The Unconscious as Infinite sets: An Essay on Bilogic*, Duckworth, London.

Meissner, W.W. (1981). Metapsychology: who needs it? *Journal of the American Psychoanalytic Association*, 29, 921–938.

Meissner, W.W. (1995). The economic principle in psychoanalysis: economic and energetics, *Psychoanalysis and Contemporary Thought*, 18, 197–226

Meissner, W.W. (2008a). Narcissism and self: psychoanalytic consideration, *Journal of the American Academy of Psychoanalysis and Dynamic Psychiatry*, 36, 461–494.

Meissner, W.W. (2008b). Narcissism as motive, *The Psychoanalytic Quarterly*, 77.755–798.

Meltzer, D. (1978) *The Kleinian Development,* Part 1, The Freudian Development, Pertgshire, Clunie Press.

Merleau-Ponty, M. (2003). *Course Notes from the College de France*, trans. R. Valier, Northwestern University Press, Everson, IL.

Mitchell, S. (1995). Interaction in the Kleinian and Interpersonal tradition, *Contemporary Psychoanalysis*, 31, 65–91.

Modell, A.H. (1981). Does metapsychology still exist? *International Journal of Psychoanalysis*, 62, 391–402.

Novick, J. (1997). Termination conceivable and inconceivable, *Psychoanalytic Psychology,* 14, 401–412.

Perelberg, R.L. (2006). Controversial discussions and the apre-coup, *The International Psychoanalytic Journal of Psychoanalysis*, 87, 1199–1220.

Piaget, J. (1970). *Structuralism*, Harper Colophon Books, New York.

Piaget, J. (1997). *The Moral Judgment of the Child*, The Free Press, New York (first published 1934).

Politzer, G. (1928/1994). *Critique of the Foundation of Psychology*, trans. A. Appry, Duguene University Press, Pittsburgh, PA.

Quinodoz, D. (2003). Words that touch, *Journal of Clinical Psychoanalysis*, 12, 131–136.

Rabin, R.M. (1995). The liberating effect on the analysis of the paradigm shift in psychoanalysis, *Psychoanalytic Psychology*, 12, 467–482.

Rangell, L. (1991). Castration, *Journal of the American Psychoanalytic Association*, 39, 3–23.

Rappaport, D. (1951). The conceptual model of psychoanalysis, in: *Psychoanalytic Psychiatry and Psychology, Clinical and Theoretical Papers*, eds R.P. Knight & C.R. Fiedman, International Universities Press, New York.

Rappaport, D. and Gill, M. (1959). The points of view and assumptions of metapsychology, *International Journal of Psychoanalysis*, 40, 153–162.

Renik, O. (1992). A case of premenstrual distress: bisexual determinants of a woman's fantasy of damage to her genital, *Journal of the American Psychoanalytic Association*, 40, 195–210.

Renik, O. (1995). The ideal of the anonymous analyst, *Psychoanalytic Quarterly*, 64, 466–495.

Renik, O. (1996). The perils of neutrality, *Psychoanalytic Quarterly*, 65, 495–517.

Renik, O. (1998a). Getting real in psychoanalysis, *Psychoanalytic Quarterly*, 67, 566–593.

Renik, O. (1998b). The subjectivity and the objectivity of the psychoanalyst, *International Journal of Psychoanalysis*, 79, 487–497.

Richards, A. (1984). Narcissism: Psychoanalytic Essays: By Béla Grunberger, *Journal of the American Psychoanalytic Association,* 22, 199–204.

Richards, A.K. (1996). Primary femininity and female genital anxiety, *Journal of the American Psychoanalytic Association,* 44 S, 261–281.

Ricoeur, P. (1970). *Freud and Philosophy: An essay on Interpretation*, trans. D. Savage, Yale University Press. New Haven, CT.

Robinson, P. (1993). *Freud and his Critics*, University of California Press, Oakland, CA.

Rosenblatt, A. and Thickstun, J. (1977). Modern psychoanalytic concepts in a general psychology, *Psychological Issues*, Monograph 42/43. International Psychoanalytic Press, New York.

Rubinstein, B. (1997). Psychoanalysis and the philosophy of science, in: *Modern Psychoanalytic Concepts in General Psychology*, ed. R. Holt Monograph 62/63, International Universities Press, New York.

Sandler, J. (1988). Psychoanalytic technique and analysis terminable and interminable, *International Journal of Psychoanalysis*, 69, 335–345.

Saville, J.B. (1999). Contemporary psychoanalytic voices in North America: death of gender stereotypes and the birth of a new fiction of femininity, *Gender and Psychoanalysis*, 4, 235–252.

Smith, D.L. (1985). Freud's developmental approach to narcissism: a concise review, *International Journal of Psychoanalysis*, 66, 489–497.

Spencer, H. (1850). *Social Statics.* Kindle edition, Amazon Books.

Spencer, H. (1862). *The First Principle*, Kindle edition, Amazon Books.

Stephen, M. and Aron, L. (1999). *Interpersonal Psychoanalysis: Vol. 1 The Emergence of a Tradition*, Routledge, New York.

Stolorow, R. and Atwood. G. (1992). The three realms of the unconscious, in: *Relational Psychoanalysis*, eds S. Michel & L. Aron, Analytic Press, Hillside, NJ.

Stolorow, R. and Atwood, G. (2002). *Context of Being: The Intersubjective Foundation of Psychological Life*, Routledge, New York.

Strachey, J. (1957a). Editor's note on papers on metapsychology, *Standard Edition*, 14, 104–107, Hogarth Press and the Institute of Psychoanalysis, London.

Strachey, J. (1957b). Editor's note, *Standard Edition*, 2, 194, Hogarth Press and the Institute of Psychoanalysis. London.

Swanson, D. (1977). A critique of psychic energy as an explanatory concept, *Journal of the American Psychoanalytic Association*, 25, 603–633.

Thoma, H. and Cheshire, N. (1991). Freud's Nachtraglichkeit and Strachey's 'deferred action': trauma, constructions and the direction of causality, *The Internal Review of Psychoanalysis*, 18, 407–427.

Tripp, E. (1970). *The Meridian Handbook of Classical Mythology*, New American Library, New York.

Van Der Leeuw, P. (1969). On Freud's theory formation, *International Journal of Psychoanalysis, 50*, 573–581.

Vygotsky, L. (1962). *Thought and Language*, trans. and eds E. Hanfmann & G. Vakar, The MIT Press, Cambridge, MA.

Waelder, R. (1941–1942). On the psychoanalytic technique: five lectures, in: S. Guttmann & I. Guttmann with the assistance of I.K. Guttmann, *Psychoanalytic Quarterly*, 46, 1–68.

Wallerstein, R. (1989). One psychoanalysis or many? *International Journal of Psychoanalysis*, 69, 5–21.

Wallerstein, R. (2005). Will psychoanalytic pluralism be an enduring state of our discipline? *International Journal of psychoanalysis*, 80, 623–626.

Zetzel, E. (1968). The so called good hysteric, *International Journal of Psychoanalysis*, 49, 256–260.

INDEX

Freud and his works are discussed throughout the book and are not fully itemized in the index.